The Only Medicare Book You Need!

Critical Steps To Making Medicare As Simple As 1-2-3

Greg Gurbikian

HSD VENTURES™

HSD Ventures, LLC
10008 N Dale Mabry Highway
Suite 200
Tampa, FL 33618

This book is not connected with or endorsed by the U.S. government or the federal Medicare program. The materials contained in this publication represent the opinions of the authors and editors and should not be construed to be the view or opinions of the companies with whom such persons are – or may be – in partnership with, associated with, or employed by.

ISBN: 9798778538566

TABLE OF CONTENTS

Introduction

How I Became An Expert On Medicare

My first glimpse into the world of Medicare came by way of my parents. My father was already on Medicare, but my mother had kept working and held off on taking her Medicare at the age of 65. I learned that the age of 65 was not just a major life milestone; it was also a major health coverage milestone. Currently, the majority of Americans will first be eligible for Medicare at the age of 65 if they did not receive it earlier due to a disability.

As I began to attempt to help my mother make an important decision on what she was going to do about her Medicare coverage, I realized that *they* did not make this easy. The *they* that I am referring to is Medicare, insurance companies, and lastly insurance agents. Between all the alphabet letters, additional insurance company offerings, and a barrage of mailings and solicitations, I began the task of trying to simplify the process for my mother.

The ironic twist is that it led me to join the industry and make it my mission to simplify the process so anyone could understand it and become a Medicare expert. That mission led me to co-founding the company Healthcare Solutions Direct, and our tag line became Simple As 1-2-3.

With over a decade in the Medicare industry, I have heard the frustration from those going onto Medicare. What seemed like an exciting idea of joining Medicare a year before turning 65 became a nightmare about six months out. Not only did Medicare not make any sense, the mailings and phone calls felt like they would never stop.

The problem with Medicare is that it is not a one size fits all, and what makes the problem even worse is that most people never get to talk to a Medicare expert that can help them with this problem. It seems like every mailing, advertisement, and phone call is designed to sell something without properly educating the individual about Medicare.

I remember talking to a gentleman that owned his own law firm that was primarily involved in international law. I remember him telling me how he spent his entire career not only becoming familiar with the laws of the United States, but he also had to know all the laws of every country internationally. He told me that looking into Medicare was so confusing and had him questioning his own competence.

I told him not to worry. He had a Medicare expert that would help him understand Medicare first and then we would look into his additional options. When we got done going over the basics of Medicare and then explained what his options were, he told me, "That's it. This is really easy. I feel better now because I was starting to question myself. Why doesn't everyone explain it like this?"

That was a great question. I left the conversation thinking the same thing. Why does everyone not explain Medicare in a simple, easy to understand format? My answer to that question is this: Companies and insurance agents are not paid to explain Medicare, they are paid to *sell* you something.

This book that you are holding is going to help educate you on Medicare first so that you understand the foundation of this healthcare system. I have written it in a way that will help you understand the four parts of Medicare: Part A, B, C, and D. Before the builder puts up the walls and roof to a home, they must make sure that the foundation is solid.

In order to understand Medicare and how insurance companies and insurance agents play a role in it, you must understand the basics of Medicare. Medicare uses alphabet letters to identify the different parts of Medicare. It is extremely important that you understand each *PART* of Medicare before we talk about additional coverage options. Additional coverage options are called *PLANS* so you can see how you can get very confused if you do not fully understand the foundation of Medicare.

This book is different than anything you will ever read because the goal is to first make sure that we keep each part of Medicare separate so that you understand the basics. In keeping each part separate, you will learn what each part costs, each part covers, and each part doesn't cover. We will then look at the different enrollment periods, and most importantly a step-by-step of how to enroll into Medicare with real examples that will help you.

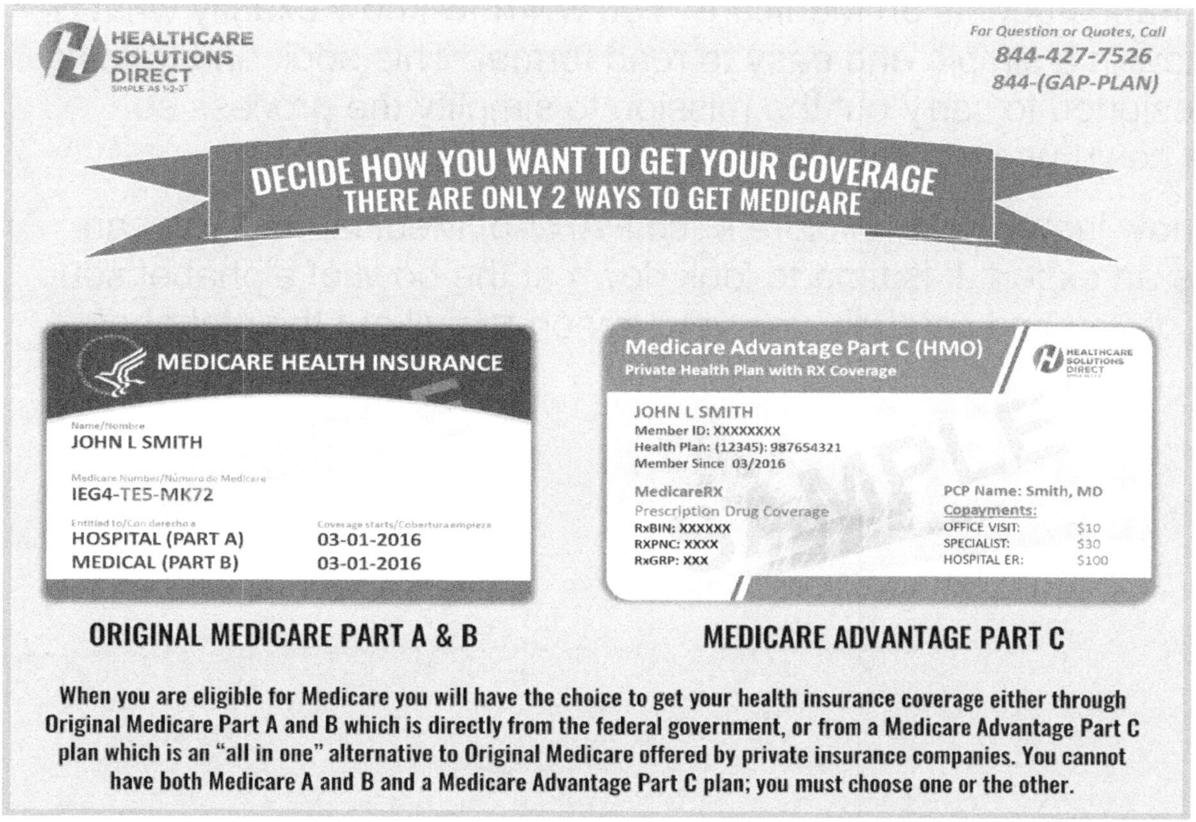

If you are looking to become a Medicare expert, it first comes down to this; you must understand that there are only two options when you are eligible for Medicare. You will get your health insurance coverage either through Original Medicare, which is directly from the federal government, or from a Medicare Advantage Part C plan, which is offered by private insurance companies. You are now one step closer to becoming a Medicare expert.

Once you understand the basics and what needs to be done with your current insurance in relation to Medicare, we will talk about the different options that are available to you when it comes to filling the "gaps" of Medicare. These "gaps" could financially impact someone's life if they are not properly addressed. I have seen so many individuals over my career that made mistakes when it came to enrolling into Medicare as well as their additional coverage options. The good news is that you will not be one of them.

I have a little secret to let you in on right now. What you are holding in your hand is actually the training manual that we currently use to train our insurance agents on Medicare. You will now know exactly what they know in a simple and easy to read format. This book and training were designed to carry out the mission to simplify the process so anyone could understand it and become a Medicare expert.

Let us now jump in and explore each *PART* of Medicare so you can become an expert. It is time to look down at the bowl of alphabet soup in front of you and carefully use your spoon to pull out the alphabet letters A, B, C, and D.

Chapter 1

Basics of Medicare —
Everything You Need To Know

What is Medicare?

- Medicare is a federal health insurance program that is offered by the federal government for those who are either turning 65 or older, under the age of 65 with certain qualifying health conditions or diagnosed with end stage renal disease (ESRD), which is permanent kidney failure requiring dialysis or a transplant.
- The Centers for Medicare and Medicaid Services (CMS) is the federal agency that oversees the federal health insurance program. Since they run the Medicare program, everything goes through CMS when someone is looking to choose their benefits.

Medicare Only Has Two Options

- When someone is eligible for Medicare, they will have the choice to get their health insurance coverage either through Original Medicare, which is directly from the federal government, or from a Medicare Advantage Part C plan, which is offered by private insurance companies.
- Someone *cannot* have Original Medicare Part A and B *and* a Medicare Advantage Part C plan; they must choose one or the other.

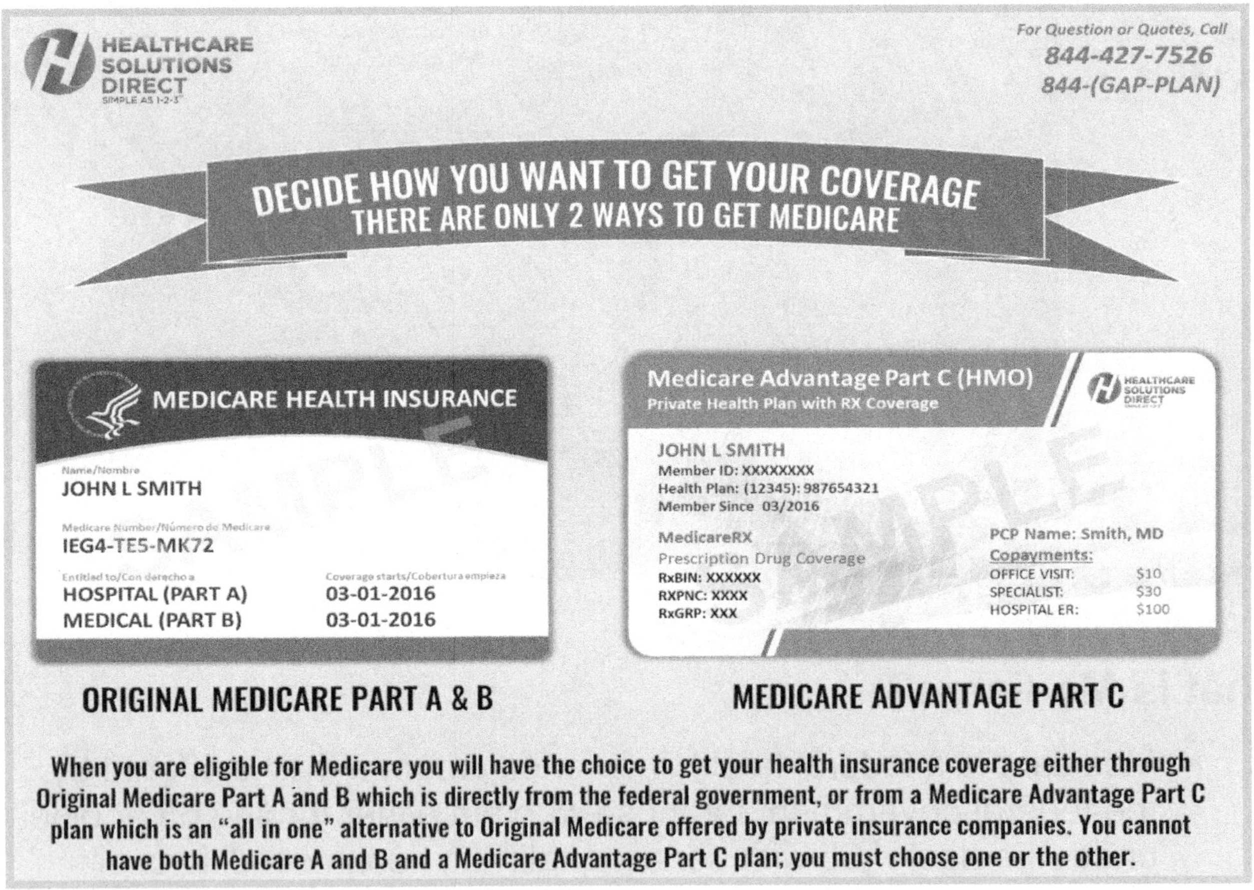

Brief History of Medicare

- Created in 1965, Medicare is a federal entitlement program providing national health insurance coverage for those who were 65 and over regardless of their income and medical history.
- In 1945, President Harry Truman first sent a message to Congress, which called for a national health insurance fund that all Americans would have access to that would be paid for through a payroll tax.

- Many saw his plan as universal health care that looked a lot like the beginning of socialism. Although Truman fought hard to get something passed, he was unsuccessful and later acknowledged that it was one of the biggest regrets of his presidency.
- In early 1960, President John F. Kennedy made the same attempt after learning that over half of all Americans over the age of 65 had no health insurance coverage at all. With the average life expectancy around 69 years old during that time, the idea of providing universal health care overseen by the federal government for those 65 and over became much more popular.

Medicare Signed Into Law

- On July 30, 1965, President Lyndon Johnson signed Medicare into law, providing hospital and medical coverage to those 65 and older. He issued the first Medicare card to none other than Truman. As a tribute to Truman, Medicare was signed into law at the Truman Library.
- In the first year alone, nearly 20 million Americans took advantage of the new plan.

Courtesy of https://www.medicareresources.org/basic-medicare-information/brief-history-of-medicare/

How Medicare Has Changed Over The Years

- When Medicare first began, only two parts existed — Part A for hospital services that was free and carried a small annual deductible, and Part B for medical services that charged a small monthly premium. The first Medicare customers paid a $40 annual deductible for Part A (hospital) and a $3 per month premium for Part B (medical).
- As of 2022, those costs are now:
    - $1,556 for the Part A deductible and
    - $170.10 per month or higher, depending on your income, for Part B.

New Additions After Medicare Became Law

- Medicare was only supposed to cover those 65 and older, but in 1972 President Richard Nixon expanded it to include certain people under that age who had long-term disabilities or ESRD.
- In the 1980s, additions to what Medicare covers expanded to include home health and hospice services. In 1980, Medicare Supplement insurance, known as Medigap, which we will go over later, was born via the Omnibus Reconciliation Act under federal oversight.
- In the 1990s, new legislation required Medicare to cover premiums for those with incomes between 100-120 percent of the national poverty level.

Medicare Part C and D Make A Late Entrance

- In 1997, Part C of Medicare was signed into law originally under the name "Medicare + Choice." In 2003, the name was later changed to what we now call Medicare Advantage. It was created as an alternative to Original Medicare to give more choices for someone under a private health insurer.
- Up until the new millennium, about 25 percent of Medicare beneficiaries had no sort of coverage for their prescription drugs. In 2003, President George W. Bush changed that when he signed the Medicare Prescription Drug Improvement and Modernization Act, enabling people to add an optional drug plan to their policies. These are offered by private insurance companies, which came to be known as Part D of Medicare.

Medicare And The Silver Tsunami

- Over 60 million Americans and almost 18 percent of the total population are covered by the many benefits available as a Medicare beneficiary.
- As of 2020, there are approximately 10,000 people a day who are turning 65 — known as the baby-boomer generation. This generation includes those who were born between 1946-1964.
- In 2011, the first of this generation started to turn 65 and age into Medicare, which will continue until 2030. By 2030, it is estimated that there will be over 80 million beneficiaries in the Medicare population.

Medicare Part A — Hospital Coverage

- Part A covers inpatient hospitalization. Think of this as the room and board when someone is admitted to the hospital.
- Part A covers:
    - Inpatient hospitalization,
    - Skilled nursing facility,
    - Home health care, and
    - Hospice care.
- Part A will also cover some blood transfusion costs.

Medicare Part A Deductible

- Part A has a deductible, which for 2022 is $1,556. This $1,556 is not an annual deductible but rather a benefit period deductible.
- This is one of the only insurances that uses a benefit period deductible and not an annual deductible.
- If someone is admitted to the hospital, this deductible is good for 60 days starting from the day they were admitted.
- Although unlikely, if someone were chronically ill and was admitted and discharged every 60 days, they could be responsible for this deductible up to six times during the calendar year.

Why "Admitted" Is Such A Big Deal

- The word "admitted" is the key word under Part A, which will trigger the deductible for a hospital stay.
- Someone who finds themselves being rushed to the hospital may only be held under "observation," which would be considered an emergency stay. This would fall under the outpatient medical services of Part B.

The Medicare 3-day Rule

- Medicare as of 2022, has a rule that you must be admitted to a hospital for three days to be eligible to receive coverage for a skilled nursing facility stay under Part A.
- "Observation" status is typically given to someone in the hospital whose condition does *not* require the need for care longer than 48 hours.

"Observation" Status Can Affect Skilled Nursing

- As of now, skilled nursing facility coverage with Medicare can only fall under Part A. Skilled nursing facility care is considered an extension of a hospital stay if someone had a serious condition that required rehabilitation before going home.
- If someone finds themselves not admitted to the hospital and under observation only, the charges will fall under what we are going to look at next, which is Part B of Medicare.

Medicare Part B — Medical Coverage

- Part B covers outpatient medical services. Part B covers almost everything medically necessary *outside* of the hospital such as:
    - Doctor visits, which include both primary care and specialists,
    - Preventative care,
    - Outpatient surgeries,
    - Durable medical equipment,
    - Expensive treatments like chemotherapy, and
    - Ambulance services.

Medicare Part B Deductible

- As of 2022, the Part B deductible is $233. This deductible is a calendar year deductible (January 1 - December 31) versus a benefit period deductible (60 days) like Part A.
- Once this deductible has been satisfied, the good news is the individual has met Medicare's Part B deductible for that entire calendar year. However, the individual is still responsible for a 20 percent coinsurance, which can be a big problem for someone with just Medicare Part A and B.

Medicare B Coinsurance

- After the Part B deductible has been met, Medicare will only pay 80 percent of all medical expenses and the individual will be responsible for the other 20 percent that calendar year.
- Unfortunately, Medicare Part B does *not* have a maximum out-of-pocket cap like most private insurance plans. The other 20 percent would be the individual's responsibility for that entire calendar year.

Medicare Part C — Medicare Advantage

- Part C is often referred to as a Medicare Advantage plan.
- These plans can be another way that someone can get their Medicare Part A and B coverage. Medicare Advantage plans are offered by private insurance companies that are approved by Medicare. Most of them will also include prescription drug coverage.
- This option has become quite popular because it allows someone to get some additional benefits not offered by Original Medicare such as prescription, dental, vision, hearing, etc.
- The plans come with another big benefit because they are required to have a limit on out-of-pocket costs each year for health care services.

Medicare Part C "All-In-One" Plan

- These types of privatized plans are sometimes referred to as "all-in-one" plans because most will include prescription drug coverage, which is *not* provided under Medicare Part A and B.

- Someone must have both Part A and B and continue to pay their Medicare Part B premium in order to enroll in a Medicare Advantage plan.

Medicare Part C Is Not A Supplement

- Most individuals think that the Medicare Advantage plan is their supplement to Medicare, but this is not the case.
- When someone enrolls in a Medicare Advantage plan, they are no longer enrolled under Original Medicare Part A and B but will always be Medicare eligible.
- The individual will always be in Medicare's system and have the right to take back their federal governments benefits.
- The Medicare Advantage plan is similar to group or individual health insurance.

Medicare Part C Will Have Its Own Card

- The individual will need to use the health insurance card that is sent to them by the Medicare Advantage plan to get their services covered since that will be their health insurance.
- The individual will want to keep their red, white, and blue Medicare card somewhere safe if they decide to switch back to Original Medicare at some point in the future.
- Original Medicare has no provider networks so an individual can go to any doctor or hospital that they want to that accepts Medicare. With a Medicare Advantage plan, the individual may need to use the health care providers in that plan's network or service area so it's important to refer to their card.
- Original Medicare Part A and B is offered by the federal government, and a Medicare Advantage Part C plan is offered by a private insurance company.

Medicare Part D — Prescription Drug Coverage

- Part D covers prescription drug coverage.
- These plans are provided by private insurance companies that are approved by Medicare to help with the cost of prescription drugs.

- Medicare never got involved in the prescription drug market but does oversee how the private insurance companies administer the prescription coverage.

There Are Two Ways To Get Prescription Coverage

- The individual will only have two options to choose from for their prescription drug coverage when they are eligible for Medicare. They can choose either a:
    - Prescription drug plan (PDP), which is referred to as a stand-alone PDP. The PDP plan will not automatically be included with Original Medicare A and B as their insurance or
    - A Medication Advantage prescription drug (MAPD) plan is through Medicare Advantage, which includes prescription drug coverage that meets the requirements of Part D.
- If someone is not taking any prescription medication, they will still need to enroll in a standalone PDP or MAPD. There will be a penalty if someone does not have credible prescription coverage and does not enroll into a prescription plan when they are first eligible for Medicare.

Chapter 2

What Medicare Costs — Everything You Need To Know

What Does Medicare Cost?

- An epic misconception is that Medicare is free and that it **will** cover **all** the health care costs.
- There are three reasons why it's not entirely the person's fault for believing that Medicare is free such as:
  1. Retirees may think that Medicare is free because they have paid into Medicare their entire life through their payroll taxes.

2. Retirees may think that Medicare is free because unless they are drawing Social Security retirement early before the age of 65, they will not receive any notice from Medicare letting them know there is a cost associated.
3. Retirees may think that Medicare is free because of the marketing and sales of Medicare Advantage plans. Many are advertised as having a $0 premium.

Better Understanding Of Why Medicare Is Not Free

- According to the Kaiser Family Foundation, the chart below shows the sources of Medicare revenue for 2018. This will help you better understand why Medicare is *not* free.

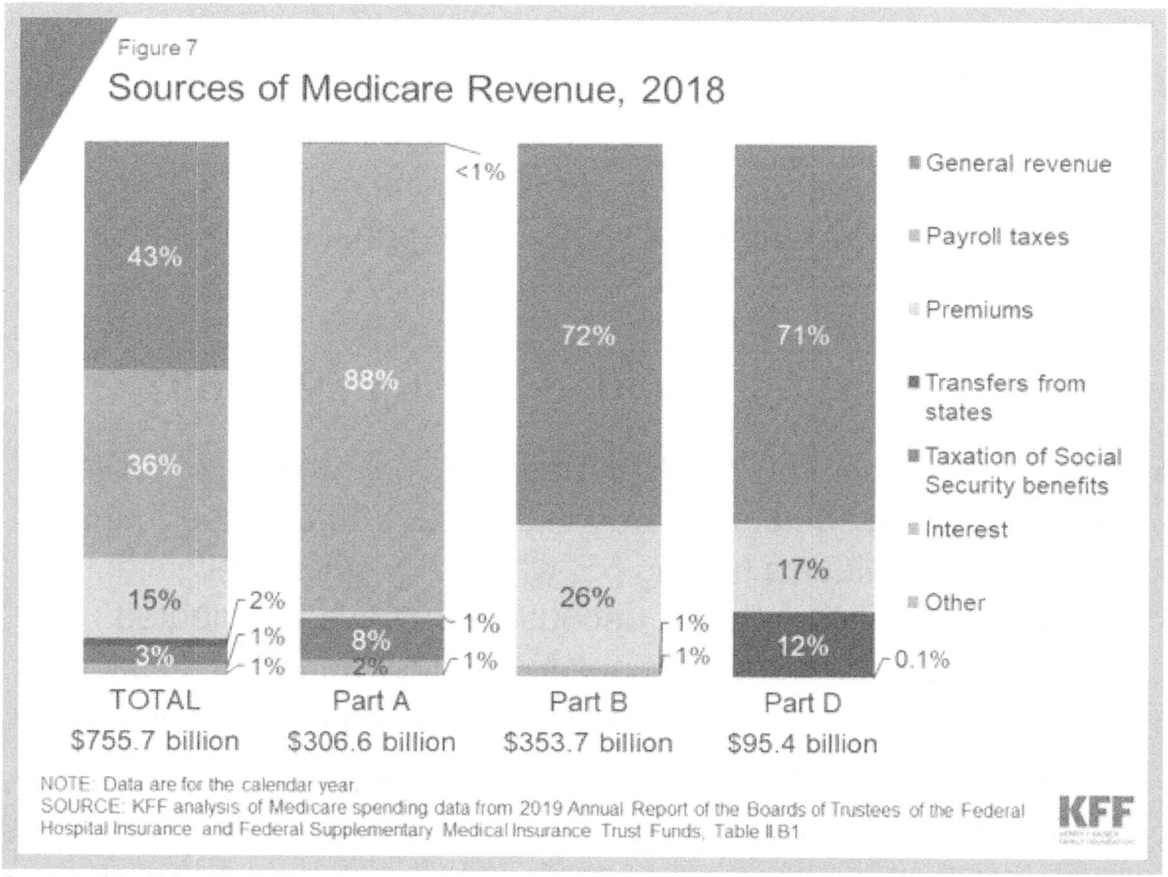

Courtesy of the Kaiser Family Foundation: https://www.kff.org/medicare/issue-brief/the-facts-on-medicare-spending-and-financing/

- Part A is 88 percent funded through payroll taxes through the Federal Insurance Contributions Act (FICA) which is withheld from wages.
- Part B is 72 percent funded from a general revenue trust fund and 26 percent is funded by Part B premiums.
- Part D is 71 percent funded from a general revenue trust fund and 17 percent is funded by Part D premiums.

How Much Is Part A?

- This part of Medicare is FREE! It is sometimes referred to as "premium-free Part A."
- Each time someone has FICA withheld from their wages, it is going to pay for the hospital insurance tax, also known as Medicare taxes.
- For 2022, the current tax rate for Medicare is 2.9 percent. This means 1.45 percent of wages are deducted for Medicare taxes, and employers will contribute and match the other 1.45 percent. If someone is self-employed, they are responsible for the full 2.9 percent.

How Much Of Part A Is Funded Through Payroll?

- Around 88 percent of Part A is funded by payroll taxes that are withheld during someone's working years. You can see that 99 percent of individuals turning 65, who are Medicare eligible, do *not* pay for Medicare Part A because they have contributed enough to payroll tax deductions to get it for free.
- Only 1 percent must pay for Medicare Part A because they did not work long enough in the United States to contribute fully to Medicare taxes.

What Does Part A Cost If You Must Pay?

- In 2022, if someone did not work the required amount of years or quarters, here is what Medicare Part A would cost:
    - Medicare taxes for less than 30 quarters, the standard Part A premium is $499 a month.
    - Medicare taxes for 30-39 quarters, the standard Part A premium is $274 a month.

Get Medicare Part A "Free" If You Did Not Work?

- Although Medicare is individual insurance, if someone's spouse did not work the full 10 years or 40 quarters than they can still get their own "premium-free Part A."
- When they turn 65, they will qualify for Medicare Part A based on their spouse's work history. Here are the requirements to get Medicare Part A for free:
    - Married: If the individual's spouse is eligible for Social Security benefits because of either the early retirement age (at least 62) or through disability, the individual will be eligible for Medicare Part A if they have been married for at least one year before applying.
    - Divorced: If the individual's former spouse is eligible for Social Security benefits because of either the early retirement age (at least 62) or through disability, the individual will be eligible for Medicare Part A if they had been married for at least 10 years. They must be currently single at the time of application to get Medicare Part A under a former spouse.
    - Widowed: If the individual's deceased spouse qualified for Social Security benefits or disability, the individual will be eligible for Medicare Part A if they were married for at least nine months before their spouse died. They must be

currently single at the time of application to get Medicare Part A under a deceased spouse. If they remarry after the age of 60, the second marriage will not be used to determine the eligibility.

Spouse Must Be 62 To Qualify For "Free" Part A

- If the non-working spouse did not work the full 10 years or 40 quarters and is older than their working spouse when they turn 65, then here is what will happen:
- If the working spouse is 62 and qualifies for Social Security retirement benefits, the non-working spouse can get "premium-free Part A" at age 65. The working spouse does not need to start drawing Social Security retirement benefits early at age 62 for the non-working spouse to get "premium-free Part A" at 65. The working spouse just needs to qualify for Social Security retirement benefits.

What Happens If Working Spouse Is Not Yet 62?

- If the working spouse is not yet 62 when the non-working spouse turns 65, then here is what will happen:
    - The non-working spouse would have to pay for Medicare Part A.
    - The non-working spouse would have to pay for Medicare Part A until the working spouse turned 62. When the working spouse turned 62, the non-working spouse would be able to get Medicare Part A for free.
- In situations like this, the working spouse will usually try to keep the non-working spouse on their working employer group coverage until they turned 62. At that point, the non-working spouse could then get the "premium-free Part A." If that is not a

possibility, then the non-working spouse may need to pay for Medicare Part A.

Another Way Non-Working Spouse Gets Part A "Free"

- If a non-working spouse or any individual develops a disability and qualifies for Social Security Disability Insurance (SSDI) benefits prior to turning 65, they will be eligible to get Medicare Part A for free *automatically* after a 24-month qualifying period.
- The federal government has what they refer to as a "waiting period" for the Medicare coverage to begin after the individual has been receiving the disability benefit checks for 24 months. On the 25th month of SSDI benefits, the individual would automatically be enrolled into Medicare.

How Much Is Part B?

- This part of Medicare is *not* free because it was never included in the FICA payroll taxes.
- There is a great difference on how the Medicare Part B is funded compared to the Part A.
- Even with someone having to pay a premium for Medicare Part B, they are only contributing 26 percent of the true cost for Part B.

The Standard Part B Premium <u>Everyone</u> Must Pay

- As of 2022, the standard monthly premium for Medicare Part B that someone will be responsible for is $170.10. Although Part B is considered voluntary, almost 92 percent of those eligible for Medicare are enrolled in Part B.
- Without Medicare Part B, someone will *not* be eligible to enroll in the alternative plan to Medicare, which is called Part C Medicare

Advantage. An individual must have both Medicare Part A and B in order to enroll in Part C.

Part B Premium History Over The Last 10 Years

- Here are the last 10 years of Medicare Part B increases:

  - 2021 Medicare Part B: $148.50
  - 2020 Medicare Part B: $144.60
  - 2019 Medicare Part B: $135.50
  - 2018 Medicare Part B: $134.00
  - 2017 Medicare Part B: $134.00
  - 2016 Medicare Part B: $121.80
  - 2015 Medicare Part B- $104.90
  - 2014 Medicare Part B: $104.90
  - 2013 Medicare Part B: $104.90
  - 2012 Medicare Part B: $99.90
  - 2011 Medicare Part B: $115.40

Part B Premium Based On Last 2 Years Of Income

- There are roughly 7 percent of individuals who will pay more for their Medicare Part B due to income. Here is a breakdown of the Medicare Part B costs by income level in 2022:

2022

The standard Part B premium amount in 2022 is $170.10. Most people pay the standard Part B premium amount. If your modified adjusted gross income as reported on your IRS tax return from 2 years ago is above a certain amount, you'll pay the standard premium amount and an Income Related Monthly Adjustment Amount (IRMAA). IRMAA is an extra charge added to your premium.

If your yearly income in 2020 (for what you pay in 2022) was			You pay each month (in 2022)
File individual tax return	File joint tax return	File married & separate tax return	
$91,000 or less	$182,000 or less	$91,000 or less	$170.10
above $91,000 up to $114,000	above $182,000 up to $228,000	Not applicable	$238.10
above $114,000 up to $142,000	above $228,000 up to $284,000	Not applicable	$340.20
above $142,000 up to $170,000	above $284,000 up to $340,000	Not applicable	$442.30
above $170,000 and less than $500,000	above $340,000 and less than $750,000	above $91,000 and less than $409,000	$544.30
$500,000 or above	$750,000 or above	$409,000 or above	$578.30

Social Security Is In Charge Of Determining Part B

- Social Security will look back at what someone has reported on their last two federal tax returns, which is provided by the Internal Revenue Service (IRS).
- For example, to determine what someone's Part B premium will be for 2022, Social Security will look back at their 2020 federal tax return.
- Social Security looks specifically at what they refer to as the modified adjusted gross income (MAGI). Although this is different from the gross income, for many the gross and MAGI will be the same.

Examples Of Modified Adjusted Gross Income

- Examples of what could be included MAGI:
    - Wages,
    - Rental income,
    - Property sale,
    - Dividends from investments,
    - Pension income, and/or
    - Another large asset.
- If the gross income or MAGI falls within the higher income tax bracket, the individual will be subjected to paying a higher amount for their Part B premium called income-related monthly adjustment amount (IRMAA).

Example Of What An Income-related Monthly Adjustment Amount Looks Like With Part B

- If you owe an IRMAA, you will receive a letter from Social Security with important information.

- A letter from a client in 2020 showed the standard Part B premium would be $148.50 for 2021. Social Security then says in the letter that this individual in 2019 filed taxes as married, filing jointly. It states that this client had an adjusted gross income of $224,094.00 plus $45,435.00 in tax-exempt interest. Social Security added these amounts together to get the MAGI of $269,529.00.
- This puts the client above $222,000 and just below $276,000. That means this individual will pay the $148.50 for the standard Part B premium in 2021 plus an additional $148.50 due to IRMA for a total monthly premium of $297.00.

$88,000 or less	$176,000 or less	$88,000 or less	$148.50
above $88,000 up to $111,000	above $176,000 up to $222,000	Not applicable	$207.90
above $111,000 up to $138,000	above $222,000 up to $276,000	Not applicable	$297.00
above $138,000 up to $165,000	above $276,000 up to $330,000	Not applicable	$386.10

Letter From Social Security Showing Income-related Monthly Adjustment Amount

- This individual will pay $297.00, which includes the standard Part B Medicare Premium in 2021 and Medicare Part B (IRMAA). This individual will still need to pay the $297.00 to Social Security even if they were to choose a Medicare Advantage plan with a $0 premium. An individual must have Part A and B in order to enroll into a Part C Medicare Advantage plan.

Social Security Administration
Important Information

Date: November 25, 2020
BNC#:

INFORMATION ONLY

JOHN L SMITH
123 SOMEWHERE LANE
GREAT TOWN, USA 54321

The Social Security Act requires some people to pay higher premiums for their Medicare Part B (Medical Insurance) and Part D (Prescription Drug Plan) based on their income. We use information the Internal Revenue Service (IRS) provides us to decide if you will need to pay these higher premiums. Based on your income, you are required to pay these higher premiums for 2021, which are called the Income-Related Monthly Adjustment Amounts (IRMAA). The IRMAA information in this letter is for one year only.

If you currently do not have Medicare Part B or Part D and enroll in 2021, those premiums will also be increased based on your income.

If you have Medicare Part B, the total 2021 premium includes:

— $148.50 for the standard Medicare premium, plus

— any surcharges you may owe for late enrollment, plus;

— $148.50 for the Medicare Part B IRMAA based on your 2019 income tax return

How We Figured Your IRMAA

IRMAA are based on your 2019 income tax return. The IRS told us that for tax year 2019 you filed your taxes as married, filing jointly. You had an adjusted gross income of $224,094.00 plus $45,435.00 in tax-exempt interest income. We added these amounts together to get your Modified Adjusted Gross Income (MAGI) of $269,529.00.

We used the following table to decide IRMAA for the Medicare Part B and Part D premiums:

If Someone Disagrees With An Income-related Monthly Adjustment Amount They Can Appeal

- Now there is good news if someone receives a letter from Social Security and does not agree with IRMAA. They can appeal the decision and file a request for reconsideration.
- The individual may amend their tax return that Social Security used to determine the IRMAA, which might help lower or remove the IRMAA or the income may have gone down since they filed the tax return. If someone had a major life-changing event and the income has gone down, they can file an appeal using form SSA-44.

Social Security Considers This A Life-Changing Event

- Social Security considers the following a major life-changing event:

INFORMATION ONLY

Page 3 of 5

If Your Income Has Gone Down

In some situations, we can make a new decision about your IRMAA. Contact us to request a new decision if your MAGI has gone down at least one range in the table above or has gone below the lowest amounts in the table since the 2019 tax year, AND the decrease in MAGI was caused by any of the following life-changing events:

- You married.
- You divorced or your marriage was annulled.
- You became a widow or widower.
- You or your spouse stopped working or reduced work hours.
- You or your spouse lost income from income-producing property due to a disaster or other event beyond your control.
- You or your spouse experienced a scheduled cessation, termination, or reorganization of an employer's pension plan, or
- You or your spouse received a settlement from an employer or former employer because of the employer's closure, bankruptcy, or reorganization.

We will use the new lower MAGI to see if we can make a new decision about your IRMAA. We cannot make a new decision if your income has changed for a reason other than those listed above, such as receiving one-time income from capital gains.

How Much Is Part C?

- An individual must have *both* Medicare Part A and B in order to enroll in Part C.
- They will still be required to pay the standard Medicare Part B premium for 2022, which is $170.10 per month.
- If someone enrolls into a Medicare Advantage plan this will include their hospital, medical, and usually prescription coverage. Even though the plan might come with a $0 premium and some additional benefits not covered by traditional Medicare, they will still need to pay the $170.10 for Part B to be enrolled in the Medicare Advantage plan.

Two Reasons Part C Requires The Part B Premium

- There are two reasons why someone must continue to pay the Part B monthly premium of $170.10.
    - First, someone is always Medicare eligible. They can always switch back to Medicare Part A and B as their primary insurance during certain enrollments during the calendar year.
    - Second, Medicare pays the private insurance companies a monthly premium to manage their health care. The average per individual is currently about $900 a month that the private Medicare Advantage company receives from the federal government to manage someone's health care.

Part C Companies Get More Based On Certain Factors

- Some Medicare Advantage companies will get much more per month than the average $900 based on the geographic location or chronic health conditions for that individual on the plan. This has unfortunately brought fraud with chronic health conditions that are improperly reported to the federal government.

What Is Medicare Part B Buy Back/Give Back?

- In certain areas in 2022, Medicare Advantage plans will choose to use some of the funding the federal government gives them to either give the member a portion or the full Part B premium of $170.10 back into their Social Security check each month.
- Finding a Medicare Advantage plan that offers the “buy back” or “give back” of someone’s full Part B premium back into their Social Security check is quite rare. Plans that do a “give back” will typically offer just a portion of the Part B premium back. Most Medicare Advantage plans will offer additional benefits rather than use the “give back” of the Part B premium.
- To be eligible for the “give back” of the Part B premium, an individual must be enrolled in Part A and B, be responsible for paying the Part B, and live in that plans service area. Individuals that receive Medicaid or any government assistance that helps to pay the Part B premium will not be eligible.
- An individual will not be sent a check. The “give back” will be added to the Social Security check. Those not drawing Social Security will get a reduction in what they must pay for Part B.
- The Part B “give back” can take 1-3 months to begin once someone has enrolled into a Medicare Advantage plan.

How Much Is Part D?

- This part of Medicare is *not* free either unless it is included as an additional benefit in the Medicare Advantage plan at no additional cost. You can see that when we earlier discussed the sources of Medicare Revenue, there is a large difference on how Medicare Part D is funded compared to the Part A.

- Even with contributing to Medicare Part D, it is only 17 percent of the true cost for Part D.
- The Medicare Insurance Trust Fund still must fund 71 percent of the Medicare Part D.

There Is No Standard Premium Set For Part D

- Unlike Part B, there is *not* a standard premium set forth for a standalone PDP. When Medicare calculates a penalty for an individual that does not have credible prescription coverage, which we will discuss later, they use a "national base beneficiary premium" of $33.37 in 2022.
- The prescription Part D drug plans are offered by private insurance companies, which are approved by Medicare. They must all follow the same guidelines that are set forth by the federal government.
- When looking at a standalone PDP, there are usually around 20 different drug plans to choose from in any given zip code. A standalone PDP will run on average between $15-$20 a month.

Income-Related Monthly Adjustment Amount Also Applies To Part D

- As part of the Affordable Care Act (ACA) in 2011, the IRMAA was implemented for Part D. If someone owes an IRMAA for Part B, they will *also* owe it for Part D.
- There are roughly 7 percent of individuals who pay more for Medicare Part B; therefore, they will also pay more for their Part D.
- Here is a breakdown of Medicare Part D costs by income level in 2022:

2022

If your filing status and yearly income in 2020 was			
File individual tax return	File joint tax return	File married & separate tax return	You pay each month (in 2022)
$91,000 or less	$182,000 or less	$91,000 or less	your plan premium
above $91,000 up to $114,000	above $182,000 up to $228,000	not applicable	$12.40 + your plan premium
above $114,000 up to $142,000	above $228,000 up to $284,000	not applicable	$32.10 + your plan premium
above $142,000 up to $170,000	above $284,000 up to $340,000	not applicable	$51.70 + your plan premium
above $170,000 and less than $500,000	above $340,000 and less than $750,000	above $91,000 and less than $409,000	$71.30 + your plan premium
$500,000 or above	$750,000 or above	$409,000 or above	$77.90 + your plan premium

Social Security Handles Income-Related Monthly Adjustment Amount For Both Parts B and D

- Social Security will look back at the individual's previous federal tax return, which is provided by the IRS just like they did for the Part B premium. For example, to determine what the Part D premium will be for 2022, Social Security will look back at the individuals 2020 federal tax return.

- In the previous example of the individual who had a MAGI of $269,529.00 in 2021, we see the breakdown below from Social Security for the added Part D IRMAA would be $31.80. Even if the individual chooses a Medicare Advantage plan with $0 premium, they would still be responsible for the $31.80 in 2021. Starting in 2022, this IRMAA would increase to $32.10 plus the cost of the Part D plan if applicable.

INFORMATION ONLY

Page 2 of 5

If you filed as:	With MAGI of:	Part B IRMAA is:	Part D IRMAA is:
Single, Head of Household or Qualifying Widow(er)	$88,000.01 - $111,000.00	$59.40	$12.30
	$111,000.01 - $138,000.00	$148.50	$31.80
	$138,000.01 - $165,000.00	$237.60	$51.20
	$165,000.01 - $499,999.99	$326.70	$70.70
	More than $499,999.99	$356.40	$77.10
Married, Filing Jointly	$176,000.01 - $222,000.00	$59.40	$12.30
	$222,000.01 - $276,000.00	$148.50	$31.80
	$276,000.01 - $330,000.00	$237.60	$51.20
	$330,000.01 - $749,999.99	$326.70	$70.70
	More than $749,999.99	$356.40	$77.10
Married, Filing Separately (if you lived apart throughout 2019, see below about Some Special Situations)	$88,000.01 - $411,999.99	$326.70	$70.70
	More than $411,999.99	$356.40	$77.10

These IRMAA are effective for 2021 only. Next year when we receive updated information from the IRS, we will make a new decision about any IRMAA owed.

Some Special Situations That May Apply To You

If your tax filing status was married, filing separately, and you lived apart from your spouse throughout the tax year we used, please call us about your living arrangement. It could lower your IRMAA. Please contact your Social Security office if you have any questions. You will need a copy of the most recent income tax return you filed with IRS.

Some May Qualify For Extra Help With Part D

- If someone qualifies for full Medicaid or those with limited income and resources, they automatically qualify for what is called "Extra

Help" Part D. For those who might not be able to qualify for full Medicaid, there are state Medicare Savings Programs (MSPs), which can help pay for premiums, deductibles, coinsurance, copayments and much more.

- If someone does not automatically qualify for either of those programs, they can still apply for Extra Help. We will go over the Extra Help in more detail when we discuss Part D. There are many individuals who are Medicare eligible that can qualify for this, but never take the time to apply for it.

How Does Someone Pay Their Premiums?

- We went over the costs that are associated with Part A, B, C, and D, so let's go over how someone is going to pay for each of these premiums.

How Does Someone Pay For Part A?

- This one is *free*; therefore, the individual will not have to worry about getting a bill or setting up a payment for their Part A.
- If someone must pay for Medicare Part A, they will get a "Medicare Premium Bill" every month from the CMS. There will be an example of a "Medicare Premium Bill" when we discuss Part B next since there are many who are Medicare eligible who get a bill for their Part B. The key to remember about Medicare Part A is that if the individual must pay for it, it will come in the form of a bill every month.

How Does Someone Pay For Part B?

- If someone is getting Social Security or Railroad Retirement Board (RRB) benefits, their Medicare Part B premium will be *automatically deducted* from their benefit check each month.

There is nothing that the individual must do to pay that premium. It will be automatically deducted each month before they deposit their monthly Social Security retirement.

- If someone is not receiving Social Security or RRB benefits, they will get a "Medicare premium bill" in the mail every *three* months.
- There are 4 ways that an individual can pay their Medicare bill:
    - Pay online through their Medicare account by credit card, debit card, or from a checking or savings account.
    - Pay directly from savings or checking account through their banks online bill payment service.
    - Sign up for Medicare Easy Pay which is a free service that deducts payments directly each month from a savings or checking account.
    - Mail the premium payment directly to Medicare.

Everyone Should Sign Up For Medicare Easy Pay

- Everyone who has Medicare Part A and B should first set up their own personal Medicare account online at MyMedicare.gov.
- An individual responsible for paying their Medicare premium since they are not drawing Social Security, should enroll in Medicare Easy Pay. It can be done easily through their Medicare account by selecting "My Premiums" and then "Sign Up" and then completing the online form.
- Medicare Easy Pay is a free service that will automatically deduct the monthly premium payments from a savings or checking account on or around the 20th of each month.
- It will appear on the bank statement as a payment to "CMS Medicare Premiums." This way the individual can pay their Medicare premium bill *monthly* instead of having to pay quarterly all at one time. This also ensures that they never miss their

payment and thus lose their Medicare Part B coverage and be put on the Medicare "naughty list."

Example Of A Medicare Premium Bill From The Centers For Medicare And Medicaid Services

- Here is a letter from a client in 2020 which shows an actual example of the first Part B Medicare premium bill sent by CMS to an individual.

U.S. DEPARTMENT OF HEALTH & HUMAN SERVICES
CENTERS FOR MEDICARE & MEDICAID SERVICES (CMS)

MEDICARE PREMIUM BILL

Part B First Bill

DATE: 10/27/2020

YOUR MEDICARE NUMBER: [redacted]

Ways to pay your bill:

- Pay online at your bank's website
- Sign up for Medicare Easy Pay
- Make a check or money order payable to "CMS Medicare Insurance"
- Use Visa, MasterCard, American Express, or Discover

Send payment with the coupon at the bottom to:
Medicare Premium Collection Center
P.O. Box 790355
St. Louis, MO 63179-0355

	Coverage Periods	Part A (Hospital Insurance) +	Part B (Medical Insurance) +	IRMAA Part D =	Total Amount
Amount due for Part A and/or Part B	12/01/2020-02/28/2021		$433.80		$433.80
Past due amount for Part A and/or Part B					
Amount due for IRMAA Part D					
Past due amount for IRMAA Part D					

Part A termination date:
Part B termination date:
Part D termination date:

Total amount due: $433.80
Payment in full due by: 11/25/2020

Please send your full payment by 11/25/2020. **Your payment is late if Medicare gets it after this date. If your bill says "Delinquent" at the top, you must pay your bill in full by this date, or you could lose your coverage and you may not be able to get your coverage back right away. Partial payment may not stop you from losing your coverage.**

Your bill shows new amounts and past amounts we didn't get by your last bill's due date.

We got your last payment of ____________ on ____________

See other side for important information, including who to contact if you have questions.

Don't send notes or letters with your payment. Cut at dotted line and return bottom with payment.

Check here if your name or address has changed or is wrong, and complete the back of this paper.

Check here if the person has died.

Amount you are paying: $

Visa/MasterCard/American Express/Discover Number:

Expiration Date: (MM/YYYY)

Credit/Debit Card Billing ZIP Code:

Signature:

Medicare Number: [redacted]

Write your Medicare number on your check or money order.

Amount due: $433.80 Due in full by: 11/25/2020

Don't send cash. **Make check/money order payable to: CMS Medicare Insurance**

Send payment to:
MEDICARE PREMIUM COLLECTION CENTER
P.O. BOX 790355
ST. LOUIS, MO 63179-0355

Everyone Should Have A Personal MyMedicare.gov

- It is strongly recommended that an individual creates a MyMedicare.gov account to pay their bill online if the premium is not being deducted from their Social Security check. It is a secure and easy way for the individual to manage their bill. Enrolling in Medicare Easy Pay will ensure that the individual can set up a monthly reoccurring payment for their Part B premium.
- It is extremely easy for someone to create their own personal secure Medicare account at MyMedicare.gov. For those not enrolled in Medicare Easy Pay, they can log in and select the "Pay My Premium" in the middle of the page. They can pay by credit/debit card, checking, or savings account. In addition, they will get a confirmation number when they make their payment. It will show on their statement as "CMS Medicare Premiums."
- An individual should consider setting up a MyMedicare.gov account even if they do not need to pay a bill so they can manage their Medicare account and view their claims.

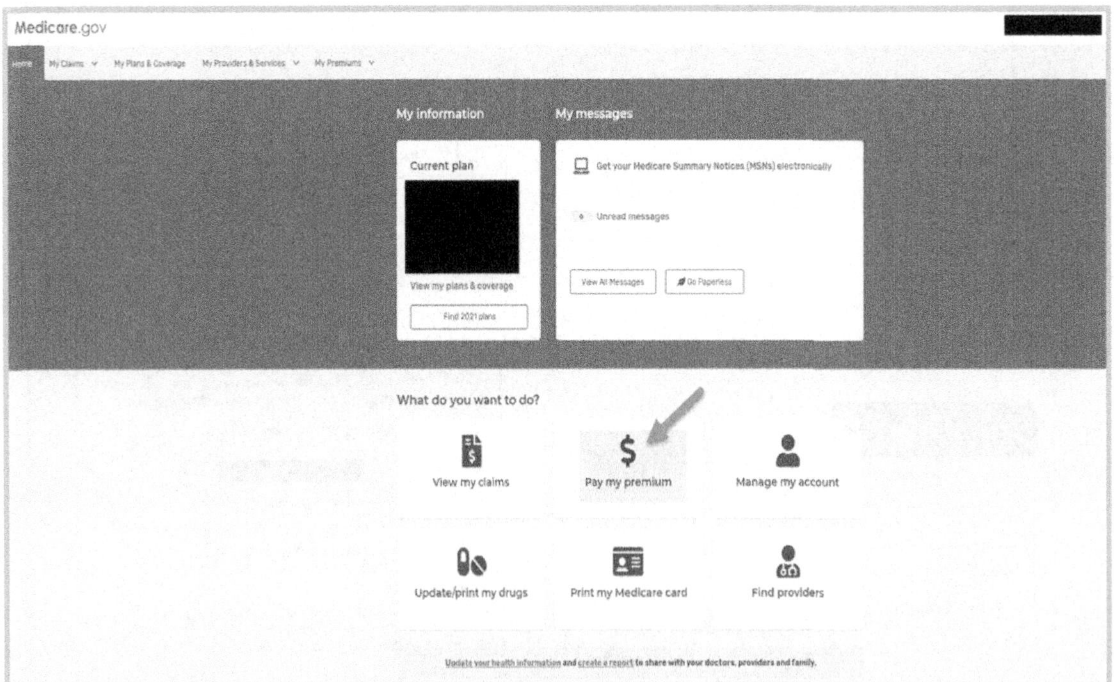

How Does Someone Pay Their IRMAA Bill?

- If someone owes IRMAA for Part B or D, they will pay that directly to Social Security. It can be automatically deducted from someone's Social Security retirement check.
- If someone is not drawing their Social Security retirement check but owe for IRMAA, they will receive a bill in the mail, or it will be added to their Medicare premium bill every three months.

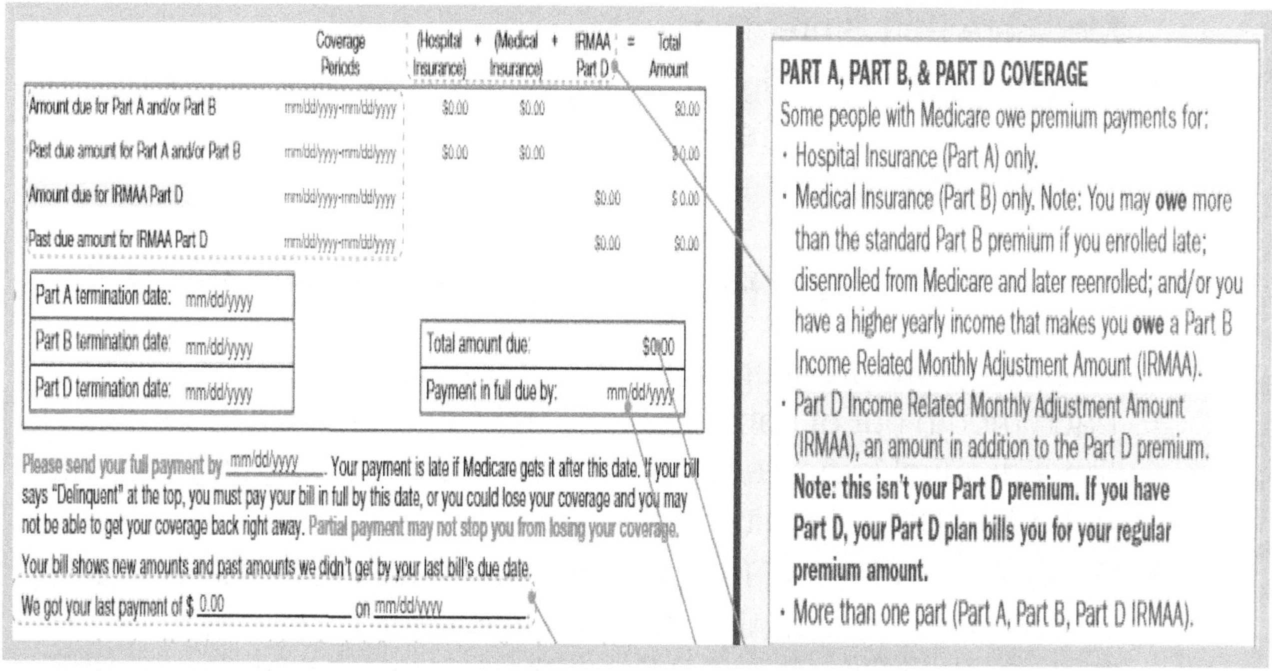

	Coverage Periods	(Hospital Insurance) +	(Medical Insurance) +	IRMAA Part D =	Total Amount
Amount due for Part A and/or Part B	mm/dd/yyyy-mm/dd/yyyy	$0.00	$0.00		$0.00
Past due amount for Part A and/or Part B	mm/dd/yyyy-mm/dd/yyyy	$0.00	$0.00		$0.00
Amount due for IRMAA Part D	mm/dd/yyyy-mm/dd/yyyy			$0.00	$0.00
Past due amount for IRMAA Part D	mm/dd/yyyy-mm/dd/yyyy			$0.00	$0.00

Part A termination date: mm/dd/yyyy
Part B termination date: mm/dd/yyyy
Part D termination date: mm/dd/yyyy

Total amount due: $0.00
Payment in full due by: mm/dd/yyyy

Please send your full payment by mm/dd/yyyy. Your payment is late if Medicare gets it after this date. If your bill says "Delinquent" at the top, you must pay your bill in full by this date, or you could lose your coverage and you may not be able to get your coverage back right away. Partial payment may not stop you from losing your coverage.

Your bill shows new amounts and past amounts we didn't get by your last bill's due date.

We got your last payment of $ 0.00 on mm/dd/yyyy

PART A, PART B, & PART D COVERAGE

Some people with Medicare owe premium payments for:

- Hospital Insurance (Part A) only.
- Medical Insurance (Part B) only. Note: You may **owe** more than the standard Part B premium if you enrolled late; disenrolled from Medicare and later reenrolled; and/or you have a higher yearly income that makes you **owe** a Part B Income Related Monthly Adjustment Amount (IRMAA).
- Part D Income Related Monthly Adjustment Amount (IRMAA), an amount in addition to the Part D premium. **Note: this isn't your Part D premium. If you have Part D, your Part D plan bills you for your regular premium amount.**
- More than one part (Part A, Part B, Part D IRMAA).

How Does Someone Pay For Part C?

- If someone has a Part C Medicare Advantage plan that has a $0 premium, they will not need to pay anything to the private insurance company they enrolled with for the coverage. If the private insurance company is charging a monthly premium for the plan, it can be deducted from the Social Security retirement check, or the individual can set up a payment plan with the private insurance company.

Medicare Premiums Must Still Be Paid With Part C

- The individual must have both Medicare Part A and B in order to enroll in a Part C Medicare Advantage.
- Although the Medicare Advantage plan is an alternative plan to Medicare through a private insurance company, the individual is still required to pay the standard Medicare Part B premium for 2022, which is $170.10 per month. This individual will still need to follow the same guidelines as outlined on how to pay the Medicare Part B premium.
- When someone is eligible for Medicare, they will always have to pay their Medicare premium regardless of what option they choose to go with for their coverage.

Medicare Premiums Follow The Same Guidelines

- The Medicare premium will either get automatically deducted each month out of someone's Social Security or RRB benefits. If the individual is *not* receiving their retirement benefits, they will get a Medicare premium bill in the mail.
- Even if the individual has a $0 premium Medicare Advantage plan that includes MAPD, they will still be responsible for IRMAA for both their Part B and D if you they are a high-income earner.
- If the Part C Medicare Advantage plan has a monthly premium, the individual can automatically have that deducted each month out of their Social Security or RRB benefits. They can also elect to have it set up as a payment plan with the private insurance company for that portion of their premium.

Part C Are Annual Contracts That Do Not Change

- Here is the reason an individual can have their Medicare Advantage plan monthly premiums and their Part B premium deducted from their Social Security check. The monthly premium is an annual contract that will not change during that calendar year. Both the Part B and/or the monthly premium charged by the Part C Medicare Advantage company are predictable.
- Always keep in mind that with Part C Medicare Advantage plans, the individual is still always responsible for the Part B premium and for IRMAA, if applicable.

How Does Someone Pay For Part D?

- If someone has a standalone PDP, they can have the monthly premium automatically deducted from their retirement benefit check each month if they are getting Social Security or RRB benefits. Many of those who are Medicare eligible choose to pay their monthly premium this way because it is convenient.
- The individual can also choose to receive a bill from the private insurance company handling their standalone PDP and pay them directly by setting up a payment plan.
- If someone owes for Part D IRMAA, they can have it deducted directly from their Social Security retirement check. If they do not receive a Social Security retirement check, they will get a Medicare premium bill which will instruct them on how to pay the premium.

Chapter 3

What Medicare Covers — Everything You Need To Know

What Does Medicare Cover?

- When someone asks what Original Medicare will cover, here is a good response: “If it is medically necessary, Medicare will cover it.”

- Now there are some things that Medicare will *not* cover that we will go over in the next section.
- To be a Medicare expert means that you must fully understand the foundation of Medicare so you can keep this simple and easy to understand.

Medicare Part A — Hospital Coverage

- Part A is the hospital side of Medicare. Think of it as the room and board when someone is admitted into the hospital. It will cover a semi-private room (will cover a private room, if medically necessary), meals, nursing, drugs as part of their stay, and other hospital services and supplies. The individual will get the treatment and coverage they need if they find themselves admitted to the hospital.
- If someone needs a blood transfusion, which has not been donated and the hospital needs to buy the blood for them, the individual will be responsible for the first three pints during that calendar year. Medicare Part A will pick up the cost after the first three pints. Most Medigap Supplement plans on the market will step in and pay for the first three pints for the individual leaving that person with no out-of-pocket costs for any blood transfusions.

Get Familiar With The 4 Things Part A Covers

- Here are the four primary things that Medicare Part A covers:
    - Hospital inpatient care,
    - Skilled nursing facility care,
    - Home health care, and
    - Hospice.

Hospital Inpatient Care

- When thinking in terms of an inpatient hospital stay, it's important to understand that the average stay is approximately 4.5 days.
- Once someone is admitted to the hospital, they will have a deductible that will be their responsibility. In 2022, the deductible for Part A is $1,556.
- Medicare Part A will cover everything for the individual's inpatient hospital stay for up to 60 consecutive days except for the $1,556 deductible.
- Hospitals are not going to keep someone in an inpatient hospital setting for 60 consecutive days. The days of being in the hospital as an inpatient for a long period of time are a thing of the past because of costs and the need for the hospital beds.

What To Always Keep In Mind About Part A Deductible

- The key to remember about Part A is that the $1,556 deductible is unique to Medicare because it is a benefit period deductible. Most all insurance deductibles are annual deductibles because they cover all aspects of health care. Medicare Part A is different because it only focuses on one thing — the hospital.
- The Part A deductible is good for 60 days starting from the day someone is admitted. If someone were admitted for 4.5 days, which is the average, then their responsibility in 2022 would be the $1,556 deductible.
- If someone were admitted again anytime during those 60 days, they would not be responsible for the $1,556 deductible again because it was within the 60-day benefit.

What If Someone Was In For More Than 60 Days?

- If an individual found themselves admitted to a hospital for longer than 60 consecutive days in 2022, here is what would happen under the Medicare Part A:
    - Days 1-60: $1,556 covers you for that benefit period.
    - Days 61-90: $389 coinsurance per day for that benefit period.
    - Days 91 and beyond: $778 coinsurance per each "lifetime reserve day" after day 90 for that benefit period (you only get up to 60 "lifetime reserve days" in your lifetime).

How The Lifetime Reserve Days Work With Medicare

- Here is how the coinsurance of $778 per day of "lifetime reserve days" works. If someone found themselves admitted to the hospital for 90 days, on day 91 Medicare would give that individual an additional 60 days in their lifetime that they could use.
- For example, if the individual were in the hospital as an inpatient for 100 consecutive days and then discharged, they would have used 10 lifetime reserve days.
    - In this example, it would leave the individual with 50 days of lifetime reserve days since they only used 10 days out of their 60-day allotment.
- If this same individual found themselves admitted again to the hospital for more than 90 consecutive days, they would have 50 days of lifetime reserve days left that they could use. If those 50 days were used, that individual in this example would be responsible for *all* costs.

Medigap Supplement Can Add An Additional 365 Days

- It is extremely unlikely that any scenario would have someone admitted to a hospital for 60 consecutive days. To be fully prepared for any scenario under the current rules, Part A will provide some coverage to anyone admitted to the hospital for almost a full consecutive five months. After five consecutive months of being in the hospital, the individual would be responsible for *all* costs.
- Here is where a Medigap Supplement plan would provide incredible coverage. A Medigap Supplement plan will cover the Part A deductible and the per day coinsurance including the lifetime reserve days. The individual would have no out-of-pocket expenses under Part A for the full consecutive five months.
- If the individual found themselves in the hospital for more than five consecutive months, the Medigap Supplement would step in and pay for an additional 365 days. Theoretically, that means someone could be in the hospital for almost a full 17 months and the hospital charges would be completely paid for by Medicare Part A *and* the Medigap Supplement company.

Skilled Nursing Facility Care

- When thinking in terms of skilled nursing facility care, it's important to understand that the average stay is approximately 28 days.
- A skilled nursing facility is an inpatient rehabilitation facility that is intended for short term use. It is designed to help someone recover from an inpatient hospital surgery or a chronic condition that will still require 24-hour care for the individual.

Skilled Nursing Facility Is Not A Nursing Home

- Many individuals confuse a skilled nursing facility with a nursing home. A nursing home is for long-term residential care, which is different from short-term skilled nursing care. What makes things sometimes confusing is that there are some nursing homes that also have a section that is used as a skilled nursing facility.
- We will discuss this more in depth in the next section, but Medicare will *not* cover care in a residential nursing home because that is not intended for short-term care.
- A skilled nursing facility is covered by Medicare Part A because it is used for a limited number of days and not for long-term care. Think of a skilled nursing facility as an extension of someone's inpatient hospital stay.

Think Of A Skilled Nursing Facility As A "Pit Stop"

- Think of the skilled nursing facility as the "pit stop" between the hospital and someone's home. It is designed to get the individual the skilled care that they still need in the form of nursing and therapy in order to get them back on their feet.
- Skilled nursing facilities will have licensed nurses, physical and occupational therapists, as well as those specializing in speech and hearing. A speech or hearing specialist might be needed for someone who had a stroke.

Difference Between "Admitted" Vs. "Observation"

- Knowing the difference between admitted vs. under observation is quite important when discussing the hospital stay. Currently, Medicare requires that someone be admitted as an inpatient in the hospital for three days in order to be covered by Part A in a skilled nursing facility.

- Here is why knowing the difference between admitted vs. under observation is so important when it comes to understanding which part of Medicare it will fall under. When an individual is admitted to the hospital, it will fall under Part A. If the individual is placed under observation, it will fall under Part B.
- At the present time in 2022, Medicare will only cover an individual's skilled nursing facility under Part A, which means they must have been admitted to the hospital.

What Goes Into How The Status Is Determined?

- There are guidelines that the hospital must follow that are outlined by Medicare as to what status the individual will fall under when they arrive at the hospital.
- To make it easy to understand, the guidelines set forth by Medicare outline that a status of admitted is viewed as a serious condition and under observation is viewed as a not serious condition. It sounds simple, but there is much more that goes into determining the status.
- When someone is under observation, the hospital has determined that the condition does not require the need for care longer than 48 hours. Someone could arrive at the hospital and be initially under observation, but then later determined that it is more serious and placed as admitted.

Skilled Nursing Facility And The "3-day Rule"

- At the present time in 2022, for Medicare to cover any part of a skilled nursing facility stay, the individual must have been admitted (serious) to the hospital. That individual must also have been admitted to the hospital for a minimum of three days, which is called the "3-day rule."

- Due to the nature of how this could affect which part of Medicare is billed for services, hospitals are required to disclose to someone if they have been admitted or just under observation.
- If someone has been admitted and meets the requirements of the 3-day rule, they will be eligible for skilled nursing facility coverage under Medicare Part A. Medicare Part A will provide 20 days at no cost to the individual for skilled nursing facility care.

What If Someone Needs Longer Than 20 Days?

- Here is what would happen if someone needed to be in a skilled nursing facility for longer than the 20 days:
  - Days 1-20: $0 for that benefit period.
  - Days 21-100: $194.50 coinsurance (2022) per day for that benefit period.
  - Days 101 and beyond: The individual is responsible for all costs.
- If the individual had a Medigap Supplement plan in 2022, it would cover the $194.50 coinsurance per day from days 21-100. This would give someone a little more than a full three months of not having to worry about any out-of-pocket costs in the skilled nursing facility. Remember, the skilled nursing facility is designed for short-term care.

Home Health Care

- When thinking in terms of home health care, it is important to understand that the average length of care for services is approximately 41.5 days.
- Here is the good news when it comes to how home health care is covered by Medicare. Medicare will cover *all* costs under either Medicare Part A or B if someone is determined that they

are homebound, which means it will be difficult for them to leave their home. Therefore, they need skilled care.

- For Medicare Part A to cover someone's home health care at no cost, they must have been admitted to a hospital for at least three consecutive days and need the home health care treatment within 14 days of being discharged from the hospital or skilled nursing facility.

How Home Health Care Is Covered Under Part A

- Medicare Part A will cover the home health care at no cost to the individual for the first 100 days if they are needing services within 14 days after being discharged from a hospital or skilled nursing facility.
- Medicare Part A will cover home health care under what they consider part-time or "intermittent" skilled nursing care. Skilled care will include assistance such as physical therapy, occupational therapy, speech therapy, etc., which are coordinated between the patient's doctor and a certified home health care agency.
- Medicare Part A or B will *not* cover home health care if it is considered personal care for assistance such as 24-hour-a-day care at home or meal delivery. Medicare will also consider things like shopping, cleaning, laundry, bathing, dressing, or using the bathroom as personal care when that is the only care the individual is needing.
- Home health care must always be predictable and have an ending point to be covered under either Medicare Part A or B.

How Home Health Care Is Covered Under Part B

- If the individual is still needing the services of home health care for more than 100 days after being discharged from the hospital or skilled nursing facility, it will automatically be covered by Part B. Medicare Part B will cover *all* costs and the person would not be responsible for the deductible or coinsurance.

- Home health care has different rules than a skilled nursing facility. Medicare Part B can still cover all costs for an individual without them having to meet the inpatient three-day hospital stay requirement.

Requirement For Home Health Care Under Part A or B

- Here are the requirements needed for Medicare to cover home health care services under Part A or B:
    - The doctor believes that the individual must be homebound and will need the part-time services of skilled nursing care in their home.
    - The patient's doctor must be the one to order the home health care services and prescribe a plan of treatment. The doctor must certify that the individual is homebound, meaning it will be too difficult for the individual to leave their home for treatment.
    - The doctor will then coordinate the care with a certified home health care agency approved by Medicare. The patient's doctor must review the plan every 60 days.
- Home health care is for part-time or intermittent skilled nursing care or therapy of usually two to three visits a week. If someone requires full-time nursing care, Medicare will not approve the home health care. The home health care must be predictable and have an ending point.

How Durable Medicare Equipment Is Covered

- If an individual needs durable medical equipment when they are receiving home health care services, it will fall under the medical side which is Part B. Medicare does *not* cover all the costs of durable medical equipment. The individual will be responsible for 20 percent of any durable medical equipment used during their home health care services.

- Here is some commonly prescribed durable medical equipment used during home health care:
  - Walkers;
  - Crutches;
  - Wheelchairs;
  - Scooters;
  - Home hospital bed;
  - Oxygen equipment;
  - Nebulizers;
  - Continuous positive airway pressure (CPAP) machines;
  - Blood sugar monitors, test strips, and lancets; and
  - Insulin pumps and insulin.

Hospice

- When thinking in terms of hospice, it is important to understand that the average stay or care for services in the United States is 77.9 days.
- Hospice is designed to cover the end-of-life care and make things as comfortable for someone with prescription drugs for symptom control or pain relief. Hospice can be provided in someone's home or at a facility.
- If it has been certified that they are terminally ill with a life expectancy of 6 months or less, Medicare Part A will cover all costs for hospice care for an individual.

Hospice Starts When Agreeing To Comfort Care

- The individual must agree to comfort care (palliative care), which means they are no longer seeking treatment for a cure to their illness.
- If an individual still requires hospice services after 6 months, they will need the doctor or a hospice doctor to confirm that they are still terminally ill for Medicare Part A to continue to cover all costs.
- Medicare Part A will take over for individuals who are in a Part C Medicare Advantage plan as soon as they have agreed to comfort care (palliative care) and are no longer seeking treatment for a cure to their illness.

Medicare Part B — Medical Coverage

- Part B is the medical side of Medicare. This part of Medicare is the most used because it covers all the outpatient medical treatment that is needed outside of the hospital.
- Here are some of the most common services that are used under Part B:
    - Doctor visits (primary and specialist),
    - Preventative care,
    - Outpatient surgeries and procedures,
    - Durable medical equipment,
    - Chemotherapy, and
    - Ambulance use.

Medicare Part B Deductible

- Medicare Part B has a deductible that must be paid *first* before Medicare pays anything for medical expenses. For 2022, the Part B deductible is only $233 and is a calendar year deductible. Medicare's calendar year runs from January 1 through December 31.

- Once the Part B deductible has been met for the calendar year, the individual will be responsible for a 20 percent coinsurance. Medicare will pay 80 percent and the individual would be responsible for the remaining 20 percent.

The Problem With Medicare's Coinsurance

- Medicare does not deal in co-payments like most group or individual plans. They operate based on coinsurance.
- The problem with Medicare is that unlike most health insurance plans available on the market, Medicare Part B does not have any annual cap or stop loss for the remaining 20 percent coinsurance. That is the individual's responsibility.

Medicare Part B Deductible Over The Years

- The Medicare Part B deductible like the monthly Part B premiums change every year due to health care costs. Here is a look back at the Part B deductible for the last 10 years:
    - 2021 Medicare Part B Deductible: $203
    - 2020 Medicare Part B Deductible: $198
    - 2019 Medicare Part B Deductible: $185
    - 2018 Medicare Part B Deductible: $183
    - 2017 Medicare Part B Deductible: $183
    - 2016 Medicare Part B Deductible: $166
    - 2015 Medicare Part B Deductible: $147
    - 2014 Medicare Part B Deductible: $147
    - 2013 Medicare Part B Deductible: $147
    - 2012 Medicare Part B Deductible: $140
    - 2011 Medicare Part B Deductible: $162

Two Types Of Services Covered Under Part B

- There are typically two types of services that Medicare Part B covers:
    - Preventative services, which prevent illness or detect health issues at an early stage.
    - Medically necessary services, which are health services or supplies that are used to diagnose and treat the medical condition.

Preventative Services

- Medicare Part B will typically pay *all* costs for all preventative services. The Part B deductible and the 20 percent coinsurance will not apply for preventative services.
- A glaucoma test is frequently listed under preventative and screening services, but Medicare does not pay all costs. If someone is at high risk for glaucoma, Medicare will cover a glaucoma test once a year, but the Part B deductible and 20 percent coinsurance will apply.

Common Preventative Services Covered By Part B

- Here is a list of some of the most common preventative services that Medicare will cover at no cost to the individual. There are more, but these are the most common.
    - One-time "Welcome to Medicare" preventative visit: This is covered within 12 months of getting Part B. This visit is to review the individual's medical history and let them know of screenings, shots, and the frequency of preventive services that are specific to their needs as they get older.
    - Yearly "wellness" visit:
      This is just a yearly checkup with the doctor for them to

recommend or update someone's prescriptions and discuss any health concerns they may be having or want to discuss with them. Routine procedures such as checking height, weight and blood pressure are performed during this visit.)

- Mammograms:
  Recommended every 12 months for women 40 or older.
- Pap tests and pelvic exams:
  Covered once every 24 months or covered once every 12 months for women at high risk.
- Prostate cancer screenings:
  Recommended every 12 months for men 50 or older.
- Colonoscopy screening:
  Recommended once every 24 months if someone is high risk. If they are not high risk, then once every 10 years.
- Bone mass measurements:
  Covered once every 24 months.
- Cardiovascular disease screenings:
  (Covered cardiovascular screening blood tests once every 5 years.
- Diabetes screenings:
  If someone is at risk for diabetes, laboratory tests will be covered up to 2 screenings per year.
- Flu shots:
  Covered oncer per year.

Primary Care and Specialist Visits

- Primary care physicians (PCPs) and specialists are covered under Medicare Part B. Currently in the United States, almost 93 percent* of all doctors accept Medicare Parts A and B. There are no referrals required to see a specialist under Original Medicare.

  *Courtesy: https://www.kff.org/medicare/issue-brief/primary-care-physicians-accepting-medicare-a-snapshot/

Outpatient Surgeries and Procedures

- Medicare Part B will cover any medically necessary outpatient surgery or procedures. Here are some of the most common:
    - Knee/hip replacement,
    - Breast biopsy,
    - Angioplasty or stent placement,
    - Physical or speech therapy, and
    - X-rays, MRI, or CT scans.

Durable Medical Equipment

- Medicare Part B will cover any medically necessary durable medical equipment that someone could medically need. Here are some of the most common:
    - Walkers;
    - Crutches;
    - Wheelchairs;
    - Scooters;
    - Home hospital bed;
    - Oxygen equipment;
    - Nebulizers;
    - Continuous positive airway pressure (CPAP) machines;
    - Blood sugar monitors, test strips, and lancets; and
    - Insulin pumps and insulin.

Chemotherapy and Part B Drugs

- Medicare Part B will cover medically necessary items such as chemotherapy and some experimental Part B drugs. Infusions such as those used for dialysis treatments at a facility or at home would also be covered.
- Any type of medically necessary shots or infusions will typically be covered under Medicare Part B, as well as vaccines.

Ambulance Services

- When it is medically necessary, Medicare Part B will cover ground ambulance transportation. Someone may need to be transported to a hospital or skilled nursing facility because traveling in any other vehicle would endanger their life.
- If it were medically necessary due to the critical nature of the situation, Medicare Part B will also cover transportation in an airplane or helicopter.

Acupuncture

- As of 2020, Medicare Part B will now cover acupuncture when it is medically necessary to treat chronic lower back pain. Until 2020, Medicare would not cover acupuncture to treat any condition. Medicare is quite specific that it must only be used to treat chronic lower back pain.
- Medicare will cover up to 12 visits in 90 days. If someone shows improvement after 12 visits, Medicare will cover another 8 visits. Medicare Part B will cover up to 20 visits in any calendar year.

Chiropractic Services

- When medically necessary, Medicare Part B will cover chiropractic services for what they call "manual manipulation of the spine," which means that the vertebrae are misaligned in the spine from its normal position, and it needs to be corrected. This is something that someone cannot do on their own to correct it.
- The PCP or specialist will order an X-ray to determine whether someone needs chiropractor services to realign their spine. If the services or tests are ordered by the chiropractor, Medicare will *not* cover them.

- Medicare will *not* cover chiropractic services used for maintenance or preventative services.

Cataract Surgery

- When it is medically necessary, Medicare Part B will cover cataract surgery. Cataract surgery can also be classified under outpatient surgeries and procedures.
- Medicare does *not* cover routine eye exams, glasses or contact lenses, which we will talk about in the next section. However, Medicare will pay for one pair of eyeglasses with standard frames or one set of contact lenses after someone's cataract surgery.
- Cataracts occur when there is a clouding of the eye's natural lenses as you get older making it feel like you are looking through a fogged-up window.

Cataracts And Lasik Surgery Are Not The Same

- During the outpatient cataract surgery, the ophthalmologist will replace the natural lens with an artificial one. Medicare will cover the exams and surgery and pay for basic traditional lenses to be implanted to remove the cataracts.
- Many ophthalmologists might recommend a newer upgraded lens that is not considered medically necessary by Medicare or most insurance companies. It's almost like getting a cataract and Lasik surgery at the same time. For those who decided to go with the upgraded lenses that are not covered by Medicare, it will be on average about $1,500 per eye.

Hearing and Balance Exams

- Medicare Part B will cover diagnostic hearing and balance exams if someone's doctor feels it is medically necessary for them to see if medical treatment is required for a condition.

- Typically, this exam is used to check for hearing loss or to diagnose the cause of either dizziness or vertigo.
- Unfortunately, if it is determined that someone could use hearing aids in order to help with hearing loss, Medicare will not cover the cost of hearing aids, which we will discuss in the next section.

Medicare Part C — Medicare Advantage

- Part C Medicare Advantage plans are required by law to offer the same if not better coverage than Medicare Part A and B.
- Medicare Advantage plans are offered by private insurance companies approved by Medicare and must provide both hospital and medical coverage in any plan that they offer.
- Most Medicare Advantage plans will also offer prescription drug coverage at no additional cost within the plan, making them like group and individual health insurance.

The Difference Between Part C and Original Medicare

- The main difference between Part C Medicare Advantage is that copayments, deductibles, and coinsurance are not standardized like they are with Original Medicare Part A and B.
- Every Part C Medicare Advantage plan offers different plans and benefits with their own out-of-pocket costs specific to that plan and geographic area that it services.
- Although Part C Medicare Advantage plans are network based like health maintenance organizations (HMOs) or preferred provider organizations (PPOs), they will cover someone out of network for an emergency.

Most Part C Will Cover Prescription Coverage

- Part C Medicare Advantage plans on the market may also offer prescription drug coverage as an additional benefit within the plan. Although they are not required to do so by law, most plans will offer it.

- Those plans that do cover prescription drugs are referred to as Medicare Advantage Prescription Drug (MAPD) and those that do not are referred to as Medicare Advantage (MA).
- Many of the Part C Medicare Advantage plans will also offer some extra benefits that you do not get with Original Medicare Part A and B, which can make them attractive.

Most Part C Will Cover Some Additional Benefits

- Additional benefits that are included in many Medicare Advantage Part C plans will be some of the following:
  - Vision benefits
  - Dental benefits
  - Hearing benefits
  - Transportation benefits
  - Meal delivery benefits
  - Fitness benefits, and
  - Over-the-counter benefits

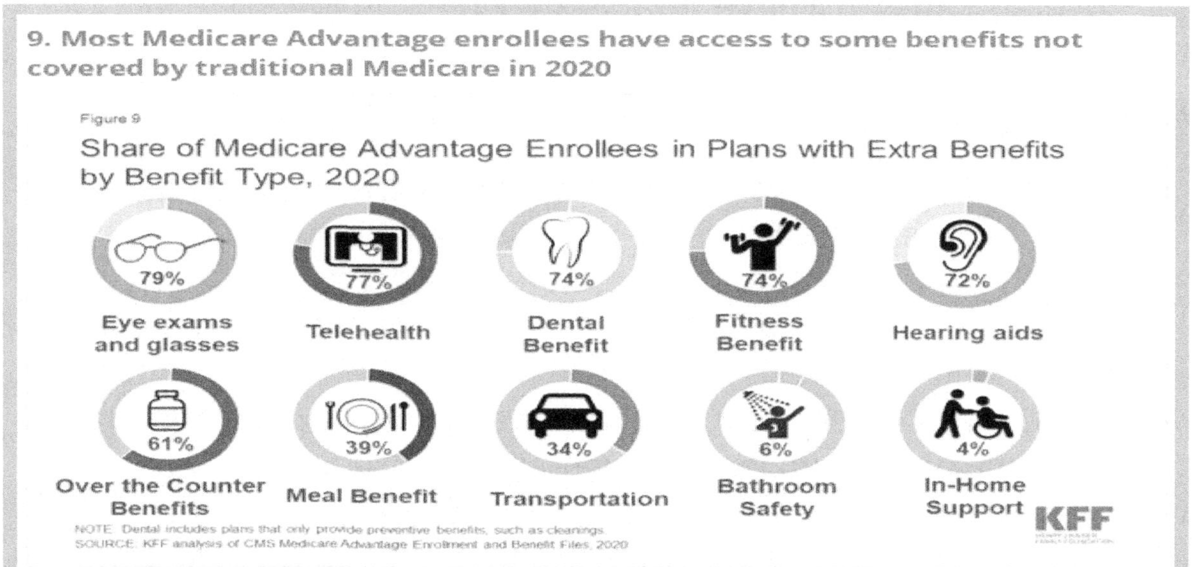

Figure 9: Share of Medicare Advantage Enrollees in Plans with Extra Benefits by Benefit Type, 2020

Courtesy of Kaiser Family Foundation: https://www.kff.org/medicare/issue-brief/a-dozen-facts-about-medicare-advantage-in-2020/

Medicare Part D — Prescription Drug Coverage

- Part D is the drug side of Medicare, which helps cover most of the prescribed medications that someone will take on a regular basis at home outside of a hospital setting.
- The two things that Part D will typically cover for someone will be oral pills and insulin.
- The Part D plans are provided by private insurance companies that are approved and overseen by Medicare to provide someone with prescription drug coverage.

Part D Is Offered In One Of Two Ways

- Medicare Part D is offered through private insurance companies as either one of the following:
  - PDP or
  - MADP.
- An individual that has Original Medicare Part A and B will select a standalone PDP. For an individual who enrolls into a Medicare Advantage Part C plan that includes prescription drug coverage, they will have what is known as an MAPD.

What Is Typically Covered Under Part D

- All Part D drug plans will typically cover both the brand name and the generic medications; however, the brand name medications will cost someone more out-of-pocket. Whenever possible, it is most cost effective for someone to be prescribed the generic version.
- Part D plans must cover an extensive list of prescriptions that are commonly taken by those who are on Medicare. Each plan will have what is called a "formulary" that will show all the prescription drugs that are covered on the plan. Most of the time the individual will find their prescription on the formulary

list. If not, there will be a similar medication they can be prescribed.

- Part D companies are required to provide at least two drugs minimum in each of the commonly prescribed drug categories. If a prescribed medication is not on the formulary and there is not a generic version or equivalent, someone can request an exception for that medication since there is nothing else that they can take that is equivalent.

Chapter 4

What Medicare Does Not Cover — Everything You Need To Know

What Medicare Does Not Cover?

- If something is medically necessary, the odds are that Medicare Part A and/or B will cover it for the individual. However, there are things that you should be aware of that Medicare Part A and/or B will *not* cover.

- There are seven core services that Medicare Part A and/or B will not cover.

7 Services Medicare Does Not Consider Necessary

- Here are seven services in 2022 that Original Medicare Part A and/or B do not currently consider medically necessary:
    - Long-term care (also called custodial care),
    - Most dental care,
    - Eye exams related to prescribing glasses,
    - Dentures,
    - Cosmetic surgery,
    - Hearing aid and exams for fitting them, and
    - Routine foot care.

Medicare Is Always Looking To Improve Its Services

- Medicare is always looking at ways to improve the health care services that it covers; therefore, we may see some of the seven services that are not currently covered as medically necessary available in the future.
- Up until 2020, Medicare would not cover acupuncture to treat any condition because they did not feel it was medically necessary. If it is medically necessary to treat chronic lower back pain, it is now covered.
- Medicare Part A and/or B will not cover any of the seven services we discussed; however, there are always circumstances where Medicare will consider it “medically necessary” and cover it.
- Some of these seven services might be provided as additional benefits under a Medicare Advantage plan, which could be an attractive option to consider. Long-term nursing home care is *not* covered under Medicare Part A or B or through a Part C Medicare Advantage plan. If an individual cannot afford nursing

home care, they would need to look at Medicaid for financial assistance.

Medicare Part A — Hospital Coverage

- As we discussed earlier, Medicare Part A is the hospital side of Medicare. Medicare is different than group, individual, or a Part C Medicare Advantage plan, which include all their health care services in an all-in-one plan. Medicare Part A is known for inpatient hospitalization and will also cover other services such as skilled nursing facility care, home health care, and hospice care.
- Let's look at some services that currently Medicare Part A does *not* cover unless determined medically necessary.

Skilled Nursing Facility Admitted "3-Day Rule"

- It is worth going over again the admitted vs. under observation rule when it comes to the Medicare Part A.
- In the previous section, we discussed that a skilled nursing facility must be viewed as a direct extension of the inpatient hospital stay. We referred to as the pit stop between the inpatient hospital stay and being able to go home and not needing 24-hour care.
- Medicare currently as of 2022, requires that an individual be admitted as an inpatient to the hospital for at least three days in order to be covered under Part A at a skilled nursing facility. If the individual is placed under observation during their hospital stay, it will not fall under Part A.
- This hospital stay would fall under Part B, which would not cover a skilled nursing facility stay regardless if the individual had spent three days in the hospital. For Medicare to cover a skilled nursing facility stay, it must fall under Part A.

Private Room — Hospital or Skilled Nursing Facility

- If someone is admitted to the hospital because of an unfortunate situation to treat an illness or injury, Medicare Part A will not cover a private room. The same will hold true if an individual went to a skilled nursing facility. Medicare will try to save on costs; therefore, the individual will more than likely be in a room with a roommate.
- If it is determined that it is medically necessary for the individual to have a private room, Medicare Part A will cover it. There is always an exception to the private room, but someone cannot just request or expect that Medicare Part A will cover a private room.
- Medicare Part A will not cover private doctors or nursing care. The doctors and nurses that are assigned to someone will also be treating other patients in that hospital or facility.
- Personal items like razors, deodorant, toothbrush, toothpaste, and slippers are typically not covered by Medicare Part A. Any type of toiletry will be the responsibility of the individual in a hospital or skilled nursing facility.

First Three Pints Of Blood

- Medicare Part A will *not* pay for the first three pints of blood unless the blood bank does not charge them for it, or someone has donated the blood specifically for an individual.
- One pint of blood can typically save up to three lives. If for some reason someone needed more than one pint, it would more than likely be a critical situation. The cost for a pint of blood is usually sold to a hospital for around $150.
- A benefit to a Medigap Supplement plan is that it will cover the first three pints that Medicare Part A will not cover.

Foreign Travel

- Foreign travel is usually not covered under either Medicare Part A or B; however, there are some exceptions to this rule such as:
    - If the individual was onboard a ship that was in territorial waters joining U.S. land.
    - A foreign hospital is closer than the nearest U.S. hospital.
- It is important to always keep in mind that Original Medicare was designed for treatment and coverage in the U.S. and not for foreign travel.

Get Foreign Travel Insurance When Going Abroad

- When an individual is going to be traveling abroad, the best advice is to look at additional foreign travel coverage. An individual should contact their credit card company to see what existing coverage they may have for foreign travel as a member.

Many credit cards will have built in travel insurance, which might be enough coverage for that individual.

- If the credit card does not offer the coverage that is needed for that individual, there are some additional policies someone can purchase by just searching “travel insurance policies for seniors” on the computer.

How Foreign Travel Works With Other Insurance

- Medigap Supplement Plans C, D, F, G, M and N will offer foreign travel emergency care as an additional benefit not offered by Original Medicare.
- There is a lifetime benefit of $50,000 offered under the plan, which can be used during the first 60 days of each foreign trip. There is an initial $250 calendar year deductible, and the individual is responsible for 20 percent coinsurance up to the $50,000 lifetime benefit.
- Some Medicare Advantage plans may also offer some additional benefit for emergency foreign travel.

Nursing Home Care

- Nursing home care is the biggest and most misunderstood topic when it comes to what Medicare will *not* cover. Nursing home care always comes up as the first thing that Medicare Part A will not cover. It is usually listed as long-term care or custodial care.
- Medicare will cover part-time or intermittent care services such as a skilled nursing facility and home health care because they are predictable and have an ending point. Medicare will not cover what the dictionary defines as a nursing home — a private institution providing residential accommodations with health care, especially for elderly people.

Better Understanding Of Nursing Home Care

- A nursing home is for someone who will need help with everyday activities such as dressing, feeding, bathing, and toileting and will need their meals provided for them because they cannot do it on their own.
- The costs associated with a nursing home can be quite expensive. The average nursing home cost can be around $8,000 a month or higher.
- If someone cannot afford the cost of a nursing home, they would need to liquidate their assets and exhaust their savings in order to qualify for assistance under their state's Medicaid program. Medicaid is the most common way to pay for nursing home care for an individual who does not have the means to afford the care.

Medicare Part B — Medical Coverage

- As we discussed earlier, Medicare Part B is the medical side of Medicare. Medicare is different than group, individual, or a Part C Medicare Advantage plan, which include all their health care services in an all-in-one plan. Medicare Part B typically covers doctor visits, including primary and specialist, preventative care, outpatient surgeries and procedures, durable medical equipment, chemotherapy, and even ambulance service.
- Let us look at some services that currently Medicare Part B will *not* cover unless determined medically necessary.

Dental Care

- Medicare will *not* cover any preventative, basic, or major dental services, which is probably the biggest concern for those going onto Medicare. Services that many individuals have been accustomed to such as preventative routine checkups, cleanings, and X-rays are not covered by Medicare.

- Basic dental services such as fillings, tooth extractions, root canals are also not covered. Major dental services such as crowns, bridges, and tooth implants are also not covered.
- If someone is needing coverage for dental services when they're Medicare eligible, there are typically two ways that an individual can get coverage.
  - There are many Medicare Advantage plans that will include some sort of dental coverage for the member.
  - The other option available is to purchase a standalone dental plan. Many standalone plans will also include dental, vision, and hearing coverage referred to as a dental, vision, and hearing plan (DVH) for approximately $30 a month.

Dentures

- Medicare will *not* cover dentures, which would fall under the category of dental care and Part B. This is an area that can be quite costly since dentures can run upwards of $3,000.
- If someone is needing coverage for dentures when Medicare eligible, there are typically two ways that an individual can get coverage.
  - There are many Medicare Advantage plans that will include some sort of coverage for dentures for the member.
  - The other option available is to purchase a standalone dental plan. Many standalone plans will also include dentures in their dental coverage along with vision and hearing referred to as a DVH plan for approximately $30 a month.

Eye Exams, Eyeglasses, And Contact Lenses

- Medicare will *not* cover routine eye exams, eyeglasses, or contact lenses, which would fall under Part B. The one exception to the rule is that Medicare will pay for one set of glasses or one set of contact lenses when someone has cataract surgery.

- If someone is needing coverage for vision when Medicare eligible, there are typically two ways that an individual can get coverage.
    - There are many Medicare Advantage plans that will include some sort of coverage for vision for the member.
    - The other option available is to purchase a standalone vision plan that will cover routine eye exams, eyeglasses, or contact lenses. Many standalone plans will also include dental, vision, and hearing coverage referred to as a DVH plan for approximately $30 a month.

Cosmetic Surgery

- Medicare will *not* cover cosmetic surgery, which would typically fall under Part B unless medically necessary.
- Medicare would consider something medically necessary like breast reconstruction if someone had a mastectomy due to breast cancer.
- There are some Medicare Advantage plans in some areas that will offer additional benefits, which could be used for certain elective cosmetic surgeries.

Hearing Aids And Exams For Fitting Them

- Medicare will *not* cover hearing aids or the exams needed to fit them, which would fall under Part B. Medicare will only cover a diagnostic hearing and balance exam if someone's doctor felt it was medically necessary for them to see if treatment were needed for a condition.
- Hearing aids can be expensive and cost anywhere from $1,000 to almost $6,000.

- If someone is needing coverage for hearing aids when Medicare eligible, there are typically two ways that an individual can get coverage.
    - There are many Medicare Advantage plans that will include some sort of coverage for hearing aids for the member.
    - The other option available is to purchase a standalone hearing plan, which will cover hearing aids and the exams for fitting them. Many standalone plans will also include dental, vision, and hearing coverage referred to as a DVH plan for approximately $30 a month.

Routine Foot Care

- Medicare will *not* cover routine foot care, which could be classified as pedicures, toenail clippings, or the removal of corns and calluses, which would fall under Part B.
- If an individual needed to see a podiatrist for treatment related to diabetes or never damage with their feet, that would be something Medicare Part B would consider medically necessary. Medicare would also consider conditions such as foot injuries, bunions, heel spurs, and hammer toe as medically necessary.

Massage Therapy

- Medicare will *not* cover massage therapy, which would fall under Part B. It would be difficult to find this as an additional benefit offered by any Medicare Advantage plan.

Medicare Part C — Medicare Advantage

- Part C Medicare Advantage plans are required by law to offer the same, if not better, coverage than Medicare Part A and B. Medicare Advantage plans can also offer additional benefits that Original Medicare Part A and B will not cover.

- Part C Medicare Advantage plans are *not* standardized like Medicare A and B. Many will offer additional benefits like dental, vision, and hearing that someone will not find covered by Original Medicare Part A and B.

Medicare Part A and B Gives A Baseline To Follow

- Being familiar with what Medicare Part A and B will not cover now gives an individual a baseline to follow when it comes to comparing some of the additional benefits offered by a Part C Medicare Advantage plan.
- The individual must then take into consideration the pros and cons of the additional benefits offered by the Medicare Advantage plan compared to that of Original Medicare Part A and B.
- Whether an individual has their coverage through Medicare Part A and B or through a Part C Medicare Advantage plan, the one thing that they typically have in common is that *neither* will provide coverage for nursing home care.
- This is usually standard when looking at either Medicare Part A and B or Part C for health care coverage due to the ongoing costs associated with providing continued care through a nursing home facility.

Medicare Part D — Prescription Drug Coverage

- Part D is the drug side of Medicare, which will help cover most of the prescribed medications such as oral pills and insulin that an individual will take on a regular basis at home outside of a hospital setting.
- Medicare Part D plans will decide which medications will not be covered on their formulary; however, here is a list of some that are typically *not* covered by most plans:
    - Fertility drugs,
    - Erectile dysfunction drugs,

    - Anorexia, weight loss, or weight gain drugs,
    - Cosmetic drugs for hair growth, and
    - Over-the-counter medications.
- Over the years, vitamin B-12 injections have become popular for weight loss, but are typically not covered by Medicare Part D or Part B.

Medicare Advantage May Offer Over-The-Counter Medications

- Part D will typically *not* cover over-the-counter medications to treat conditions such as cold or cough symptoms. It must be prescribed by a doctor or physician for it to be covered under Part D.
- Here are some popular over-the-counter vitamins and minerals that typically are *not* covered by Part D:
    - Vitamin C, D, and E;
    - Fish oil;
    - Hair, skin, and nails with biotin;
    - Aspirin and pain relievers; and
    - Cough and cold medicines.
- Some Medicare Advantage plans will offer an additional benefit of a monthly allowance for popular over-the-counter medications. This could be a helpful benefit for some of the medications that are not covered by Part D.

Chapter 5

The Medicare Enrollment Periods — Everything You Need To Know

Original Medicare Enrollment Periods

- When it comes time for someone to enroll into Medicare, there are only three enrollment periods available that someone can use to get Medicare Part A and/or B:
    - Initial Enrollment Period (IEP),
    - Special Enrollment Period (SEP), and
    - General Enrollment Period (GEP).

Become An Expert In The Three Enrollment Periods

- In order to become an expert in Medicare, it is extremely important to get familiar with each one of the three enrollment periods for Medicare Part A and B.
- Original Medicare will be the foundation to the federal health insurance program.
- Without Original Medicare, an individual cannot purchase a Medigap Supplement or choose to go with the alternative Medicare Advantage plan.

Medicare Always Has An Effective Date Of The First Of The Month

- When an individual is eligible for Medicare and decides to enroll into Medicare Part A and/or B, the federal government will *always* set the effective date for the 1st of the month.
- Medicare will never assign an effective date for Medicare Part A and/or B coverage that does not fall on the 1st of the month.

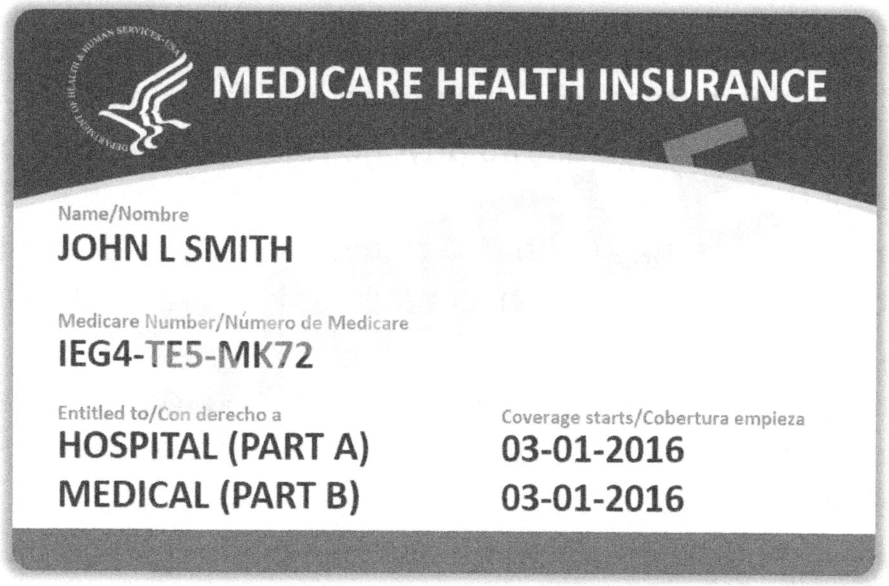

Medicare 7-Month Initial Enrollment Period

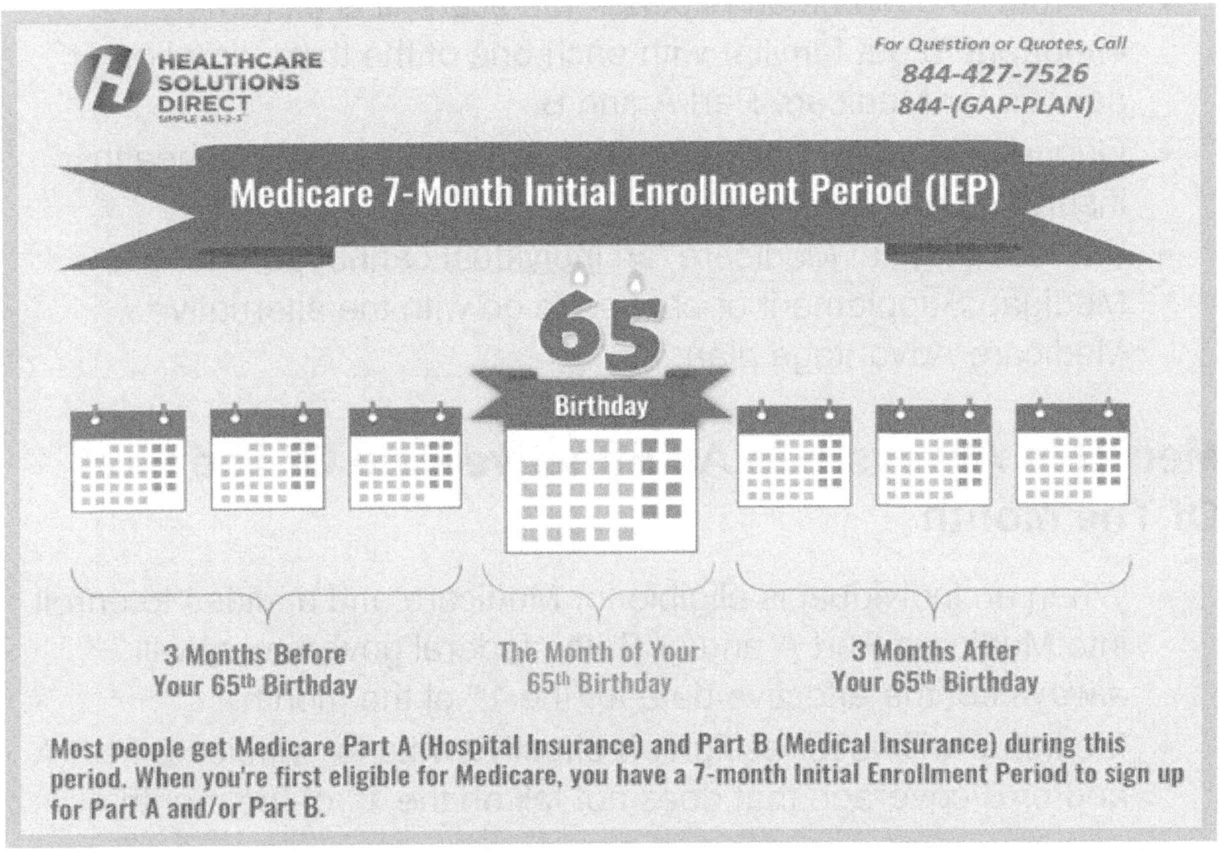

- First time eligibility for Medicare will typically be when an individual is turning 65. This period is referred to as a 7-month IEP, which allows anyone to enroll into Medicare Part A and/or B.
- If an individual has not been granted Medicare eligibility early because of a disability, this enrollment period will be extremely important.
- During the IEP, the individual will not need to provide any documentation in order to enroll into Medicare Part A and/or B.
- If the individual is turning 65 and has worked 10 years in the U.S., it entitles them to their Medicare benefits.

Most Individuals Should Enroll During Their Initial Enrollment Period

- This enrollment period is when everyone who is first eligible for Medicare Part A and/or B should enroll. Here is why this enrollment period is so important even to those who are still working and covered by employer group health insurance:
    - There is no paperwork required.
    - There is no delay to Part A and B.
    - There is no penalty for delaying Part B.

Not Enrolling During The Initial Enrollment Period Could Be Stressful

- If an individual delays enrolling into their Medicare Part A and/or B during the 7-month IEP, they could find themselves in the following situation:
    - Paperwork may be required to enroll.
    - Delays in the Medicare effective date.
    - Being responsible for a lifetime penalty.

Working With Employer Group Should Still Enroll

- Many individuals who are still working and covered by their employer group plan may feel that delaying their Medicare Part B is a better idea because they have credible coverage.
- The first thing someone should do is look at the foundation of Medicare, which is that Part A is free. And as of 2022, the standard Part B premium is $170.10. Original Medicare will cost an individual a total of $170.10.
- Here is why delaying Part B could be a mistake financially as well as a headache for an individual later:

- Paperwork will be needed from the employer, which could delay an individual from being able to enroll into Part A and/or B.
- Most individuals who apply for Part B *after* their IEP need the coverage to start within 30 days, and that is typically not enough time to process the request.
- Original Medicare with a Medigap Supplement or enrolling into a Medicare Advantage could be much more cost effective and better coverage than the employer group plan.

7-Month Initial Enrollment Period Is Automatic With Retirement Benefits

- The 7-month IEP is the easiest and most efficient way for an individual who is Medicare eligible to enroll into their Medicare Part A and B.
- If the individual is drawing Social Security or RRB, they will automatically be enrolled into Medicare Part A and B on the 1st day of their 65th birth month.
- Individuals are *automatically* enrolled because the federal government can easily withhold the standard Part B premium of $170.10 (2022) from their retirement benefits. There is no need for the individual to set up a payment plan.

When Will Medicare Card Arrive When Automatic?

- The Medicare card will arrive automatically in the mail approximately three months (90 days) *before* the individual's effective date. There is nothing that needs be done to enroll or request Medicare Part A and B when turning 65.

- Medicare's rule is that if an individual is born on the 1st of the month, their Medicare Part A and B effective date will start the first of the previous month.
  (Example: An individual born on July 1 would have an effective date for their Medicare Part A and B of June 1.)

Understand When To Apply During The 7-Month Initial Enrollment Period

- If an individual needs to enroll into Medicare Part A and/or B because they are not receiving Social Security retirement benefits at the age of 65, they will need to apply during the 7-month IEP.
- Medicare can be applied for over the phone by calling Social Security, but the federal government does not recommend that. It is recommended that the individual apply online for their Medicare benefits at www.ssa.gov anytime during the 7-month period as follows:
  - Enroll as early as three months (90 days) before the month turning 65.
  - Enroll the month turning 65.
  - Enroll up to three months (90 days) after the month turning 65.

Enroll As Soon As Possible During 90-Day Initial Enrollment Period Window

- Medicare Part A and/or B effective date will be effective the 1st day of someone's 65th birth month regardless of how early or late someone enrolls in the 90-day window leading up to their 65th birthday.
- Since it can take 3-4 weeks to get the Medicare Part A and/or B card in the mail, it is highly recommended that an individual

enrolls as soon the 90-day window is first available. The individual cannot anticipate natural disasters or extenuating circumstances, which could cause a delay. The sooner someone enrolls, the better it is for them.

- For those individuals who wait to enroll until their actual 65th birth month, or anytime in the 3 months after will find that their Medicare Part A and/or B will be delayed.

Rules for Initial Enrollment Period Delayed Start

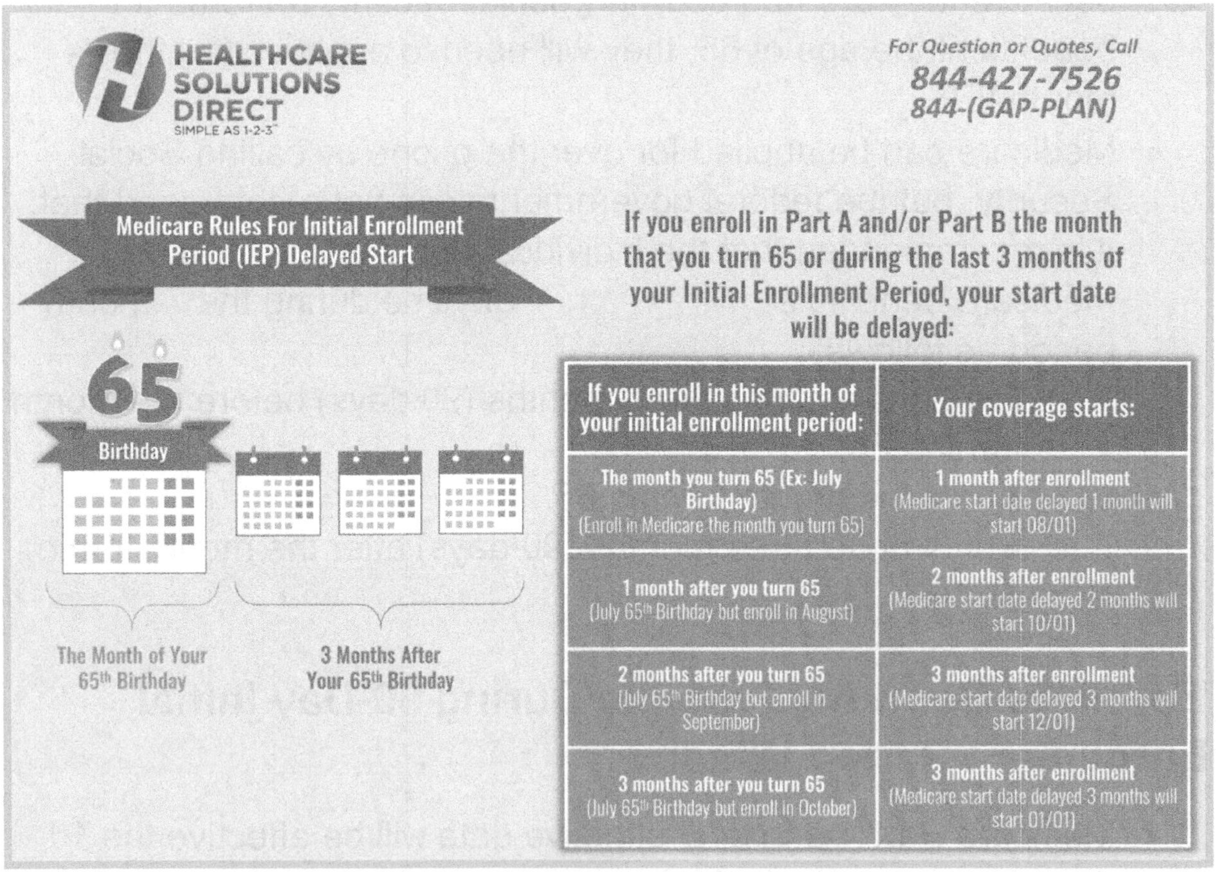

If you enroll in this month of your initial enrollment period:	Your coverage starts:
The month you turn 65 (Ex: July Birthday) (Enroll in Medicare the month you turn 65)	1 month after enrollment (Medicare start date delayed 1 month will start 08/01)
1 month after you turn 65 (July 65th Birthday but enroll in August)	2 months after enrollment (Medicare start date delayed 2 months will start 10/01)
2 months after you turn 65 (July 65th Birthday but enroll in September)	3 months after enrollment (Medicare start date delayed 3 months will start 12/01)
3 months after you turn 65 (July 65th Birthday but enroll in October)	3 months after enrollment (Medicare start date delayed 3 months will start 01/01)

- If an individual enrolls in Medicare the month that they turn 65 or anytime during the last three months of their IEP, they will find that their Medicare Part A and/or B start date is delayed.

- This Medicare rule does not make sense, but it is overseen by CMS, and they will not bend it. Medicare has some weird rules, and this is one of them.
- Medicare will delay an individual's start date based on the month that they decide to enroll. It is always best to enroll in Medicare during the 90-days prior to turning 65 so as not to delay the coverage start date.

Breaking Down Delayed Start For Initial Enrollment Period

If you enroll in this month of your initial enrollment period:	Your coverage starts:
The month you turn 65 (Ex: July Birthday) (Enroll in Medicare the month you turn 65)	**1 month after enrollment** (Medicare start date delayed 1 month will start 08/01)
1 month after you turn 65 (July 65th Birthday but enroll in August)	**2 months after enrollment** (Medicare start date delayed 2 months will start 10/01)
2 months after you turn 65 (July 65th Birthday but enroll in September)	**3 months after enrollment** (Medicare start date delayed 3 months will start 12/01)
3 months after you turn 65 (July 65th Birthday but enroll in October)	**3 months after enrollment** (Medicare start date delayed 3 months will start 01/01)

- If an individual enrolls into Medicare Part A and/or B during the month that they turn 65, their Medicare will start on the 1st of the next month.

- If an individual enrolls into Medicare Part A and/or B one month after they turn 65, their Medicare will start on the 1st of the 2nd month.
- If an individual enrolls into Medicare Part A and/or B two months after they turn 65, their Medicare will start on the 1st of the 3rd month.
- If an individual enrolls into Medicare Part A and/or B three months after they turn 65, their Medicare will start on the 1st of the 3rd month.

Medicare Special Enrollment Period

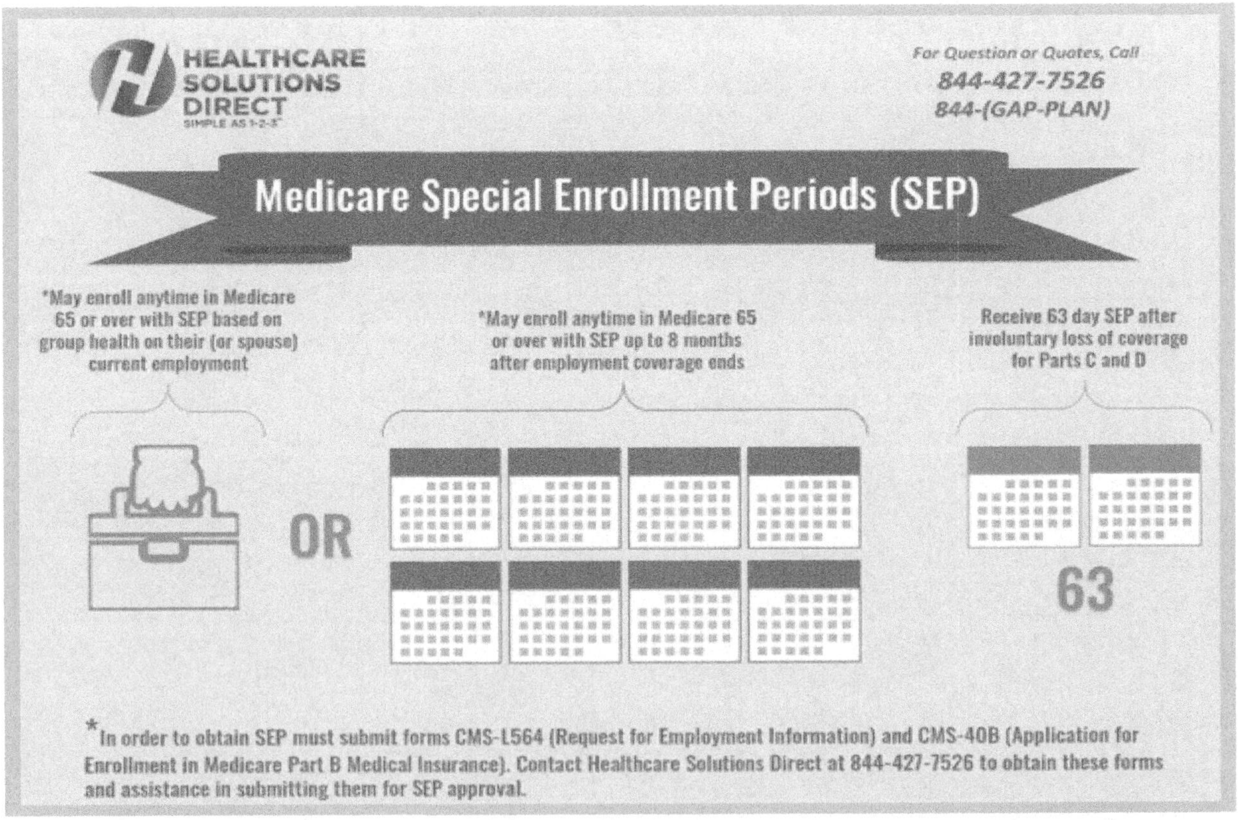

- The Medicare SEP is for an individual who did *not* enroll during the 7-month IEP, but has a valid reason that is recognized by the federal government.

    - The only valid reason the federal government will accept is that the individual or their spouse was working, and they were covered by their current employers group insurance.
- Many individuals have found themselves without an SEP because they thought that they could keep a previous employers group insurance past the age of 65 and that would count as credible coverage.
- The key wording by the federal government is that it must be based on the current employer's group insurance.

Special Enrollment Period Requires Documentation

- An individual who wants to enroll after their 7-month IEP must provide valid documentation to Social Security that is accepted for enrollment into an SEP.
- The requirement that CMS has in place for a SEP is that the individual must be covered by a group health insurance plan that is based on their current employment if the following are satisfied:
    - The individual or their spouse (or family member if they are disabled) is working.
    - The individual is covered by a group health insurance plan through that employer or union that is based on where they are working.
- Social Security will require that a form be filled out by the current employer showing that the individual or spouse was currently working for the company and was covered by the group health insurance plan.

Two Reasons Why Someone Might Want To Delay Initial Enrollment Period

- It is highly recommended that an individual enrolls into Medicare Part A and /or B during their 7-month IEP. Those individuals who might want to consider waiting to enroll during an SEP would be for one of the two following conditions:
  - A dependent under the age of 65 is on the group health insurance coverage and would be affected or
  - The individual is taking high-cost brand name or specialty medication, which is more cost effective under the group employer insurance plan.
- If the individual does *not* have one of these two conditions, it is highly recommended to enroll during the 7-month IEP.

Reasons Enrolling During Special Enrollment Period Should Be Last Resort

- The first reason an individual should enroll during their 7-month IEP is that the standard Medicare Part B premium for 2022 is only $170.10 per month.
- It could be more cost effective for the individual to pay the $170.10 per month and choose a $0 premium MAPD plan or purchase a Medigap Supplement with a standalone PDP.
- Enrolling during the 7-month IEP will also avoid having to get the necessary documents together through the current employer for an SEP.
- It will also avoid the problems and stress of having to rely on Social Security to process the documents in time for the effective date that the individual will need it to start. Frequently an individual applying for an SEP needs the coverage to start within 30 days.

How To Apply For A Special Enrollment Period With Social Security

- The individual can request an SEP anytime within the 90-day window prior to the month that they want their Medicare Part A and/or B effective date.
- The individual does not need to wait to enroll into an SEP just because their employer group coverage is ending. The individual can enroll with a valid SEP anytime they would like their effective date to start.
- Medicare provides a valid SEP up to 8 months after the individual's employment or coverage ends.

How To Submit The Forms To Social Security For Special Enrollment Period

Already Enrolled in Medicare

If you already have Medicare, you can get information and services online. Find out how to manage your benefits.

If you are already enrolled in Medicare Part A and you want to enroll in Part B, please complete form CMS-40B, Application for Enrollment in Medicare – Part B (medical insurance). If you are applying for Medicare Part B due to a loss of employment or group health coverage, you will also need to complete form CMS-L564, Request for Employment Information.

You have three options to submit your enrollment request under the Special Enrollment Period. You can do **one** of the following:

1. Go to "Apply Online for Medicare Part B During a Special Enrollment Period" and complete CMS-40B and CMS-L564. Then upload your evidence of Group Health Plan or Large Group Health Plan.
2. Fax your CMS-40B and employer-signed CMS-L564 to 1-833-914-2016.
3. Mail your CMS-40B and employer-signed CMS-L564 to your local Social Security office.

Note: When completing the CMS-L564

- State on the form "I want Part B coverage to begin (MM/YY)" in the remarks section of the CMS-40B form or online application.
- If possible, your employer should complete Section B.
- If your employer is unable to complete Section B, please complete that portion as best as you can on behalf of your employer without your employer's signature and submit one of the following forms of secondary evidence:
    - Income tax form that shows health insurance premiums paid;
    - W-2s reflecting pre-tax medical contributions;
    - pay stubs that reflect health insurance premium deductions;
    - health insurance cards with a policy effective date;
    - explanations of benefits paid by the GHP or LGHP; or
    - statements or receipts that reflect payment of health insurance premiums.

- Currently, Social Security requires an individual to provide a Request for Employment Information (CMS-L564) form filled out by the employer benefits coordinator and a signed Application for Enrollment in Medicare Part B Medical Insurance (CMS-40B) form by the individual in order to qualify for a valid SEP.

- There are three ways that someone can provide these forms to Social Security. Uploading the forms is highly recommended and the most convenient:
    - Upload the CMS-L564 form and electronically fill out the CMS-40B form.
        - In the remarks section state, "I want Part B coverage to begin MM/YY, by going to www.ssa.gov and choosing "Medicare Enrollment" and clicking on "Apply Online for Medicare Part B During a Special Enrollment Period".
    - Fax the forms to Social Security.
    - Mail the form to the local Social Security office.

63-day Special Enrollment Period Is Not For A Medicare Enrollment Option

- The 63-day SEP has *nothing* to do with enrolling into Medicare with Social Security. It is important for an individual to be aware of this if they have a Medicare Advantage plan or standalone PDP.
- When someone is already enrolled in both Medicare Part A and B, they may be eligible for what is referred to as the 63-day SEP after involuntary loss of coverage for a Medicare Advantage Part C or standalone Part D.
- The reason this enrollment period is important is that there is a penalty if someone goes without credible prescription drug coverage for a continuous period of more than 63 days.
- The 63-day SEP is a protection that CMS gives an individual to ensure they always have coverage in place for prescription drug coverage if they move or there is an involuntary loss of coverage.

Examples Of 63-day Special Enrollment Period For Loss Of Coverage

- If an individual moves out of the coverage area of their Medicare Advantage plan or the plan stopped offering coverage in that individual's area, the individual will have
  63 days to enroll into another MAPD, MA, or a standalone PDP. (Example: An individual moves from Florida to Texas; therefore, their current plan would be out of the coverage area.)
- If an individual moved out of the coverage area of their standalone PDP, this would also give them 63 days to enroll into another standalone PDP plan that would cover that area.
- To make it easy, an individual cannot go without one of the following for more than 63 days.
  - Standalone Medicare Part D or
  - MAPD.

Medicare General Enrollment Period

- If an individual who is eligible for Medicare did *not* enroll in their Medicare Part B during the 7-month IEP and do not have a valid SEP, they will have one last enrollment period available to them.
- To make this easy to remember, you can think of the GEP as the naughty list.
- This can be referred to as the naughty list because the individual would have a lifetime late enrollment penalty for their Part B premium of 10 percent for each full year they delayed signing up. They would also have a delay in when their Medicare Part A and/or B effective date would start.

General Enrollment Period Available Every Year

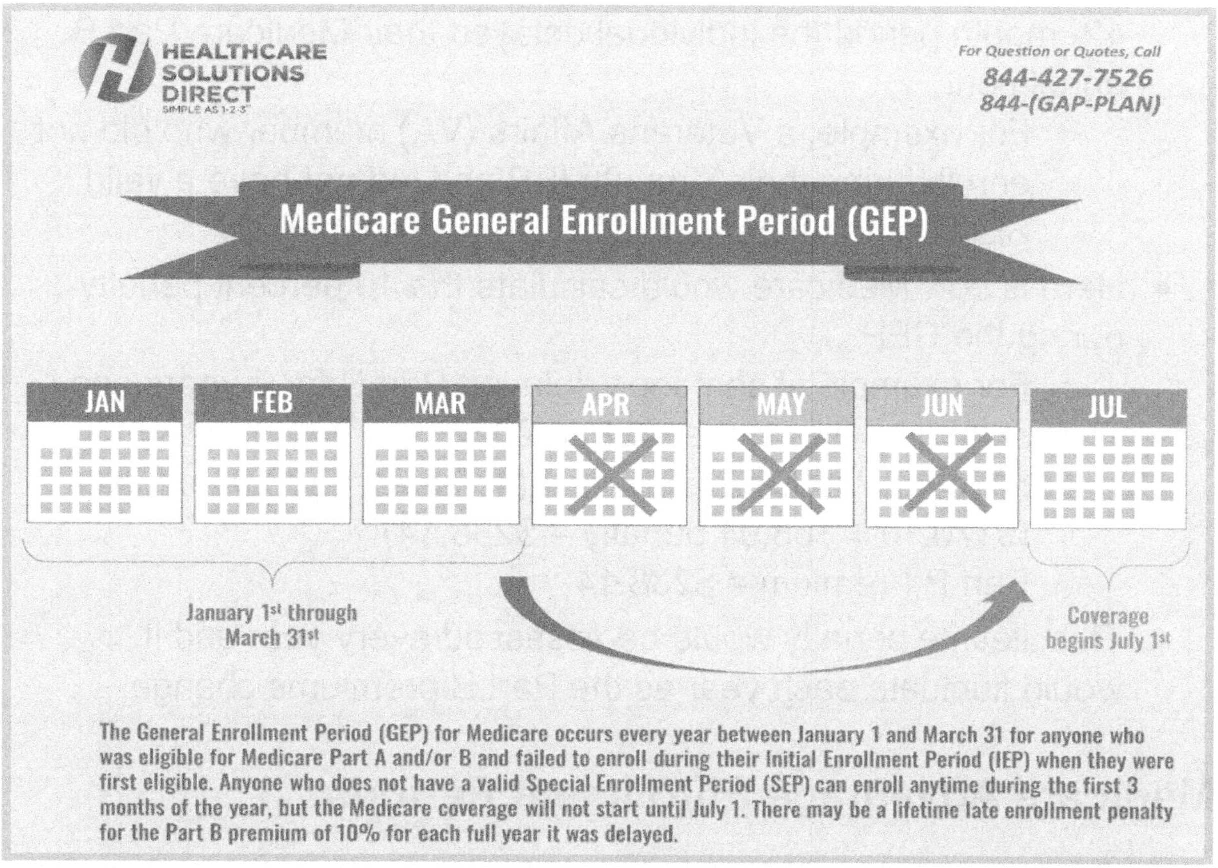

- Every year, the GEP runs for enrollment into Part B between January 1 through March 3 with an effective date of July 1.
- This enrollment period is typically for someone over the age of 65 who never enrolled into Medicare Part B during their 7-month IEP, and they do not have a valid SEP. This affects about 1.5 percent of Medicare beneficiaries.
- There is no supporting documentation that is required for someone to enroll during the first three months of each calendar year during the GEP.

Understanding How The Part B Penalty Works

- The GEP would have a 10 percent penalty for each 12- month period the individual delayed their Medicare Part B enrollment.
    - For example, a Veterans Affairs (VA) member who did not enroll during their 7-month IEP and did not have a valid SEP would be penalized the 10 percent penalty.
- Here is how Medicare would calculate the 10 percent penalty during the GEP.
    - For example, if someone delayed Part B for 4 years and signed up during the GEP in 2022.
    - $170.10 Part B premium x .4 (4 years) = $68.04 penalty ($170.10 + $68.04 penalty = $238.14)
    - Part B Premium = $238.14
- This lifetime penalty would be assessed every year and it would fluctuate each year as the Part B premiums change.

Medicare Advantage Enrollment Periods

- Once an individual is enrolled into Medicare Part A and B, they will have the option to enroll into an alternative plan such as an HMO or PPO through a private insurance company.
- Part C Medicare Advantage plans will have annual contracts with that private insurance company since they are an alternative to Medicare Part A and B.
- An individual who wants to join or make changes to their Part C Medicare Advantage plan will need to be aware of the two annual enrollment periods that are available to them, which they can do every year.
- These enrollment periods are constant and do not change.

The Two Medicare Advantage Enrollment Periods

- There are two enrollment periods that happen every year that are primarily dedicated to Part C Medicare Advantage plans. These two enrollment periods occur like clockwork and are available to someone who is already in Medicare's system.
- Here are the two enrollment periods that are available:
  - Medicare Open Enrollment Period (OEP): October 15-December 7 and
  - Medicare Advantage OEP: January 1-March 31.

Medicare Open Enrollment Period

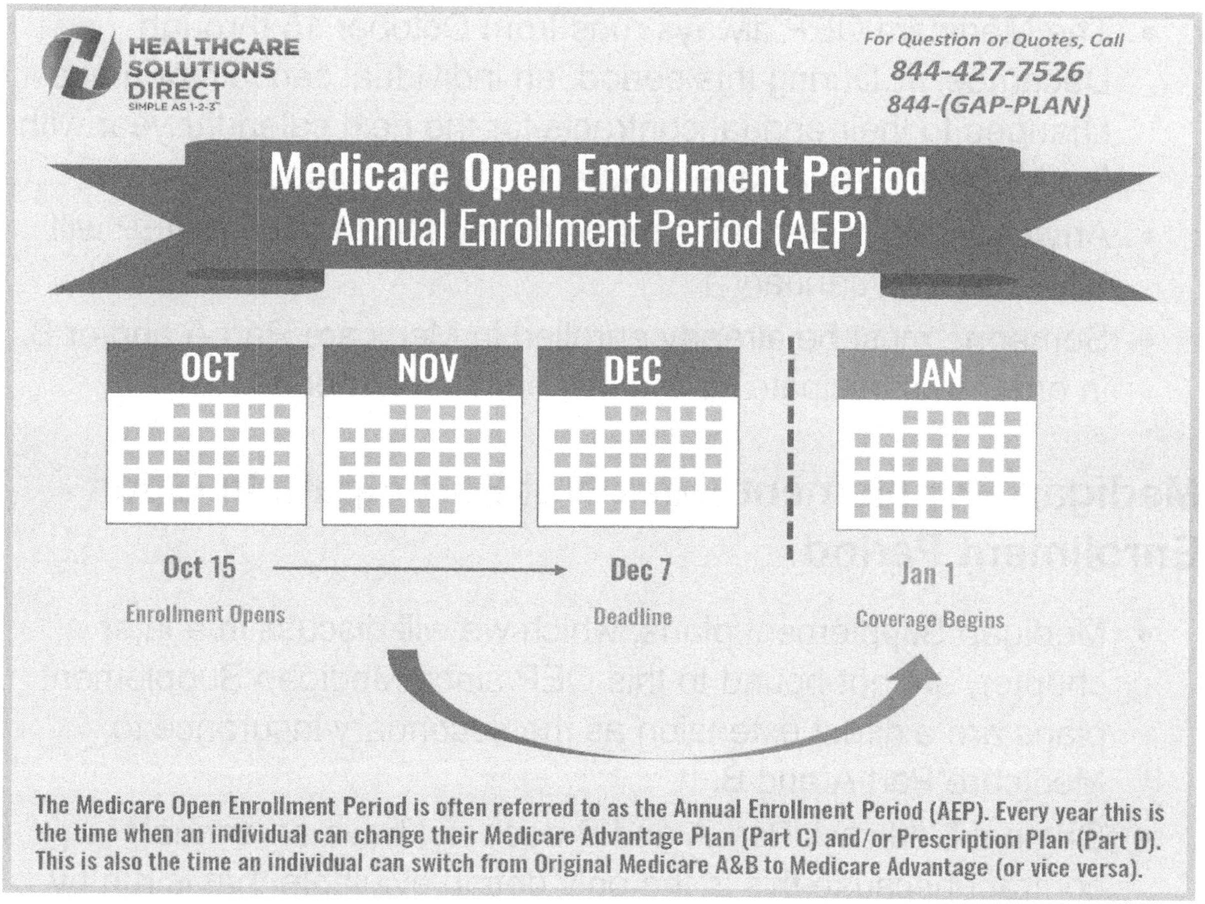

- Recently, Medicare started referring to this period as the OEP. If you hear it called the AEP, which it was commonly referred to as previously, these are both the *same* enrollment periods.
- Medicare does not make sense sometimes in how they decide to word things. This is another reason why looking at the different options that Medicare has to offer can be quite confusing.
- Medigap Supplement plans also have an enrollment period called the OEP, which is typically only available once during someone's lifetime and has nothing to do with this annual enrollment period.

Medicare Open Enrollment Period Occurs Every Year

- The Medicare OEP always runs from October 15 through December 7. During this period, an individual can join or make changes to their annual contracts for the next calendar year with the Medicare Advantage private insurance company.
- Any changes or decisions made during this Medicare OEP will take effect on January 1.
- Someone must be already enrolled in Medicare Part A and/or B in order to participate during this enrollment period.

Medigap Supplement Does Not Participate In Open Enrollment Period

- Medigap Supplement plans, which we will discuss in a later chapter, are not bound to this OEP since Medigap Supplement plans are a direct extension as the secondary insurance to Medicare Part A and B.
- Original Medicare Part A and B does *not* have an annual contract because this is the only option available that is run by the federal government.

- On the other hand, Part C Medicare Advantage plans are run by different private insurance companies, which have several different options available to them.

Here Is What Someone Can Do During The Open Enrollment Period Each Year

- During the OEP, which runs from October 15 - December 7, an individual can make the following changes to their coverage:
    - Change to a Medicare Advantage plan from Original Medicare,
    - Change to Original Medicare from a Medicare Advantage plan,
    - Change from one Medicare Advantage plan to another, regardless if they have drug coverage, and/or
    - Enroll or drop a standalone PDP.

Two Requirements To Enroll In A Medicare Advantage Plan

- If an individual would like to enroll in a Medicare Advantage plan during the OEP, here are the only two requirements:
    - The individual must be enrolled in both Medicare Part A and B and
    - They must live within the plans service area or network.

What To Do During The Open Enrollment Period If Content With Coverage

- If the individuals current MA, MAPD, or PDP plan is still available in their area and they do *not* want to make any changes during the Medicare OEP, they do not need to do anything.

- The coverage will automatically renew for the next calendar year at midnight on December 7. The individual will be able to continue to use their current insurance cards.

What To Do If Current Coverage Is Not Available

- If the individual's Medicare Advantage plan is not available for the next calendar year, they will receive a notice before the beginning of the Medicare OEP.
- The individual will want to select another Medicare Advantage plan during this period so they will have coverage on January 1. If the individual does not select a new plan, they will go back to Original Medicare Part A and B as of January 1.
- If the individual did not select a new plan during the Medicare OEP, they will still have an opportunity to do so when the coverage ends on January 1. The individual can use the 63-day SEP available to them because the coverage ending involuntarily.

Medicare Advantage Open Enrollment Period

- The Medicare Advantage OEP is only available to those individuals who are already enrolled into a Medicare Advantage plan with or without drug coverage.
- Some refer to this enrollment as a "buyer's remorse" period.
- This period is set aside for those who would still like to make some changes to their current Medicare Advantage plan.

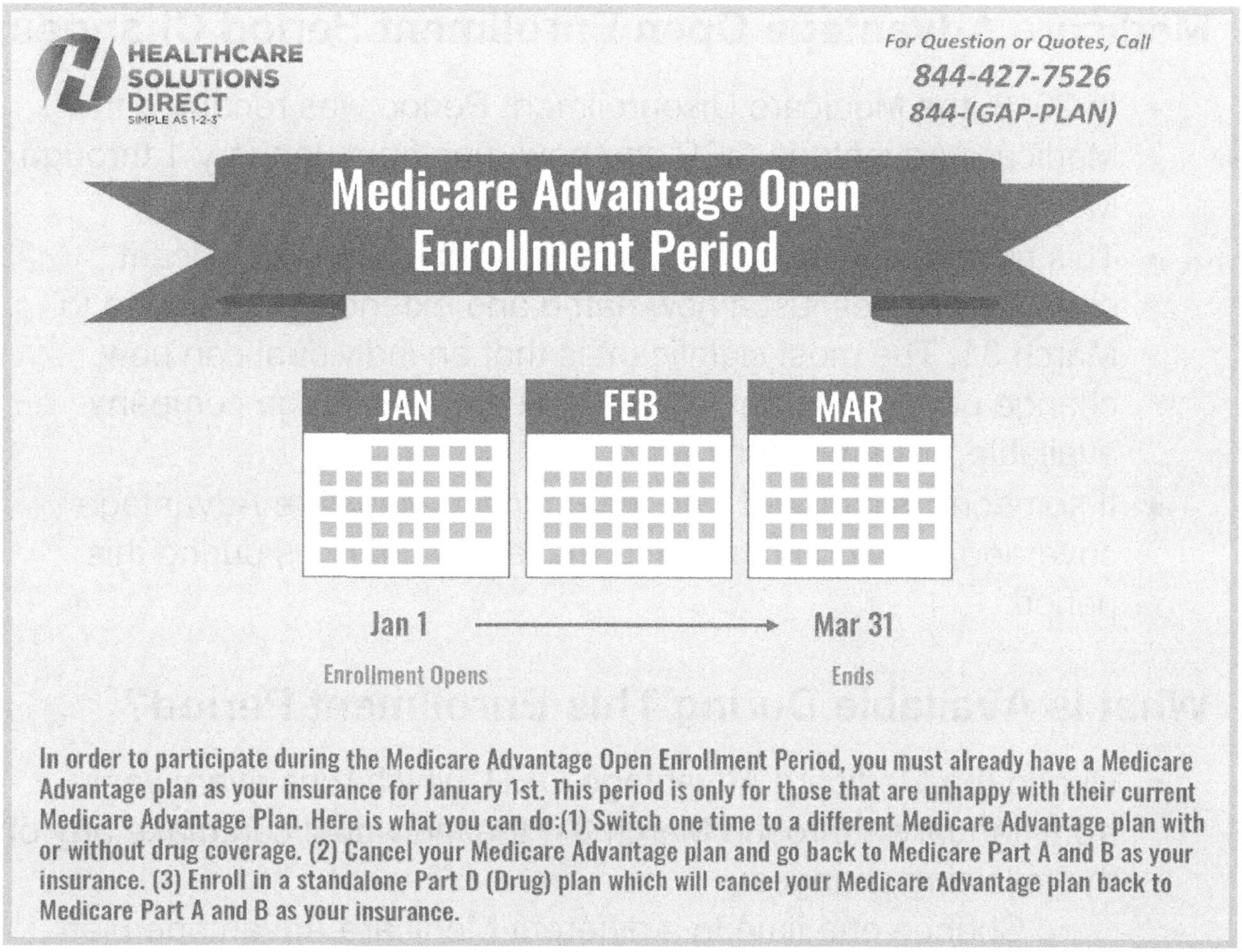

Originally Called The Medicare Disenrollment Period

- Until 2019, the Medicare Advantage OEP was called the Medicare Disenrollment Period, which ran from January 1 through February 14. Obviously, this was a shorter time period than the current period of January 1 through March 31.
- During the Medicare Disenrollment Period available prior to 2019, the only thing someone could do with their Medicare Advantage plan was to enroll into a standalone PDP. This would allow someone to get out of their current Medicare Advantage plan contract and return back to Original Medicare Part A and B as their primary insurance.

Medicare Advantage Open Enrollment Period Changes

- In 2019, the Medicare Disenrollment Period was renamed the Medicare Advantage OEP and now runs from January 1 through March 31.
- This new enrollment period brought with it some significant changes besides just a new name and extending the period to March 31. The most significant is that an individual can now change one time to any other Medicare Advantage company available to them in their area.
- If someone is satisfied with their current Medicare Advantage coverage, they do not need to make any changes during this period.

What Is Available During This Enrollment Period?

- During the Medicare Advantage OEP, which runs every year from January 1 through March 31, the individual can make <u>any</u> of the following changes:
    - Change one time to a different Medicare Advantage plan with or without drug coverage,
    - Cancel the Medicare Advantage plan and return to Original Medicare Part A and B, or
    - Enroll in a standalone PDP, which cancels the current contract with the Medicare Advantage plan and returns the individual to Original Medicare Part A and B.

Enrollment Period Provides Someone More Options

- The new Medicare Advantage OEP provides someone with more options and the ability to get out of their current contract. Any changes that are made during this enrollment period will start on the first of the next month.

- For example, if someone makes any changes to their coverage in the month of February, their new coverage will start on March 1.
- No changes can be made to someone's Medicare Advantage plan *after* the March 31 midnight deadline until that calendar years next Medicare OEP, which will run from October 15 through December 7.

Chapter 6

How To Enroll In Medicare — Everything You Need To Know

Everything You Need To Know To Enroll In Medicare

- If an individual is needing to enroll into Medicare at 65 or older, it can be quite stressful. This section will provide step- by-step instructions on what an individual needs to do in order to enroll into their Medicare Part A and B.
- Enrolling into Medicare should be a onetime event for someone who is eligible for Medicare. The individual does *not* need to

renew their Medicare coverage every year. Once enrolled into Medicare Part A and B, they are now in the Medicare program.

- Enrolling into Medicare will only be stress free if an individual knows exactly what they need to do. After you are done with this section, you will know exactly what needs to be done in order to simply complete the enrollment process.

Who Is Eligible For Medicare?

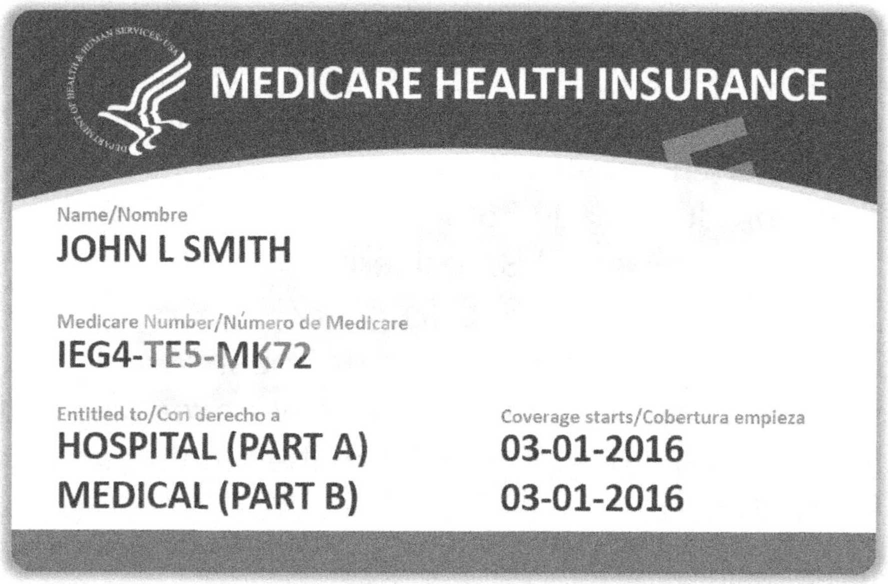

- Before we look at the Medicare enrollment process, it is important to go over who is eligible for Medicare. We can then look at who gets Medicare automatically, and who must enroll in Medicare.
- Here are the requirements needed in order to be eligible to receive Medicare Part A and B.
    - Age 65 or older,
    - Disabled,
    - ESRD, or
    - Lou Gehrig's disease or ALS.

Age 65 or Older

- The majority of those who are first eligible for Medicare will fall into the category of age 65 or older. In the insurance industry when someone is turning 65, these individuals are often referred to as T-65, which means turning 65.
- When someone is turning 65 no matter what their current insurance is at that time, they have the option to enroll into Medicare Part A and/or B.

Simple Requirements For Medicare At 65 Or Older

- Here are the *only* requirements that CMS has in place when someone is turning 65 or older:
    - The individual is age 65 or older,
    - The individual is a U.S. resident,
    - The individual is a U.S. citizen, and
    - The individual is an alien who has been lawfully admitted for permanent residence and has been residing in the U.S for five continuous years prior to the month that they apply for Medicare.

Requirement Of Permanent Residence For 5 Years

- The last scenario of requiring permanent residence in the U.S. for the last five years is typically when a family moves a parent over from another country to live with them permanently in the U.S. Once that family member is admitted for permanent residence, it will be five years before they can buy into Medicare.
- This would be a good example of an individual that would fall into the one percent of having to pay for their Medicare Part A.

Disabled

- In order to get Medicare prior to the age of 65, you must qualify based on permanent disability.
- An individual must apply with Social Security and be granted what is known as SSDI, which means that they are asking the federal government to pay them a benefit each month because they are permanently disabled and can no longer work.

Social Security Determination For Disability

- Social Security will *only* pay out benefits if they have determined that an individual cannot work due to a disability for at least one year or it will result in the individual's death. Social Security will use the following basic requirements to determine if someone could qualify:
    - Are you working?
    - Is your condition severe?
    - Is your condition found in the list of disabling conditions?
    - Can you do the work you did previously?
    - Can you do any other type of work?

Payments Are Only Offered For Permanent Disability

- This is a lengthy process as the doctors and disability specialists must be involved in ensuring that the individual is unable to work and perform the basic duties of lifting, standing, walking, sitting, or the individual has cognitive issues that affects their impairment.
- Social Security does *not* offer short-term disability, but they do offer total permanent disability. They are making the decision to financially take care of the impact the individual will have because they can no longer contribute to the workforce.

Once Granted Disability Medicare Is Not Immediate

- Once someone is granted permanent disability, they will begin to receive SSDI benefits each month after a five-month waiting period.
- The SSDI will be paid on the sixth full month after the date that the disability was approved. Medicare, however, will not be automatic for the individual that first month when they start receiving their SSDI payments.

24-Month Social Security Disability Insurance Waiting Period Before Medicare Starts

- Social Security has what they call a Medicare waiting period of 24 months of SSDI benefits before someone will qualify for Medicare Part A and B.
- Once someone has received SSDI benefits for at least 24 months, their Medicare Part A and B will start automatically on the 25th month.
- The Medicare card will arrive in the mail about three months prior to the effective date of the 25th month of SSDI benefits. The individual does not need to apply for their Medicare.

End Stage Renal Disease

- Someone will qualify for Medicare if they have ESRD that results in permanent kidney failure, which requires dialysis or a kidney transplant.
- An individual that meets these requirements will need to apply for Medicare Part A and B. It will not be automatic just because they received the diagnosis of ESRD.

End Stage Renal Disease Guidelines Required To Apply For Medicare

- Here are the general guidelines and rules to get Medicare started when an individual meets the ESRD requirements:
    - If an individual is receiving dialysis at an inpatient or outpatient facility for at least three months, they are eligible for Medicare on the 1st day of their fourth month of treatment.
    - If an individual decides to begin at home dialysis, they may be eligible for Medicare on the 1st day of the month that their program begins.
    - If an individual is receiving a kidney transplant, they are eligible for Medicare starting the 1st day of the month that they will be admitted to the hospital for the transplant. If the kidney transplant is successful, their Medicare will end 36 months after they have the kidney transplant.

Lou Gehrig's Disease

- Amyotrophic lateral sclerosis or ALS is most referred to as Lou Gehrig's disease, which would be considered a permanent disability according to Social Security.
- An individual would still have the five-month waiting period before receiving their SSDI benefit payments.

Lou Gehrig's Disease Has No Waiting Period Before Medicare Starts

- What is different with this type of permanent disability, is that the 24-month waiting period for Medicare is waived. Medicare will start the first month that the individual begins to receive their SSDI benefit payments.

- The Medicare card will arrive automatically in the mail about three months prior to the effective date of the first month of SSDI benefit payments.

Medicare Automatically vs. Needing To Apply

- It is important that every individual knows whether they will receive their Medicare Part A and B card in the mail automatically or if they need to apply for it.
- Breaking down which category the individual falls into will help to greatly reduce any stress when needing to know exactly what to do.

Who Gets Medicare Card In The Mail Automatically?

- If an individual is getting their retirement benefits from Social Security or the RBB at least four months prior to turning 65, the individual will *automatically* receive their Medicare card in the mail. There is nothing they need to do to apply for Medicare Part A and B.
- This will also apply to someone who is receiving SSDI. There is nothing that they need to do to apply for Medicare because it will be automatically mailed to them.

Here Is What To Expect In The Mail From Centers for Medicare and Medicaid Services

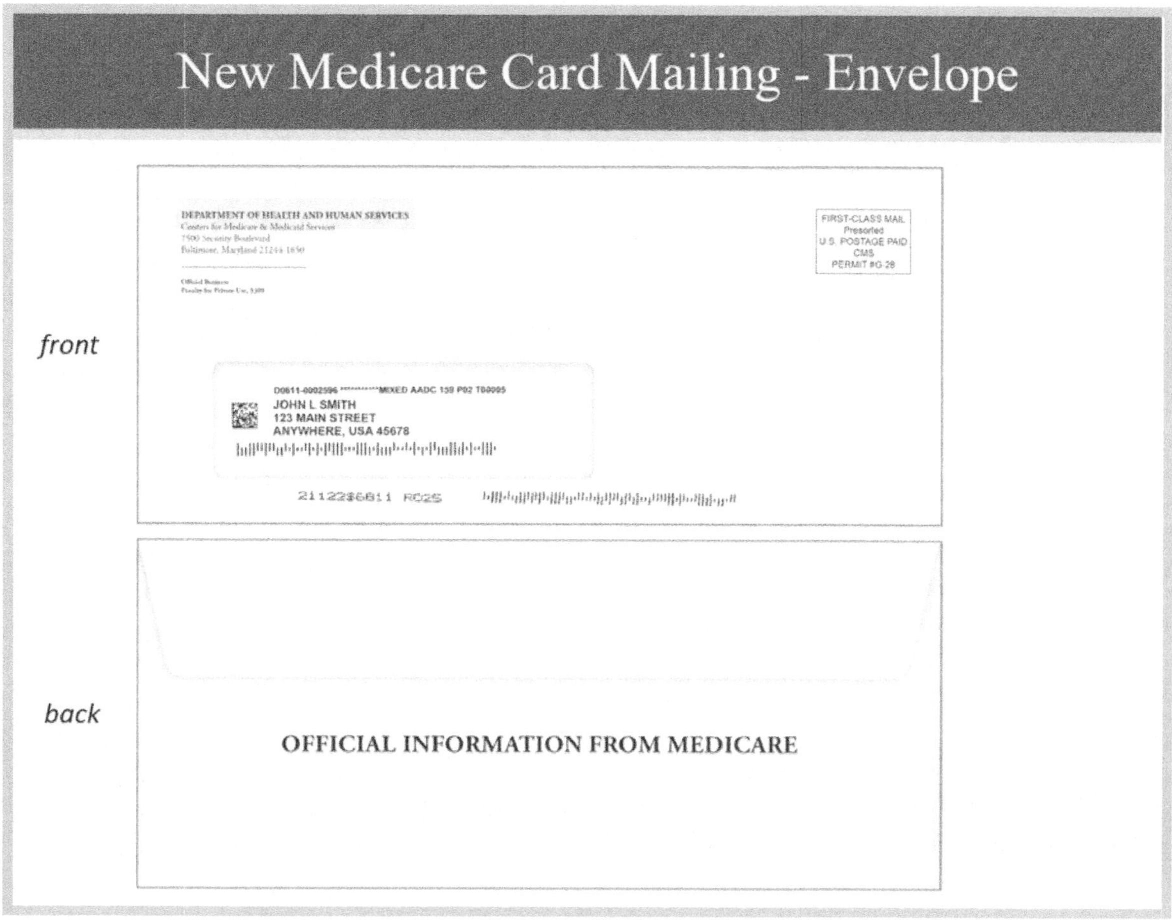

- The individual will receive a letter in the mail from CMS with their Medicare card enclosed.
- Currently, the front of the envelope says, “Department Of Health And Human Resources” and the back says, “Official Information From Medicare.”
- The Medicare Part A and B card that is enclosed is a paper card and does not carry any weight to it like a credit card. Unfortunately, there are those who will dismiss this correspondence as junk mail and throw it away.

Medicare Card Mailing Insert In The Envelope

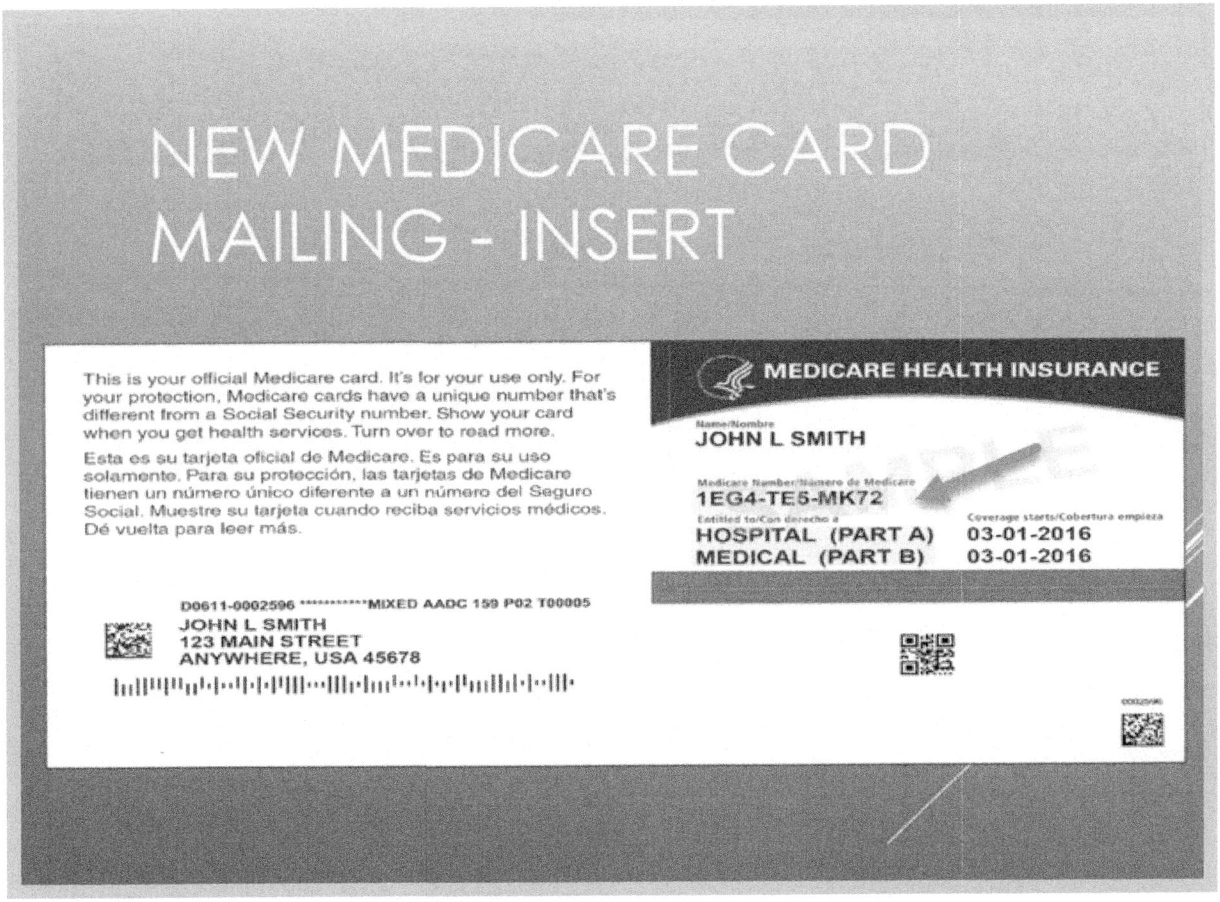

- The Medicare card that is enclosed in the envelope from CMS will have a unique Medicare number on it for that individual. It will also clearly show the Part A and B effective dates.
- The individual will need that unique Medicare number in order to sign up for a Part C Medicare Advantage plan. In order to enroll in an alternative plan to Medicare with a private insurance company, the individual must first be in the Medicare system.

Medicare Arrives 90 Days Prior To Effect Date

- An individual who is turning 65 and is automatically enrolled into Medicare should expect to have the letter with their Medicare card at least 90 days prior to their Medicare effective date.
- Medicare Part A and B will go into effect on the 1st day of the individual's 65th birth month. If the individual happens to be born on the 1st of the month, their Medicare will start the first of the prior month.
    - For example: If someone turned 65 of July 1, their effective date for Medicare would be June 1.

Who Must Enroll In Order To Get Their Medicare?

- If someone is not receiving their benefits from Social Security or the RBB at least four months prior to turning 65, the individual will need to apply with Social Security or the RBB in order to get their Medicare card.
- Those diagnosed with ESRD who have met the requirements of eligibility for Medicare will also need to apply with Social Security or the RBB.

Social Security Must Set Up Payment Plan For Part B

- The individual must enroll in Medicare when not receiving benefits from Social Security or the RBB because the federal government does not have a means to automatically deduct the standard Part B monthly premium of $170.10 (as of 2022).
- The individual must request their Medicare card and set up a payment plan for the standard Part B monthly premium of $170.10 (as of 2022).
- The best way to enroll into Medicare is by applying online through Social Security at www.ssa.gov. Our company has an incredible department called the Client Experience Group that

will take the time to walk anyone through the online steps in order to ensure the enrollment is successful. They understand that it can be stressful for someone enrolling for the first time and will virtually hold their hand throughout the process.

Steps To Enroll In Medicare When Not Automatic At 65

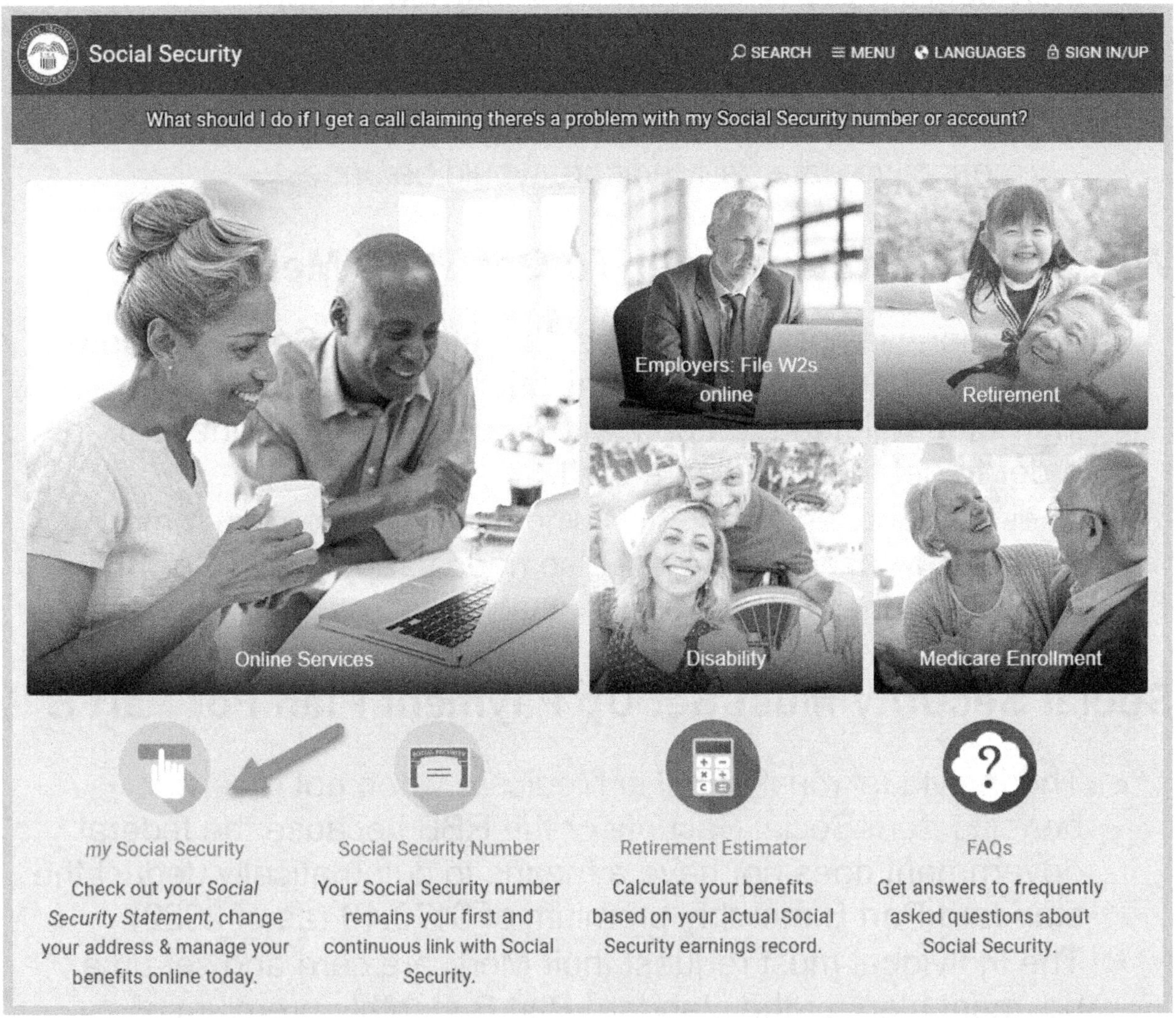

- Many times, an individual needing to enroll into Medicare Part A and/or B are not given clear instructions.

- We are going to go through step-by-step instructions on what an individual needs to do in order to successfully enroll into Medicare themselves and apply online.
- Social Security handles the enrollment and cards for Medicare. The first place the individual needs to go is to www.ssa.gov to begin the enrollment process.

Must Have A My Social Security Account To Enroll

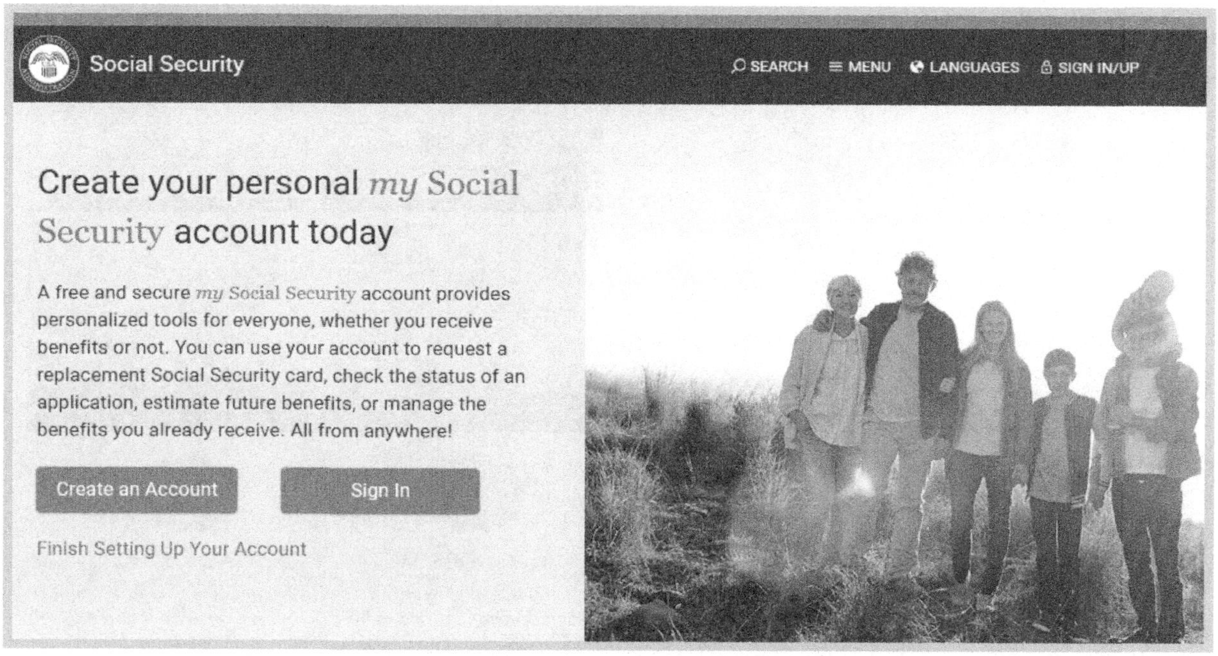

- In order to enroll into Medicare, the individual will first need to log into or create an account through Social Security called 'my Social Security.'
- My Social Security account is a free and secure account that will help to identify that the individual is eligible for Medicare Part A and B. The benefit of my Social Security is the individual can log into their account anytime and request a replacement Social Security card, check the status of a submitted application, and manage their benefits.

- My Social Security is not just for those who are eligible for Medicare. Everyone should create a personal account so they can manage their social security and retirement information.

Next Steps When Someone Has My Social Security

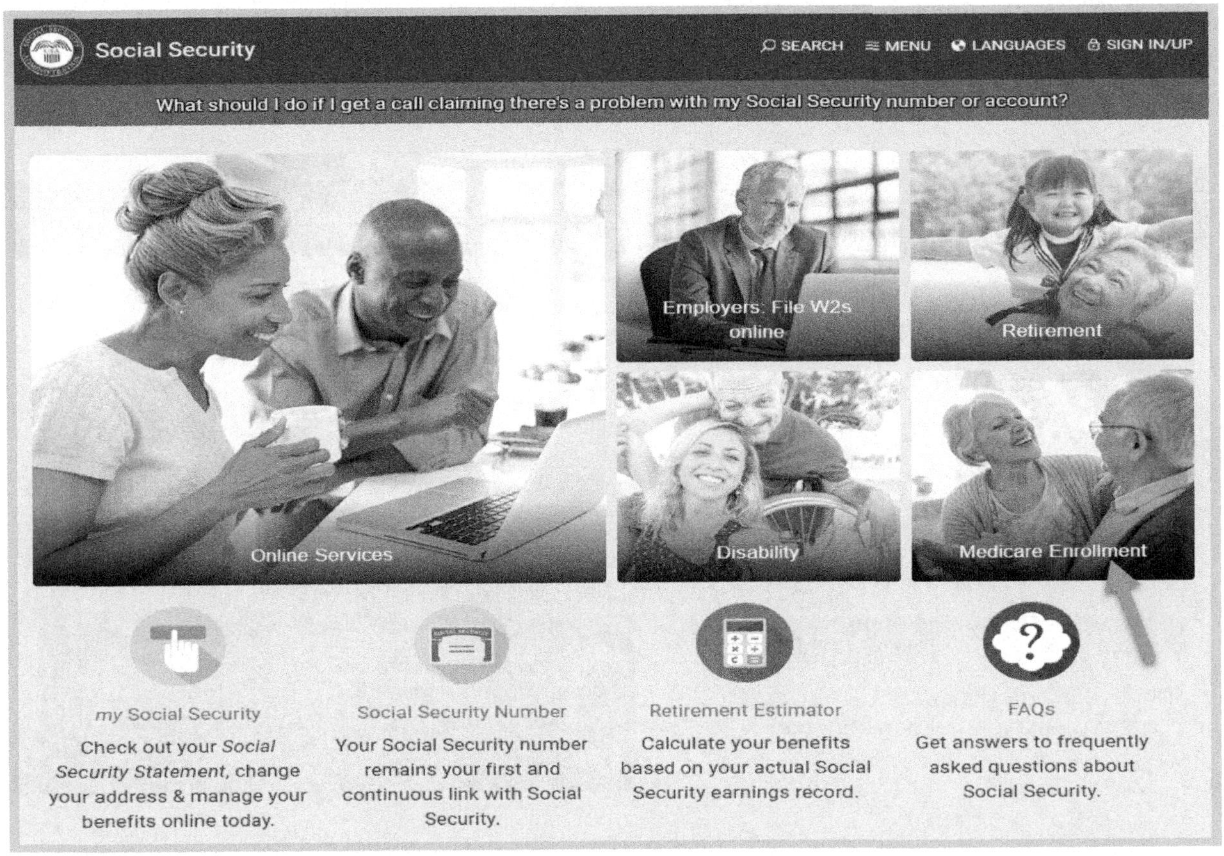

- Once an individual has their log in information for my Social Security or they have created their personal account, they are now ready to begin the process of enrolling into Medicare for their Part A and/or B. On the front page of Social Security, they individual will select "Medicare Enrollment."
- What will happen next is the individual will then be directed to the Medicare benefits page, which will explain to them the parts of Medicare.

- The individual will want to scroll down to the middle of the page until they see a big blue button, which says, "Apply for Medicare Only."

Applying For Medicare Takes Less Than 10 Minutes

Special Enrollment Period (SEP)

If you have medical insurance coverage under a group health plan based on your or your spouse's **current employment**, you may not need to apply for Medicare Part B at age 65. You may qualify for a "Special Enrollment Period" (SEP) that will let you sign up for Part B during:

- Any month you remain covered under the group health plan **and** you, or your spouse's, employment continues.
- The 8-month period that begins with the month after your group health plan coverage or the employment it is based on ends, whichever comes first.

How To Apply Online For Just Medicare

If you are within three months of age 65 or older and not ready to start your monthly Social Security benefits yet, you can use our online retirement application to sign up just for Medicare and wait to apply for your retirement or spouses benefits later. It takes less than 10 minutes, and there are no forms to sign and usually no documentation is required.

Apply for Medicare Only

Return to Saved Application | Check Application Status | Replace Medicare Card

To find out what documents and information you need to apply, go to the Checklist For The Online Medicare, Retirement, and Spouses Application.

- For an individual who is holding off on their Social Security retirement benefits, but will still need their Medicare Part A and/or B, this is the most convenient way to enroll into Medicare.
- An individual turning 65 will *not* be required to sign any forms or need to provide any documentation.

Must Agree Applying For Medicare Benefits

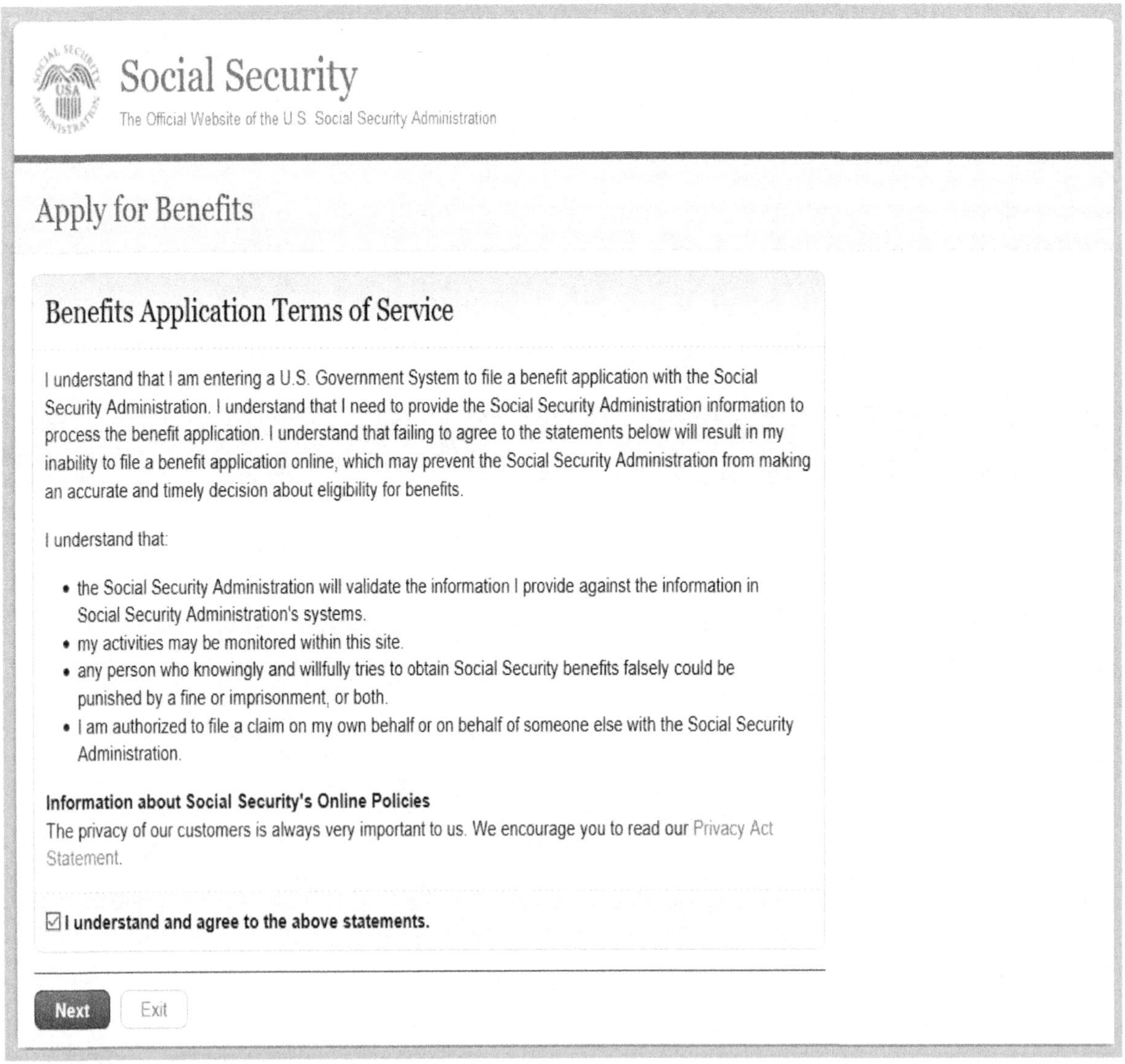

Social Security

The Official Website of the U.S. Social Security Administration

Apply for Benefits

Benefits Application Terms of Service

I understand that I am entering a U.S. Government System to file a benefit application with the Social Security Administration. I understand that I need to provide the Social Security Administration information to process the benefit application. I understand that failing to agree to the statements below will result in my inability to file a benefit application online, which may prevent the Social Security Administration from making an accurate and timely decision about eligibility for benefits.

I understand that:

- the Social Security Administration will validate the information I provide against the information in Social Security Administration's systems.
- my activities may be monitored within this site.
- any person who knowingly and willfully tries to obtain Social Security benefits falsely could be punished by a fine or imprisonment, or both.
- I am authorized to file a claim on my own behalf or on behalf of someone else with the Social Security Administration.

Information about Social Security's Online Policies

The privacy of our customers is always very important to us. We encourage you to read our Privacy Act Statement.

☑ **I understand and agree to the above statements.**

Next Exit

- The individual will be directed to the Benefits Application Terms of Service page where they will agree to the statements that they are applying for their Medicare benefits.

Individual Is Now Ready To Start A New Application

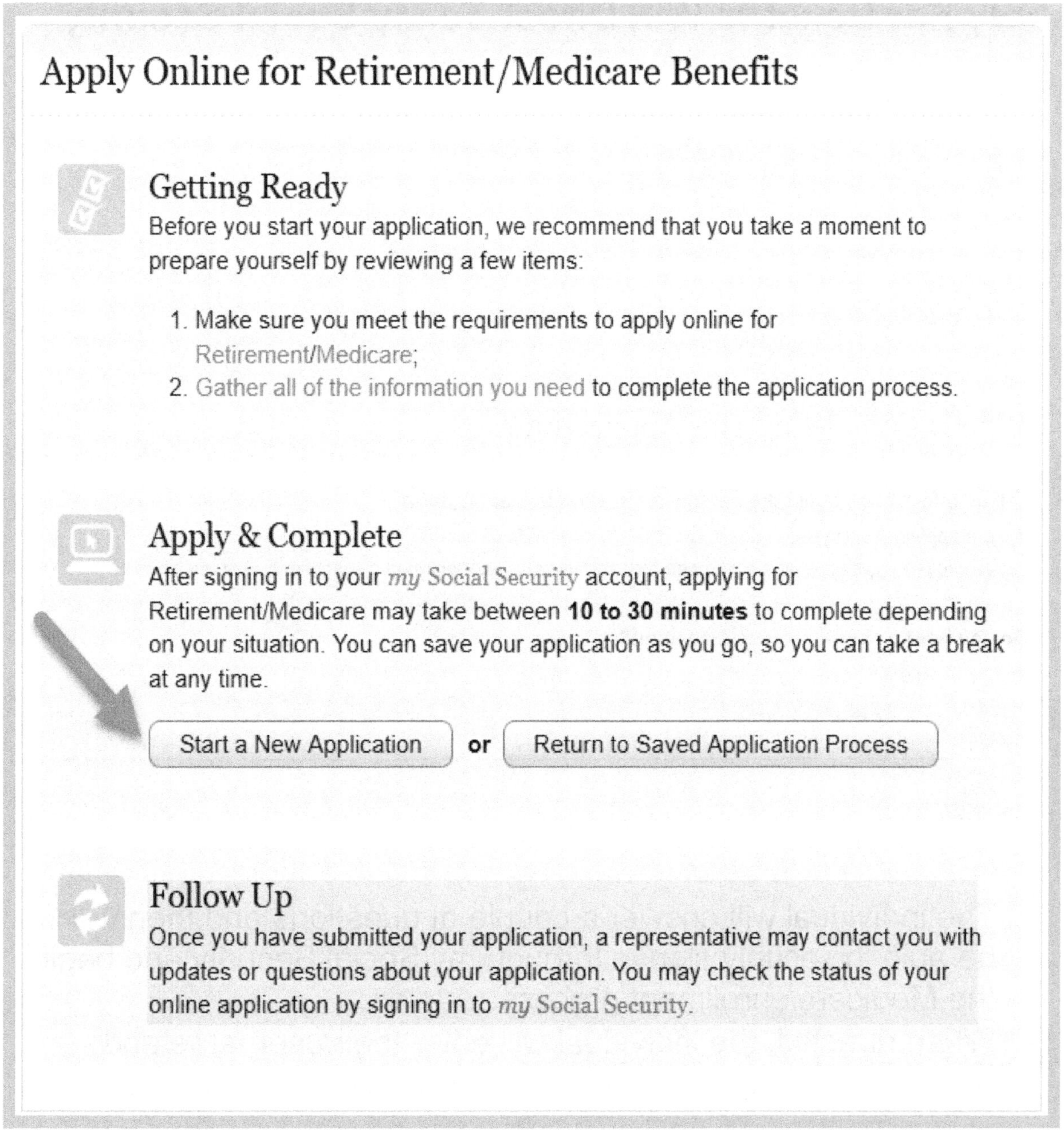

Apply Online for Retirement/Medicare Benefits

Getting Ready

Before you start your application, we recommend that you take a moment to prepare yourself by reviewing a few items:

1. Make sure you meet the requirements to apply online for Retirement/Medicare;
2. Gather all of the information you need to complete the application process.

Apply & Complete

After signing in to your *my* Social Security account, applying for Retirement/Medicare may take between **10 to 30 minutes** to complete depending on your situation. You can save your application as you go, so you can take a break at any time.

Start a New Application **or** Return to Saved Application Process

Follow Up

Once you have submitted your application, a representative may contact you with updates or questions about your application. You may check the status of your online application by signing in to *my* Social Security.

- The individual is now ready to apply online for their Retirement/Medicare Benefits by clicking on “Start a New Application.” Once submitted, they can always follow up and check the status of their application by signing into their personal my Social Security account.

Apply For Benefits Will Direct To My Social Security

- The individual will answer a couple of questions and then will be able to securily sign in through my Social Security and begin the Medicare enrollment process.
- When directed, the individual will enter their username and password and sign in through my Social Security.

Key Questions On The Application For Medicare

- The “Identification” tab will ask the individual if they would like to apply for Medicare only or for their retirement cash benefits as well. If applying for Medicare only, the individual will answer “Yes” and click on the next button.

- The “General” tab will ask the individual if they would like to enroll in Medicare Part B, which they will answer “Yes.”

Confirmations Indicate Application Is Complete

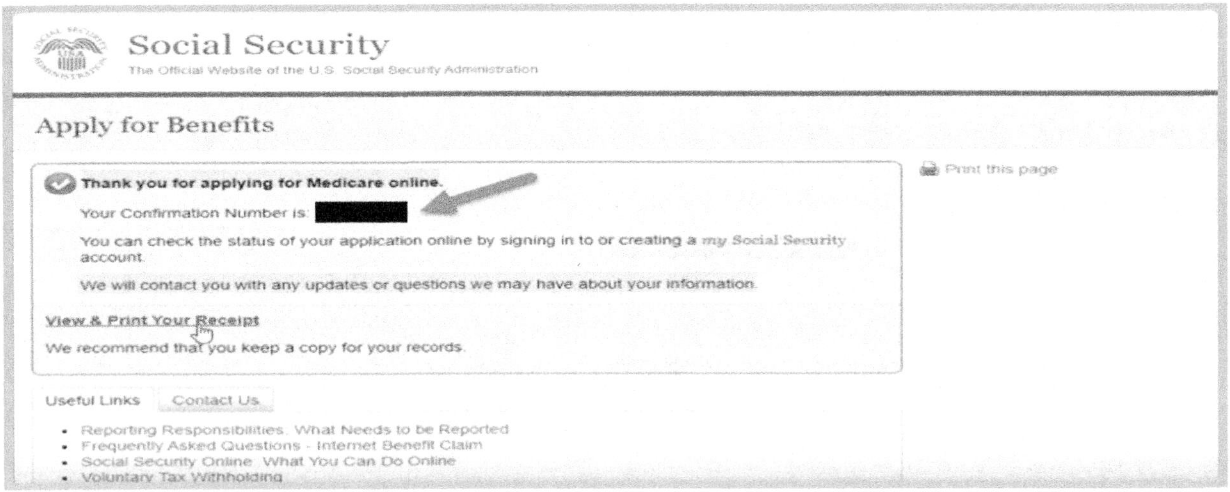

Social Security
The Official Website of the U.S. Social Security Administration

Apply for Benefits

Print this page

Thank you for applying for Medicare online.

Your Confirmation Number is: [redacted]

You can check the status of your application online by signing in to or creating a *my Social Security* account.

We will contact you with any updates or questions we may have about your information.

View & Print Your Receipt

We recommend that you keep a copy for your records.

Useful Links | Contact Us

- Reporting Responsibilities: What Needs to be Reported
- Frequently Asked Questions - Internet Benefit Claim
- Social Security Online: What You Can Do Online
- Voluntary Tax Withholding

- Once the individual has reviewed and electronically signed the application, they will get a "Thank you for applying for Medicare online." The application is now complete.

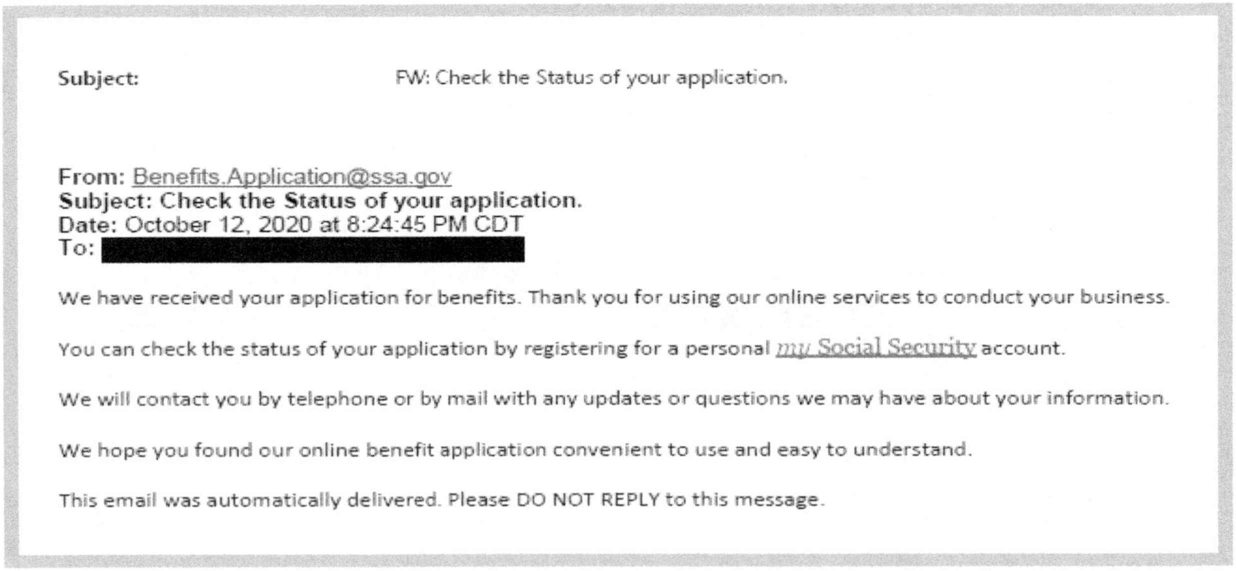

Subject: FW: Check the Status of your application.

From: Benefits.Application@ssa.gov
Subject: Check the Status of your application.
Date: October 12, 2020 at 8:24:45 PM CDT
To: [redacted]

We have received your application for benefits. Thank you for using our online services to conduct your business.

You can check the status of your application by registering for a personal *my Social Security* account.

We will contact you by telephone or by mail with any updates or questions we may have about your information.

We hope you found our online benefit application convenient to use and easy to understand.

This email was automatically delivered. Please DO NOT REPLY to this message.

- The individual should receive an email confirmation once they have submitted the application to Social Security for their Medicare, letting them know the application has been received.

Access Medicare Number Online Right Away

Social Security Administration
Benefit Verification Letter

Date: October 26, 2020
BNC#:
REF:

INFORMATION ONLY

JOHN L SMITH
123 SOMEWHERE LANE
GREAT TOWN, USA 54321

You asked us for information from your record. The information that you requested is shown below. If you want anyone else to have this information, you may send them this letter.

Date of Birth Information

The date of birth shown on our records is January 13, 1956.

Medicare Information

You are entitled to hospital insurance under Medicare beginning January 2021.

You are entitled to medical insurance under Medicare beginning January 2021.

Your Medicare number is 1EG4-TE5-MK72 . You may use this number to get medical services while waiting for your Medicare card.

If you any questions, please log into Medicare.gov, or call 1-800-MEDICARE (1-800-633-4227).

Suspect Social Security Fraud?

Please visit http://oig.ssa.gov/r or call the Inspector General's Fraud Hotline at 1-800-269-0271 (TTY 1-866-501-2101).

If You Have Questions

We invite you to visit our web site at www.socialsecurity.gov on the Internet to find general information about Social Security. If you have any specific questions, you may call us toll-free at 1-800-772-1213, or call your local office at 1-866-572-2492. We can answer most questions over the phone. If you are deaf or hard of hearing, you may call our TTY number, 1-800-325-0778. You can also write or visit any Social Security office. The office that serves your area is located at:

SOCIAL SECURITY
10824 N.CENTRAL EXPWY
DALLAS TX 75231

See Next Page

- The individual will typically receive a letter from Social Security called the "Benefit Verification Letter" within 10 business days, showing they were approved for their Medicare.
- It is highly recommended that the individual log into my Social Security under "Benefits & Payments" and select "Get a Benefit Verification Letter." They can print this letter with their unique Medicare number and effective dates so they have it right away. It will take about three to four weeks to get the Medicare card in the mail so this will be useful to have this letter immediately.

Enroll Online With A Special Enrollment Period

Already Enrolled in Medicare

If you have Medicare, you can get information and services online. Find out how to manage your benefits.

If you are enrolled in Medicare Part A and you want to enroll in Part B, please complete form CMS-40B, Application for Enrollment in Medicare – Part B (medical insurance). If you are applying for Medicare Part B due to a loss of employment or group health coverage, you will also need to complete form CMS-L564, Request for Employment Information.

You have three options to submit your enrollment request under the Special Enrollment Period. You can do **one** of the following:

1. Go to "Apply Online for Medicare Part B During a Special Enrollment Period" and complete CMS-40B and CMS-L564. Then upload your evidence of Group Health Plan or Large Group Health Plan.
2. Fax or mail your CMS-40B, CMS-L564, and secondary evidence to your local Social Security office (see list of secondary evidence below).

Note: When completing the forms CMS-40B and CMS-L564

- State "I want Part B coverage to begin (MM/YY)" in the remarks section of the CMS-40B form or online application.
- If possible, your employer should complete Section B.
- If your employer is unable to complete Section B, please complete that portion as best as you can on behalf of your employer without your employer's signature and submit one of the following forms of secondary evidence:
  - Income tax form that shows health insurance premiums paid.
  - W-2s reflecting pre-tax medical contributions.
  - pay stubs that reflect health insurance premium deductions.
  - health insurance cards with a policy effective date.
  - explanations of benefits paid by the GHP or LGHP.
  - statements or receipts that reflect payment of health insurance premiums.

- If an individual is applying during a SEP, they should also apply online through Social Security. On the front page of Social Security, they will select Medicare Enrollment. They will scroll to the middle of the page where it says, "Already Enrolled in Medicare."
- The individual will then select "Apply Online for Medicare Part B During a Special Enrollment Period."

Uploading Documents To Social Security Is Easy

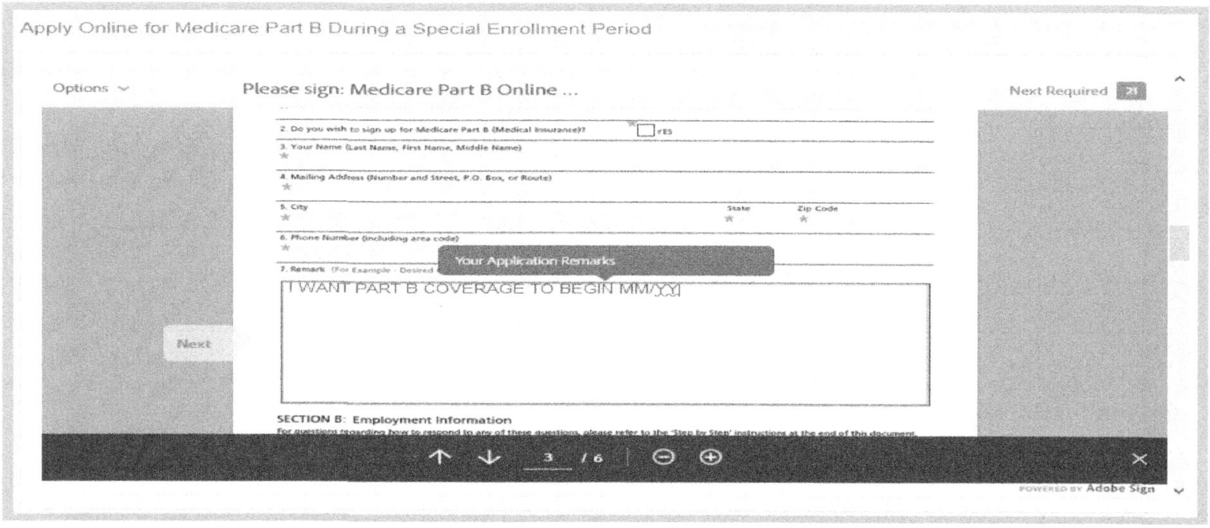

- The individual will be directed to the Medicare Part B Enrollment during a SEP. They will fill out form CMS-40B and in the remarks section say, “I want Part B coverage to begin MM/YY.”

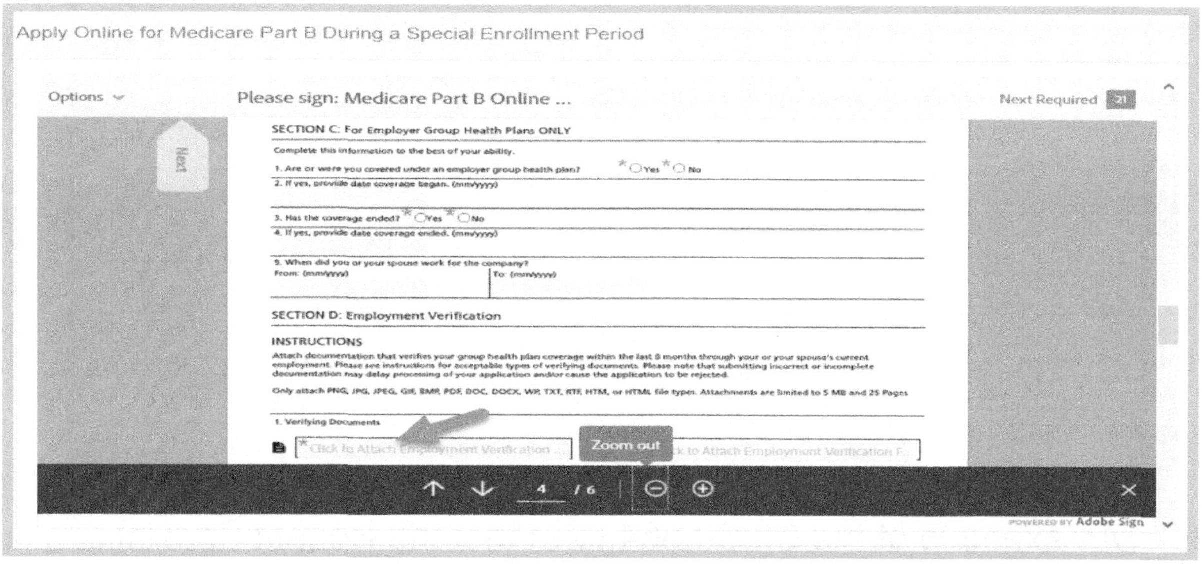

- The form CMS-L564 that the Benefit Specialist filled out can be easily uploaded during the application process.

Request For Employment Information CMS-L564

DEPARTMENT OF HEALTH AND HUMAN SERVICES
CENTERS FOR MEDICARE & MEDICAID SERVICES

Form Approved
OMB No. 0938-0787

REQUEST FOR EMPLOYMENT INFORMATION

SECTION A: To be completed by individual signing up for Medicare Part B (Medical Insurance)

1. Employer's Name
2. Date __ __ / __ __ / __ __ __ __
3. Employer's Address

City | State | Zip Code

4. Applicant's Name
5. Applicant's Social Security Number __ __ __ – __ __ – __ __ __ __
6. Employee's Name
7. Employee's Social Security Number __ __ __ – __ __ – __ __ __ __

SECTION B: To be completed by Employers

For Employer Group Health Plans ONLY:

1. Is (or was) the applicant covered under an employer group health plan? ☐ Yes ☐ No
2. If yes, give the date the applicant's coverage began. (mm/yyyy) __ __ / __ __ __ __
3. Has the coverage ended? ☐ Yes ☐ No
4. If yes, give the date the coverage ended. (mm/yyyy) __ __ / __ __ __ __
5. When did the employee work for your company?
   From: (mm/yyyy) __ __ / __ __ __ __ To: (mm/yyyy) __ __ / __ __ __ __ Still Employed: (mm/yyyy) __ __ / __ __ __ __
6. If you're a large group health plan and the applicant is disabled, please list the timeframe (all months) that your group health plan was primary payer.
   From: (mm/yyyy) __ __ / __ __ __ __ To: (mm/yyyy) __ __ / __ __ __ __

For Hours Bank Arrangements ONLY:

1. Is (or was) the applicant covered under an Hours Bank Arrangement? ☐ Yes ☐ No
2. If yes, does the applicant have hours remaining in reserve? ☐ Yes ☐ No
3. Date reserve hours ended or will be used? (mm/yyyy) __ __ / __ __ __ __

All Employers:

Signature of Company Official | Date Signed __ __ / __ __ / __ __ __ __

Title of Company Official | Phone Number (__ __ __) __ __ __ – __ __ __ __

According to the Paperwork Reduction Act of 1995, no persons are required to respond to a collection of information unless it displays a valid OMB control number. The valid OMB control number for this information is 0938-0787. The time required to complete this information collection is estimated to average 15 minutes per response, including the time to review instructions, search existing data resources, gather the data needed, and complete and review the information collection. If you have comments concerning the accuracy of the time estimate(s) or suggestions for improving this form, please write to: CMS, 7500 Security Boulevard, Attn: PRA Reports Clearance Officer, Mail Stop C4-26-05, Baltimore, MD 21244-1850.

Form CMS L564/R297 (08/20) 2

- An example of the CMS-L564 form that the Benefit Specialist must fill out for an individual is shown as an example. Once this form is completed, it can be uploaded to Social Security as previously indicated during the SEP.

Confirmation Emails Are Sent During SEP Enrollment

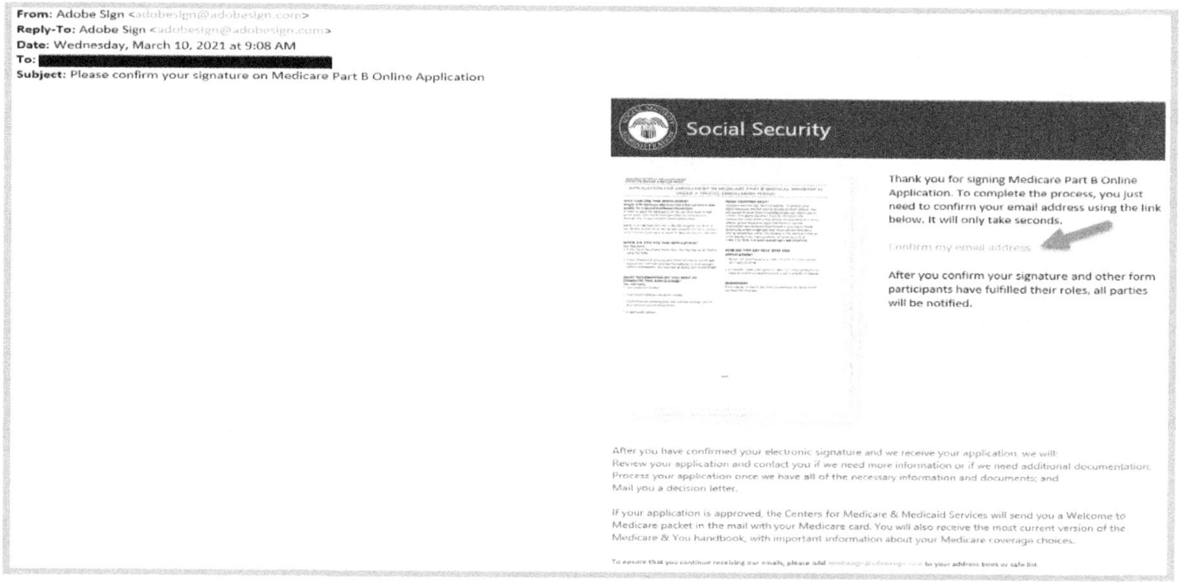

From: Adobe Sign <adobesign@adobesign.com>
Reply-To: Adobe Sign <adobesign@adobesign.com>
Date: Wednesday, March 10, 2021 at 9:08 AM
To:
Subject: Please confirm your signature on Medicare Part B Online Application

Social Security

Thank you for signing Medicare Part B Online Application. To complete the process, you just need to confirm your email address using the link below. It will only take seconds.

Confirm my email address

After you confirm your signature and other form participants have fulfilled their roles, all parties will be notified.

After you have confirmed your electronic signature and we receive your application, we will:
Review your application and contact you if we need more information or if we need additional documentation;
Process your application once we have all of the necessary information and documents; and
Mail you a decision letter.

If your application is approved, the Centers for Medicare & Medicaid Services will send you a Welcome to Medicare packet in the mail with your Medicare card. You will also receive the most current version of the Medicare & You handbook, with important information about your Medicare coverage choices.

- Once the application has been submitted electronically to Social Security the individual will get an email. The individual will need to confirm their email address.

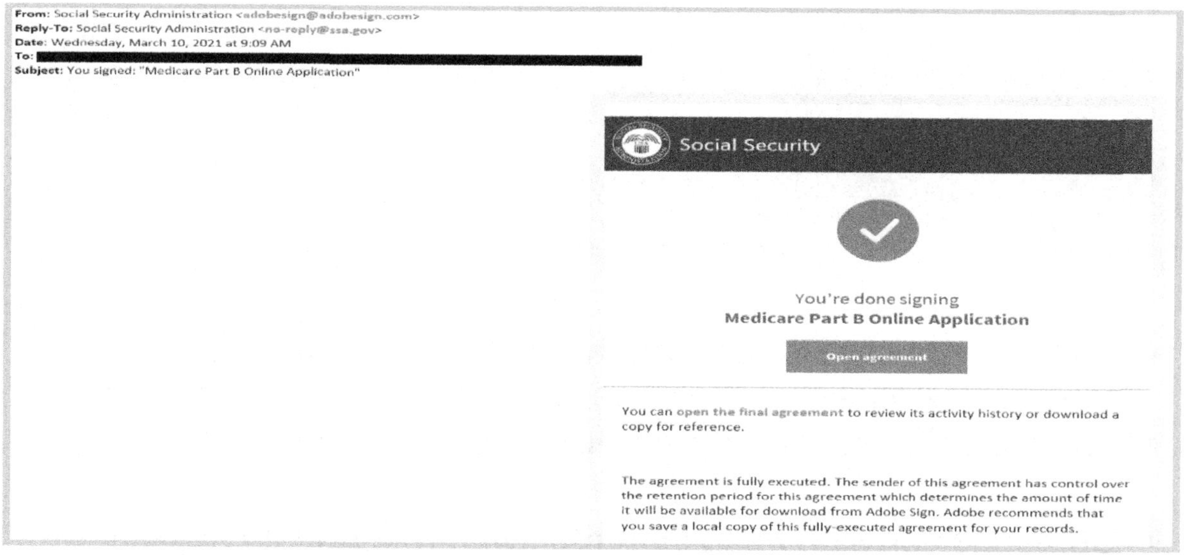

From: Social Security Administration <adobesign@adobesign.com>
Reply-To: Social Security Administration <no-reply@ssa.gov>
Date: Wednesday, March 10, 2021 at 9:09 AM
To:
Subject: You signed: "Medicare Part B Online Application"

Social Security

You're done signing
Medicare Part B Online Application

Open agreement

You can open the final agreement to review its activity history or download a copy for reference.

The agreement is fully executed. The sender of this agreement has control over the retention period for this agreement which determines the amount of time it will be available for download from Adobe Sign. Adobe recommends that you save a local copy of this fully-executed agreement for your records.

- Once the email has been confirmed, they will get another email confirming that everything has been signed and completed.

When Should You Take Social Security Benefits?

When Should I Take Social Security Retirement Benefits?

BIRTH YEAR	YOUR FULL RETIREMENT AGE (FRA)	Reduced Benefit At Age 62
1937	65	20.00%
1938	65 and 2 months	20.83%
1939	65 and 4 months	21.67%
1940	65 and 6 months	22.50%
1941	65 and 8 months	23.33%
1942	65 and 10 months	24.17%
1943 – 1954	66	25.00%
1955	66 and 2 months	25.83%
1956	66 and 4 months	26.67%
1957	66 and 6 months	27.50%
1958	66 and 8 months	28.33%
1959	66 and 10 months	29.17%
1960 and later	67	30.00%

- This is a decision that someone will need to make for themselves based on their needs. Currently, every individual has the option to take Social Security retirement benefits anytime between the ages of 62 through 70.
- Someone can sign up to start receiving retirement checks from the federal government as early as age 62, however, their payments will be reduced by taking it early before their full retirement age.

- An individual turning 65 in 2022 will have been born in 1957, which will make age 66 and 6 months their full retirement age.

Retirement Benefits Will Be Reduced If Taken Early

- An individual turning 65 in 2022 who decided to start their retirement benefits early at the age of 62, would have seen their benefits reduced by 27.50 percent.
- Social Security retirement benefits are intended to provide income for the rest of someone's life; therefore, taking it early can be an important decision.

Three Reasons For Taking Retirement Benefits Early

- There are three reasons why it may be beneficial for someone to take their retirement as early as 62.
    - The first reason may be due to income concerns of having to leave the workforce earlier than anticipated and not being able to find employment.
    - The second reason could be that even with the reduced benefits, it will help make up the difference in the loss of income if the individual retires early.
    - Lastly, it might be due to health concerns. The individual believes it would be more beneficial to take retirement benefits early based on life expectancy.

The Most Popular Ages People Claim Social Security

- In 2018, USA Today published a study that discussed the most popular ages to take Social Security retirement benefits. The two most popular ages are 62 and 66.
- The reason 66 is quite popular is because that is now the full retirement age to claim without reduction in Social Security

benefits. We will probably see age 67 in the next four years become increasingly popular as well.

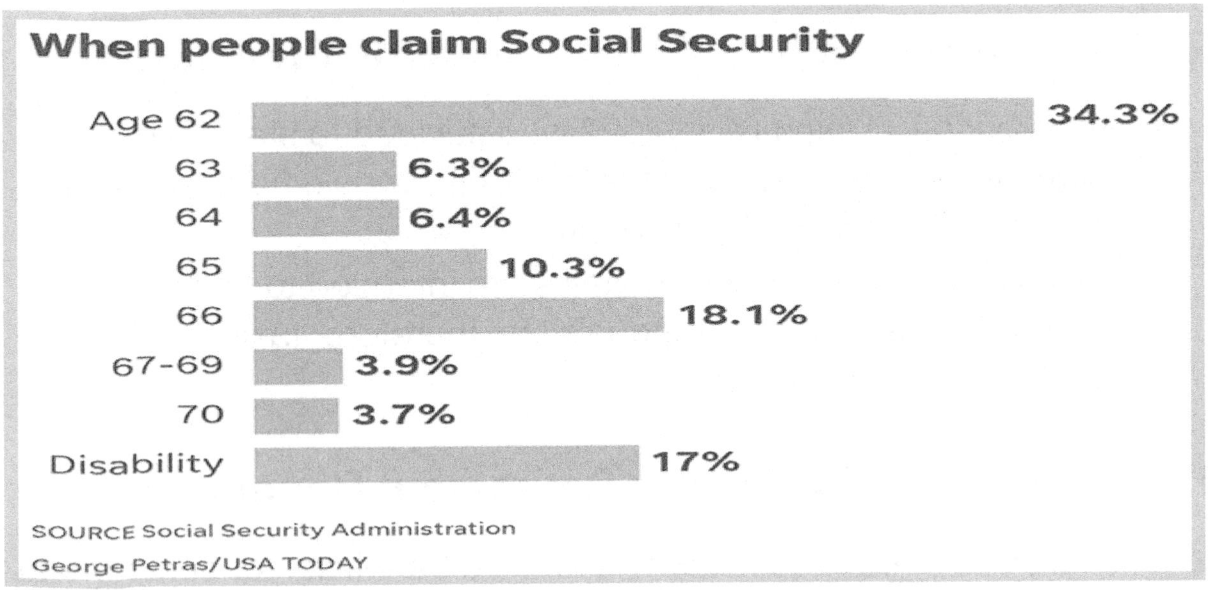

Courtesy of:
https://www.usatoday.com/story/money/personalfinance/retirement/2018/06/19/whats-most-popular-age-to-take-social-security/35928543/

Retirees Decide To Take Retirement Benefits Early

- In 2018 according to USA Today, almost half of retirees are taking their Social Security retirement benefits prior to the age of 65.
- The bad news for those individuals is that they will be receiving less Social Security retirement benefits.
- The good news for those individuals is that they will receive their Medicare Part A and B card automatically in the mail and do not need to apply for it.

Benefits To Waiting Until Full Retirement Age

- There are benefits to waiting until the full retirement age or later to start drawing Social Security benefits.

- If someone waits until their full retirement age, they will get 100 percent of the benefits that Social Security calculated for them based on their lifetime earnings.
- There is also a big benefit to those who wait until age 70 to start drawing their Social Security retirement benefits. For every year past someone's full retirement age, Social Security will give an additional 8 percent increase in their Social Security payments.

Calculating Your Retirement Age Is Based On Needs

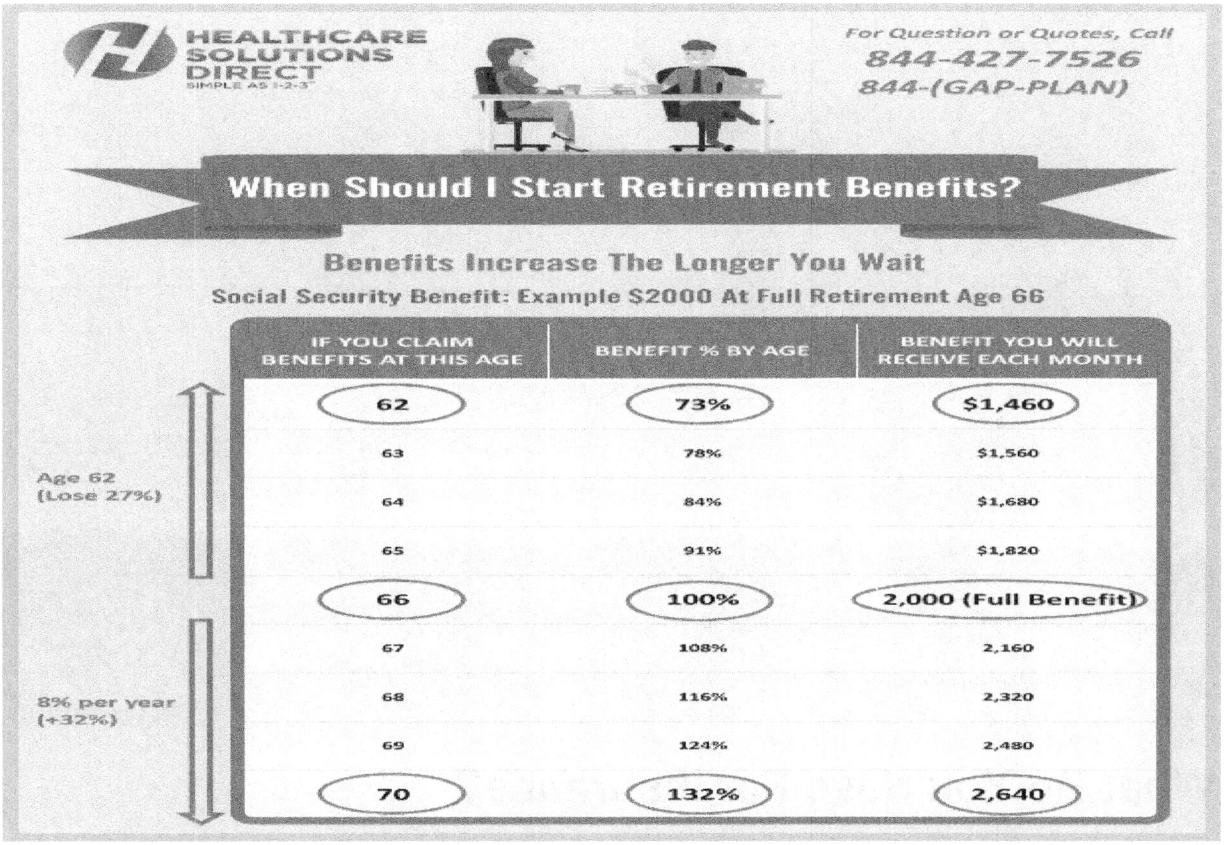

IF YOU CLAIM BENEFITS AT THIS AGE	BENEFIT % BY AGE	BENEFIT YOU WILL RECEIVE EACH MONTH
62	73%	$1,460
63	78%	$1,560
64	84%	$1,680
65	91%	$1,820
66	100%	2,000 (Full Benefit)
67	108%	2,160
68	116%	2,320
69	124%	2,480
70	132%	2,640

- There is no right or wrong answer when it comes to when someone draws their Social Security retirement benefits. Everyone must take the time to evaluate what is best for their needs as they enter retirement.

Chapter 7

How Medicare Works With Insurance — Everything You Need To Know

What Do You Have For Insurance?

- When it comes time for someone to look at Medicare, their current insurance plays a big role in their decision-making process. Sometimes it is rather cut and dry with what someone should do. However, at other times it is not.

- Unfortunately, there are many licensed insurance agents that do not know what to do or what plan to recommend. This makes looking into the Medicare process even more frustrating.
- This section is crucial to understanding how each insurance will work with Medicare and it will also provide suggestions on exactly what to do. Once the individual and insurance agent identify which insurance they currently have, both will be better prepared to know what steps need to be taken to solve the problem.
- This section is dedicated to making this as easy as possible so that everyone understands exactly what they need to do when it comes to their current insurance and whether they should take Medicare Part A and/or B.

The Mindset Everyone Should Have About Medicare

- Here should be the mindset of both the individual and the insurance agent when someone is turning 65:

"The individual must take Medicare when first eligible."

- As of 2022, Medicare will only cost $170.10 for the standard Part B premium. Taking Medicare when first eligible could be more cost effective, but more importantly it will save on the stress of paperwork or a penalty in the future.
- It is so important when someone is turning 65 that the insurance agent helps the individual make the right decision. The mindset that everyone needs to enroll in Medicare will ensure that the process is the same for everyone and each person gets the undivided attention they deserve.

Insurance Agent Needs To Find This Out Immediately

- We are now going to look at each possible insurance that an individual could have when they are retiring or turning 65 and discuss what they and the insurance agent should focus on so both parties are being respectful of the other's time.
- Early in the conversation, the insurance agent should be in the habit of starting the discovery process by uncovering three crucial pieces of information so they are focusing on the needs of the individual who is eligible for Medicare. The three crucial pieces include:
    - Current or past employment,
    - Current or past health insurance, and
    - Current or past monthly premium for health insurance.

Exploring The Three Pieces Of Crucial Information

- **What did or does the individual do for a living?**
    - This question will start the process of helping to identify what the individual has for insurance. A self-employed individual is likely to have an individual plan through the health marketplace, but that is *not* always the case.
    - The individual might be married or in a civil union and on their group insurance plan.
    - The insurance agent should follow up by asking what the individual has for insurance so that everyone is on the same page. More importantly the insurance agent should be asking about employment to get to know the other person if they expect to develop a lifetime relationship as their trusted advisor.
- **What does the individual currently have for health insurance?**

    - This question really starts the process of being a trusted advisor and ensuring the individual needs to enroll in Medicare Part A and/or B. An individual who is a federal employee with federal employee health benefits, might not need to enroll in Medicare Part A and/or B. This question is extremely important in identifying what the individual should do first about Medicare before advising them on any other coverage.

- **What does the individual currently pay each month for their health insurance?**
    - This question starts the process of uncovering what the individual's financial needs are in relation to Medicare benefits. If they should be looking at qualifying for Extra Help or an MSP (Medicare Savings Program) due to financial reasons, the individual does not need to purchase a Medigap Supplement.
    - What an individual is paying for their current health insurance is not always indicative of enrolling in a Medicare Advantage or a Medigap Supplement, but it does give a baseline of where the individual is at currently.
    - To be a trusted advisor, a full needs analysis should be completed by the insurance agent.

Do Not Move Forward Until Uncovering Crucial Information

- An insurance agent should not be advising an individual on what they should do for their insurance needs *until* they have the answers to those three important questions stated above. If an insurance agent starts recommending something right away, they are making it about them and not the other person.

- We are going to look at every possible form of insurance that an individual might have when they are retiring or turning 65 and eligible for Medicare.
- It is important to always keep in mind as you begin the process of looking at the different insurance options that the standard Medicare Part B premium for 2022 is *only* $170.10. This could be the only premium an individual might need to pay if they decide to enroll into a $0 premium MAPD. An individual who is interested in a Medigap Supplement plan will only need to invest an additional $100 a month.

Remember: Medicare Part B Monthly Premium for 2022 = $170.10

Individual Marketplace — The Affordable Care Act

- Individual health insurance is provided through the marketplace known as ACA to anyone who does not have access to a group health insurance plan through a current or previous employer. Many have also come to refer to this as Obamacare.
- Plans that are provided by health insurance companies on a short-term basis, which are not part of the ACA would also be considered individual health insurance plans.
- Individual health insurance was meant to provide coverage to someone prior to the age of 65 who did not have access to group health insurance until they were eligible for Medicare.

Can Someone Keep Individual Insurance After 65?

- Prior to ACA someone turning 65 who was on individual health insurance was automatically cancelled and could not keep it after they turned 65.

- Most insurance companies will still cancel the insurance when someone turns 65, but it is not always automatic. The individual must call the insurance company the month before they go onto Medicare and let them know that they want it cancelled. The individual is the only one that can cancel their insurance, so let us look at why it is advised that they do that.

Individual Insurance Has Tax Subsidies That Expire

- When the ACA was passed, it came with tax subsidies for individual health insurance for those with incomes between 100 percent to 400 percent of the federal poverty level.
    - In 2022, this would translate to an individual whose income was roughly between $12,880 to $51,520. If the individual did not have access to affordable health coverage through an employer, they could receive some sort of tax subsidy for their individual health insurance through the ACA.
    - There are many individuals who could be paying less than $100 a month at the age of 64 for their individual health insurance plan because of tax subsidies.

Individual Insurance Without Subsidies Is Expensive

- Any individual who does not receive tax subsidies because they reported earnings of more than $51,520, the insurance would cost on average between $800 to $1000 a month. Any individual in 2022 that is paying less than $800 a month for their ACA plan is getting a tax subsidy.
- When someone is eligible for Medicare Part A, that individual will no longer be eligible for any tax credits or cost savings that they were getting from the individual marketplace plan no matter what income bracket they fall under.

Losing Subsidies Means All Must Take Medicare At 65

- If after the age of 65 and the individual keeps the ACA plan, two things would happen that might not be good:
  - The plan would go to full cost, which could be around $800 to $1000 a month regardless of their income.
  - The individual would miss their one-time IEP and could be faced with a big penalty in the future.
- It is strongly advised that the individual call and make sure the plan is canceled the month before they turn 65 years old.

What Happens If Tax Subsidies Stay On Plan After 65?

- It can be quite enticing to be paying less than $100 a month for health insurance at the age of 65 and decide to leave everything the same.
- If the plan is not automatically cancelled and the individual keeps the plan and the tax subsidies do not automatically go away, this will be a problem for that individual in the future.
- The federal government will eventually realize the mistake and the individual will get a big bill for the tax subsidies when they file their taxes. Any individual who turns 65 and is eligible for the "premium free" Medicare Part A, will lose all tax subsidies given to them by the federal government. This means everyone must take Medicare at 65.

Conclusion When It Comes To Individual Health

- An individual turning 65 with individual health insurance which may include those who are self-employed, must take their Medicare Part A and B and pay the standard monthly Part B premium of $170.10 (2022) in order to avoid any penalties in the future.

- This individual will need to be enrolled into Medicare Part A and B during their IEP.
- This individual should speak to an insurance agent to discuss whether a $0 premium Medicare Advantage or investing around $100 into a Medigap Supplement plan would best fit their needs.

Employer Group Health Insurance Coverage

- When it comes to employer group coverage and needing to enroll in Medicare when an individual is turning 65 is sometimes the most confusing and misunderstand part of Medicare.
- In order to attempt to help make this simple and easy, we will refer to group coverage as either working employer group insurance coverage or retired employer insurance group coverage.
- Although the insurance may be provided by the same employer, Medicare views someone who is still working and being provided group health insurance benefits by their current employer *differently* than someone who is retired and no longer working for that company.

Understanding What Medicare Considers Working

- If an individual is retired at the age of 65, but their spouse is still working and both are covered under the current employment group health insurance coverage, Medicare will still consider this working employer group health coverage.
- Even though the individual may be retired and eligible for Medicare at 65, their spouse or family member is still working and contributing to Medicare taxes.

- If one of the individuals is still working and covered by that employer's group coverage, the federal government still views the coverage as working even if the person who is eligible for Medicare at 65 is retired.

Medicare Has Different Rules For Working vs. Retired

- Medicare has different rules when it comes to enrolling into Medicare Part A and/or B for those who are enrolled into working employer group insurance coverage versus those who have retired employer group insurance coverage.
- Here is the general rule of thumb when it comes to enrolling into Medicare at the age of 65 that might help:
    - If someone is still working: they may wait or
    - If someone is retired: they *must* register.
- Since Medicare has different rules based on the size of the company, we are going to first look at working employer group insurance coverage.

Working Employer Group — Fewer Than 20 Employees

- It is important that the individual who is turning 65 and still working and covered by their employer group coverage finds out if the company has more than 20 employees.
- If the individual works for a company that has less than 20 employees, that individual must take Medicare Part A and B, or they will not be eligible for a SEP in the future.
- This is a Medicare rule that does not really make sense, but it has to do with how Medicare coordinates with the small group insurance plan.

Medicare Rule: Individual Must Take Medicare A & B

- If the company has less than 20 employees, and the individual (or their spouse) is still working and they are covered by the current employer's group coverage when turning 65, Medicare states that the individual must take their Medicare Part A and B.
- Regardless if the individual (or their spouse) can or would like to keep the current group coverage, the size of the company dictates that they must enroll in both Medicare Part A and B.
- To have a better understanding of this rule, it is important to know that small group will coordinate with Medicare differently than how the large group will coordinate benefits.

Coordinating Medicare With Small vs. Large Group Insurance

- Small group insurance is defined by Medicare as having fewer than 20 employees. Medicare Part A and B will become the primary insurance, and the small group insurance coverage will be the secondary insurance. This makes it necessary for the individual to enroll in their Medicare Part A and B at 65 regardless if they keep the small group insurance coverage or select another option like a Medicare Advantage plan or Medigap Supplement.
- Large group insurance, which is defined by Medicare as having more than 20 employees, works differently than that of a small group. The large group insurance coverage will remain the primary insurance if the individual remains working for the company regardless if they were to enroll in Medicare Part A and/or B. The group insurance always stays the primary insurance.

Small Group Should Consider Other Health Coverage

- Since the individual must take Medicare Part A and B, an individual working for a company with fewer than 20 employees should consider a Medicare Advantage plan or a Medigap Supplement.
- As of 2022, this individual will be responsible for the standard Part B monthly premium of $170.10 regardless of if they decide to keep the small group insurance coverage or not past the age of 65.
- There are only two reasons why someone working for a company with fewer than 20 employees should consider keeping their small group insurance plan even though they must enroll in Medicare Part A and B as their primary insurance.

Questions To Consider When Deciding On Coverage

- There are only two questions that an individual should ask themselves if they are still working and can keep their employer group coverage regardless of the size of the company.
    - Do they have any dependents on their group coverage? and
    - Are they taking any high-cost brand name medications?
- If there are no dependents on the group coverage who would be affected and the individual is not taking high-cost brand name medication that would be better covered under the employer group health insurance plan, that individual should look at other coverage. They should consider enrolling into a Medicare Advantage plan or look at a Medigap plan since they will be required to enroll into Medicare Part A and B.

Conclusion When It Comes To Small Group Insurance

- An individual turning 65 with small group health insurance (less than 20 employees) must take their Medicare Part A and B and pay the standard monthly Part B premium of $170.10 (2022) in order to avoid any penalties in the future.
- This individual will need to be enrolled into Medicare Part A and B during their IEP.
- This individual should speak to an insurance agent to discuss whether a $0 premium Medicare Advantage or investing around $100 into a Medigap Supplement plan would best fit their needs.

Working Employer Group — More Than 20 Employees

- If an individual (or their spouse) is turning 65 and they are working and their health insurance coverage is being provided by their current employer that has more than 20 employees, the individual can delay their Medicare Part A and/or B.
- The individual may delay their Medicare Part A and/or B until they (or their spouse) stop working, or they lose that coverage. The individual will not be penalized by Medicare for delaying their Medicare Part A and/or B.
- Medicare will grant the individual (or their spouse) an SEP when they decide to stop working or within eight months of losing their coverage.
- Let's explore why someone who is still working and covered under their current employer group coverage should still look at enrolling into Medicare Part A and B.

Reasons Why Taking Medicare Is A Good Idea

- The individual will need to get their Human Resources benefits coordinator to complete the CMS-L564 in the future when they decide to enroll into Medicare through an SEP.
- The process of requesting and getting all the paperwork necessary to submit to Social Security can be quite stressful and time consuming. During the Covid-19 pandemic, there was a major delay in processing the paperwork needed for a SEP.
- Most of the time, the individual will need their Medicare Part A and/or B coverage to start within 30 days. If there is a delay in Social Security processing the information, it could be stressful for that individual.

Medicare Can Be More Cost Effective Than Group

- As of 2022, an individual can enroll into Medicare for just the standard Medicare Part B premium of $170.10 a month. The other positive is the individual can enroll during their 7-month IEP and not need to worry about having to rush to get an SEP in the future.
- An individual could also choose to enroll in a $0 premium Medicare Advantage plan, which would be quite similar to their employer group health coverage and may even be offered additional benefits that they are not currently receiving.
- An individual could also choose to invest around $100 a month to purchase a Medigap Supplement that might give them better coverage and flexibility and could cost less than their current employer group coverage.

Questions To Consider When Deciding On Coverage

- There are only two questions that we discussed earlier when we talked about small group health insurance coverage that will still apply to someone who works for a large group company regardless if they can keep the coverage.
- An individual should still ask themselves these two questions if they are still working and can keep their employer group health insurance coverage.
    - Do they have any dependents on their group coverage?
    - Are they taking any high-cost brand name medications?
- If there are no dependents on the group coverage who would be affected and the individual is not taking high-cost brand name medication that would be better covered under the employer group health insurance plan, that individual should look at other coverage. They should consider enrolling into a Medicare Advantage plan or look at a Medigap plan since they will be required to enroll into Medicare Part A and B.

Health Savings Accounts Do Not Work With Medicare

- If an individual has an employer group insurance plan that has a high deductible plan with a health savings account (HSA), it would be advisable not to enroll into even Medicare Part A if they would like to still make contributions.
- Anyone with a HSA can no longer contribute pre-tax dollars or have any employer contribution if they enroll in any part of Medicare, which includes Part A.
- If an individual wants to continue to contribute to their HSA account after the age of 65, they must stop collecting their Social Security retirement benefits at least four months leading up to the age of 65.

Why Collecting Social Security Is A Problem For HSA

- If an individual is collecting their Social Security retirement benefits at least four months prior to 65, they will automatically be enrolled into Medicare Part A and B.
- As soon as the individual is automatically enrolled into Medicare because they were drawing their retirement benefits, they will not be able to decline the premium free Part A. This will be a problem for someone still wanting to contribute to their HSA.
- An individual can no longer contribute to an HSA if they have any part of Medicare, which includes the premium free Part A.

Stop Contributing To Health Savings Accounts 6 Months Prior To Medicare

- If an individual does not enroll in either Medicare Part A and/or B, they can continue to contribute pre-tax dollars into their HSA. Once that individual decides they want to enroll into Medicare Part A and/or B, they will need to stop contributing to the HSA account at least six months prior to their effective date. The reason is that their Medicare Part A will be backdated six months prior to the Part B effective date when they go to enroll in the future.
- If for some reason someone did not stop contributing six months prior, they may incur an income tax penalty on the funds that they contributed to their HSA with pre-tax dollars after they had been enrolled in Medicare Part A.
- An individual might find it in their best interest to stop contributing to their HSA when they are turning 65 to ensure that they do not make any mistakes in the future.

Conclusion When It Comes To Large Group Insurance

- As of 2022, an individual turning 65 with large group health insurance (more than 20 employees), may delay their Medicare Part A and/or B and not need to pay the standard monthly Part B premium of $170.10.
- This individual will be able to enroll into Medicare Part A and/or B during an SEP later in the future when they decide to stop working or within 8 months of losing their coverage.
- This individual should still speak to an insurance agent to discuss whether taking their Medicare Part A and B and looking at a $0 premium Medicare Advantage or investing around $100 into a Medigap Supplement plan would best fit their needs.

Retired Employer Group Insurance Coverage

- Retired employer group health insurance coverage is when an individual and/or their spouse is either retired or no longer working for the company, but they will still be offered the ability to continue with the employer's group health insurance coverage.
- Since the individual and/or spouse is no longer working, they will be required to enroll in both Medicare Part A and B when they turn 65 in order to avoid any penalties in the future.
- It is important to understand that this individual will not be granted an SEP since they and/or their spouse are no longer working for that company and this type of coverage will not be considered credible coverage by Medicare.
- Most retired employer group coverage that is offered today will be in the form of a group Medicare Advantage plan, which will require the individual to enroll in Medicare.

Retired Group Is Typically A Medicare Advantage

- Retired employer group insurance coverage is typically provided to someone who worked for a large company. Fortune 500 companies will many times offer their retired employees an option to continue with the company's insurance in the form of a Group Medicare Advantage plan.
- This is another reason why it is important that the insurance agent find out what the individual did for a living during the discovery process. This will begin the process of possibly determining if the individual worked for a large company and they can keep the company insurance after they retire. Companies like Exxon Mobil or Verizon are good examples of Fortune 500 companies that will provide their retires with a continued Group Medicare Advantage plan.
- This is important for the insurance agent to determine this early in the discovery process, so they are being respectful of the individual's time. Group Medicare Advantage plans will typically be offered as a PPO network and may offer additional benefits not offered to the general public. The retiree may be happy with the coverage that is being provided to them and may need to go through a third party.

Reason Most Employers Offer Medicare Advantage

- In the past, many employers would allow the retiree to keep the group insurance plan as the secondary with Medicare Part A and B as the primary. Fewer companies are still providing this as a benefit due to cost reasons.
- It saves the employer a lot of money to let a Medicare Advantage company create a plan specifically tailored to that large group of individuals. The individual will still be responsible for the Part B premium; however, the employer allows a Medicare Advantage plan to manage the retired employer group coverage.
- This is a smart business move for the employer and it gives its employees an option for their health care with some additional benefits that they might not be able to get elsewhere.

Questions Retirees Should Inquire About Coverage

- Here are some key questions that a retiree should consider about their retiree employer group coverage before they decide whether this will best fit their needs.
    - Are they happy with the plan?
    - Will Medicare Part A and B be their primary insurance?
        - Many retirees think that Medicare Part A and B will be the primary insurance without fully understanding that the group health insurance plan is a Medicare Advantage plan.
    - Do all their doctors accept the plan?
    - Do they know their maximum out-of-pocket cost?
    - Do they need to consult with a third-party administrator about the insurance?

Most Fortune 500 Companies Will Use A Third Party

- Most Fortune 500 or large companies will use a third-party administrator to help service their retirees. Some companies will give additional benefits to their retirees to go through a third-party and some will just use the third-party to help the retiree navigate their options.
- There are many third-party administrators that companies will use to help either administer or advise the retiree with their Medicare options. Companies like One Exchange and Via Benefits are popular administrators. If an individual needs to consult with a third-party administrator, they should first talk to that third-party before talking to an insurance agent.

Conclusion When It Comes To Retiree Group

- An individual turning 65 who is being offered retiree group health insurance, must take their Medicare Part A and B and pay the standard monthly Part B premium of $170.10 (2022) in order to avoid any penalties in the future.
- This individual will need to be enrolled into Medicare Part A and B during their 7-month IEP.
- This individual does not need the services of an insurance agent if they must go through a third-party administrator or they are happy with the insurance coverage.
- If the individual does not need to talk to a third-party administrator and they are not happy with the insurance coverage being offered, they should speak to an insurance agent to discuss whether a $0 premium Medicare Advantage or investing around $100 into a Medigap Supplement plan would best fit their needs.

Consolidated Omnibus Budget Reconciliation Act (Cobra) Retiree Health Coverage

- The Consolidated Omnibus Budget Reconciliation Act (COBRA) is a federal law, which will let an individual keep their working employer group coverage for a limited time after their employment ends or they lose the coverage as a dependent of that employee.
- The COBRA coverage typically applies only to large companies with 20 or more employees, but some states will require smaller companies to provide continued coverage for a limited time.
- The COBRA coverage was *never* intended to be a long-term solution or a continuation of insurance by the employer. Think of COBRA as the band-aid health insurance to get an individual back on their feet until they find other health insurance.

Consolidated Omnibus Budget Reconciliation Act Coverage Is Expensive And Only For Limited Time

- The COBRA coverage is typically only offered for 18 months and in some cases 36 months from the date the group health coverage ends. When someone turns 65, they must enroll in Medicare Parts A and B during their 7-month IEP since they are no longer working. The COBRA coverage is not considered working employer group coverage since the individual is no longer working for that company.
- The COBRA coverage allows the employee to continue the health insurance by paying the full cost of the insurance, including what the employer was contributing to the health insurance plan. It is not uncommon to see someone paying over $1000 a month for their COBRA health insurance.
- If the COBRA coverage included a spouse or dependents when someone turns 65, they may extend the coverage only to the

dependents for 36 months since the individual qualified for Medicare. This is another protection COBRA gives an individual when they are turning 65 and Medicare eligible.

Individual Must Still Enroll In Medicare With Consolidated Omnibus Budget Reconciliation Act Coverage

- For those individuals who decide to keep COBRA coverage after turning 65 due to the plan's comprehensive prescription benefit, the individuals must still enroll in Medicare Part A and B since this is considered retiree health coverage.
- The COBRA coverage will not entitle an individual to an SEP in the future since this will not be considered credible coverage.
- The majority of individuals who do turn 65 will cancel their COBRA retiree health coverage and enroll into Medicare Part A and B due to the costs associated with the health insurance coverage.

Conclusion When It Comes To Consolidated Omnibus Budget Reconciliation Act Coverage

- As of 2022, an individual turning 65 who is being offered COBRA retiree health coverage must take their Medicare Part A and B and pay the standard monthly Part B premium of $170.10 in order to avoid any penalties in the future.
- Since they will not qualify for an SEP, this individual will need to be enrolled into Medicare Part A and B during their 7-month IEP.
- This individual should speak to an insurance agent to discuss whether a $0 premium Medicare Advantage or investing around $100 into a Medigap Supplement plan would best fit their needs.

Federal Employees Health Benefits

- The Federal Employees Health Benefits (FEHB) Program is for federal employees, retirees, and their survivors.
- A federal employee is anyone who has worked for the federal government at either the local, state, or national level.
- Federal employees are among the most secure when it comes to insurance as they carry some impressive benefits that you do not see in the private sector.
- At the local level, examples can include being a police officer, firefighter, or land surveyor. At the state level examples can include being an elementary school teacher, records clerk, or civil engineer. At the national level examples can include a U.S. postal worker, Federal Bureau of Investigation agent, or an aeronautical engineer.
- Railroad workers are also considered employees of the federal government under the Federal Railroad Administration.

All Federal Employees Will Have Access To Federal Employees Health Benefits

- If an individual worked for the federal government, they would have access to FEHB. Since they already have the federal governments insurance that is being made available to them, this individual does not need to speak to an insurance agent.
- For someone to keep FEHB after they retire, they must be enrolled in FEHB for at least five years to be eligible to continue the coverage. Someone who's allowed to keep their FEHB when they turn 65 does not need to enroll in Medicare Part A and/or B.
- There are three options an individual will have with FEHB when they turn 65, which we will look at next.

First Option With Federal Employees Health Benefits When Looking At Retiring

- The first option an individual has is they can keep their FEHB as their primary insurance and continue to pay their monthly premium for the plan. They should enroll in Medicare Part A since it is free at 65 and it could help them with hospital expenses under their FEHB.
- Since the FEHB includes prescription drug coverage, there is no need for Part D. A benefit to not enrolling in Part B would be that they would save the standard $170.10 premium (2022).
- The downside is that not enrolling during the 7-month IEP, the individual would not be eligible for an SEP if they wanted their Part B later.

Second Option With Federal Employees Health Benefits When Looking At Retiring

- The second option an individual has is they can enroll in Medicare Part A and B as their primary insurance and the FEHB will be their secondary insurance like that of a Medigap Supplement plan. There will be no need for a standalone Part D since the FEHB includes prescriptions.
- As of 2022, the individual will pay the standard Medicare Part B premium of $170.10, as well as the premium for the FEHB plan. This would give the individual the most comprehensive coverage and leave them with small out-of-pocket expenses.
- This would also give the individual coverage through Medicare for things such as some orthopedic and prosthetic devices, durable medical equipment, home health care, chiropractic services, and some medical supplies that some FEHB plans may not cover.

Third Option With Federal Employees Health Benefits When Looking At Retiring

- The third and final option an individual has available to them is they can enroll in Medicare Part A and B and suspend their FEHB plan. If they cancel the FEHB plan, they will *never* be able to get it back again.
- If they ever suspend their FEHB, the individual can always take it back during their 'open season' each year, which runs between November 9 and December 14. The only reason an individual would want to suspend their FEHB would be to either join a group health insurance plan or maybe try and help lower the monthly premium with a $0 premium Medicare Advantage plan.

Conclusion When It Comes To Federal Employees Health Benefits Coverage

- As of 2022, an individual who is eligible for FEHB is not required to take their Medicare Part A and/or B or pay the standard monthly Part B premium of $170.10. However, the individual does need to decide which of the three options works best for their needs.
- This individual does *not* need the services of an insurance agent for either a Medicare Advantage or Medigap Supplement plan.

TRICARE For Life

- TRICARE is a health insurance program for uniformed military service personnel and their families that will become known as TRICARE for Life (TFL) when the individual is Medicare eligible.
- As of 2022, an individual who is turning 65 must enroll in Medicare Part A and B and pay the standard monthly Part B premium of $170.10 in order to keep their TFL.

TRICARE For Life Acts Like A Medigap Supplement

- The TFL program has incredible coverage, which becomes the secondary insurance to Medicare Part A and B. It will act similar to a full coverage Medigap Supplement plan. The TFL coverage also includes a decent PDP, which is considered credible prescription drug coverage.
- The prescription coverage with the TFL is typically much more comprehensive than Part D. There is no need for the individual to purchase a standalone Part D.
- The TFL beneficiaries are sometimes targeted by Medicare Advantage plans for some of the extra benefits like dental, vision, and hearing, which are sometimes lacking in the TFL plan.

Conclusion When It Comes To TRICARE for Life

- As of 2022, an individual who is eligible for TFL must take their Medicare Part A and B during their 7-month IEP and pay the standard monthly Part B premium of $170.10 in order to keep TFL.
- The TFL coverage will act as a *full* coverage Medigap Supplement to Medicare Part A and B.
- This individual does *not* need the services of an insurance agent for either a Medicare Advantage or Medigap Supplement plan.

Veterans Affairs (VA) Benefits

- Veterans Affairs Benefits are typically referred to as VA benefits. This health insurance is provided to an individual who actively served in the military. Typically, the requirements are that the individual must have served for 24 uninterrupted months in the military and were released or honorably discharged.

- Veterans have access to VA hospitals and clinics throughout the country at no charge, which is an incredible benefit given to a VA member.
- The problem that some VA members may encounter is that with so many veterans who need health care services, there may be long wait times to see a medical professional.
- Another problem some VA members may have is they might have a long commute to get to a VA hospital or clinic.

Veterans Affairs Will Prioritize Care By Assigning A Group Number

- In order to prioritize the care with so many veterans needing health care services, the VA will assign everyone a priority number between one through eight.
- A priority group number one will get the most attention because that will be assigned to an individual who has a service-connected disability that has been rated 50 percent or more disabled or they have been rendered unemployable.

Veterans Affairs Encourages All Veterans To Enroll In Medicare

- Since the VA does not coordinate care with Medicare, an individual who is eligible for VA coverage is not required to enroll into Medicare Part A and/or B. They are two separate programs.
- However, the VA website does encourage every VA member to enroll into *both* Medicare Part A and B as soon they are eligible during their 7-month IEP. The VA states on their website that they do not know if Congress will provide enough funding in future years to provide care for all veterans.

Veterans Affairs Members Should Enroll In Medicare Part A and B

- If a VA member is turning 65 and decides not to take their Medicare Part A and B during their 7-month IEP, they will fall into the GEP. This individual will have a penalty if they want Medicare Part B later.
- A VA member who is turning 65 should enroll into Medicare Part A and B and choose either a Medigap Supplement or Medicare Advantage plan, which will give the individual options outside the VA for hospital and medical care.
- If the VA member is assigned a priority group number eight and their health changes, it might be hard to get the level of attention that they need right away since they were not assigned a closer priority group number one. Therefore, this is another reason the VA member should enroll into Medicare.

Understanding Prescription Drug Coverage Under Veterans Affairs

- The VA will offer prescription drug coverage to all its members that will be considered credible coverage by Medicare. This is important to know because prescription drug coverage is not mandatory for a VA member who enrolls in Medicare Part A and B. The individual can always add prescription coverage during the OEP every year between October 15 through December 7.
- It might be in the best interest of a VA member who has Medicare A and B to consider a MADP or a standalone PDP. The reason is that if a VA member sees a doctor outside the VA, it will be difficult to get that prescription filled at the VA. Also, some brand name medications maybe on low supply at the VA or might not be covered.

- In some cases, a standalone PDP or MADP might save the VA member on their high-cost brand name medication.

Conclusion When It Comes To Veterans Affairs Coverage

- As of 2022, an individual who is eligible for VA benefits is not required to take their Medicare Part A and B and pay the standard monthly Part B premium of $170.10.
- An individual that is eligible for VA benefits is strongly encouraged to enroll in Medicare Part A and B during their 7-month IEP.
- The reason a VA member should consider enrolling into Medicare Part A and B is because they could experience long wait times for services or there might be a time in the future where there is not enough funding to take care of all the veteran's needs.
- This individual should speak to an insurance agent to discuss whether a $0 premium Medicare Advantage or investing around $100 into a Medigap Supplement plan would best fit their needs.

Comprehensive Health Care Benefits Program (CHAMPVA) By Veterans Affairs

- The Comprehensive Health Care Benefits Program (CHAMPVA) is a health insurance program that is administered by the VA.
- The program is provided to a spouse or widow and to the children of a veteran who did *not* qualify for TFL that was rated permanently and totally disabled due to a service-connected disability.
- The qualification could also include a veteran who died of a service-connected disability or died on active duty.

- CHAMPVA and TFL are similar, but are two separate programs.

Comprehensive Health Care Benefits Program By Veterans Affairs Is For The Family Of A Veteran

- The CHAMPVA coverage is not for the veteran themselves, but for their family. Those with CHAMPVA can use some VA facilities cost-free, but not all VA facilities are eligible due the volume of veterans they are responsible for serving.
- An individual who has CHAMPVA and is turning 65 must enroll in Medicare Part A and B in order to keep their CHAMPVA benefits.

Comprehensive Health Care Benefits Program By Veterans Affairs Will Act Like A Medigap Supplement

- The CHAMPVA is incredible coverage, which becomes the secondary insurance to Medicare Part A and B. It will act similarly to a full coverage Medigap Supplement plan. CHAMPVA also includes a good PDP that is considered credible prescription drug coverage.
- The prescription coverage with CHAMPVA is typically much more comprehensive than Part D. There is no need for the individual to purchase a standalone Part D.
- The CHAMPVA beneficiaries are sometimes targeted by Medicare Advantage plan agents for some of the extra benefits such as dental, vision, and hearing, which are sometimes lacking in this plan.

Conclusion When It Comes To Comprehensive Health Care Benefits Program By Veterans Affairs

- An individual who is eligible for CHAMPVA must take their Medicare Part A and B during their 7-month IEP and pay the standard monthly Part B premium of $170.10 (2022) in order to keep CHAMPVA.
- The CHAMPVA will act as a full coverage Medigap Supplement to Medicare Part A and B.
- This individual does not need the services of an insurance agent for either a Medicare Advantage or Medigap Supplement plan.

Indian Health Service (IHS)

- Indian Health Services (IHS) will provide *free* health care at Indian health services facilities to those individuals who are recognized by the federal government as Native American and Alaskan Natives.
- The IHS is not an insurance plan because it will only provide care at their facilities. The facilities include hospitals, health centers and health clinics run by the IHS.
- Those individuals turning 65 are eligible for Medicare Part A and B, but are not required to enroll into the Medicare program in order to continue to get care from the IHS.
- Many individuals who are eligible for IHS and decide to enroll into Medicare Part A and B will also get help from one of the MSPs at low or no cost, which will allow that individual to get care outside of the IHS.

Conclusion When It Comes To Indian Health Service

- An individual who is eligible for IHS is not required to take their Medicare Part A and B and pay the standard monthly Part B premium of $170.10 (as of 2022) in order to continue to get care from the IHS program.
- This individual does *not* need the services of an insurance agent for either a Medicare Advantage or Medigap Supplement plan.

Medicaid

- Many individuals confuse the terms Medicare and Medicaid. Both have similar names so it is easy to see how that can be confusing.
- Both programs are sponsored by the U.S. government and are designed to cover health care costs for Americans, but they are two separate programs.
- Eligibility for Medicaid assistance is based primarily on financial need. On the other hand, eligibility for Medicare *has* nothing to *do with* income level.

Medicaid Is The Largest Insurance Coverage In U.S.

- Medicaid is the single largest health insurance coverage in the U.S., currently covering over 72 million Americans. Of that number, over 7 million are low-income seniors on Medicare.
- Medicaid is extended to individuals who are at or below 133 percent of the federal poverty level. Whenever the news talks about expanding Medicaid, they are talking about raising or extending the poverty percentage guideline.
- Medicaid is for low-income assistance and is the *last* resort for health insurance for those who do not have any other means for their health insurance due to income.

Medicare And Medicaid Is Called Dual Eligible

- An individual turning 65 who has Medicaid will typically be automatically enrolled into Medicare Part A and B during their 7-month IEP since they are receiving Social Security benefits. The individual will not lose Medicaid eligibility because they are turning 65 and eligible for Medicare.
- Once the individual has Medicare and Medicaid, they will automatically qualify for Extra Help under Part D and Medicare will cover their prescriptions.
- If the income level is still below the limits, the individual may also qualify for help paying the standard monthly Part B premium of $170.10 (as of 2022) from their state through a Medicare Savings Program (MSP).
- Once the individual has both Medicare and Medicaid, they will commonly be referred to as "dual eligible."

Dual Eligible Qualifies For Special Needs Plan (SNP)

- Once the individual is eligible for Medicare, the state Medicaid program will now work with Medicare to get them all the help they qualify for through one of the four Medicare Savings Programs (MSP).
- Once the individual is dual eligible, which means they have Medicare and Medicaid, there are some excellent Medicare Advantage plans, which are designed to specifically detect, treat, and prevent a chronic condition that they may be diagnosed.
- It is estimated that almost one third of dual-eligible individuals are enrolled in some sort of SNP through a Medicare Advantage program.

Conclusion When It Comes To Medicaid

- An individual turning 65 who has Medicaid will typically be automatically enrolled into Medicare Part A and B during their 7-month IEP because they are receiving Social Security benefits.
- An individual who has Medicare and Medicaid are referred to as dual eligible.
- The individual will qualify for a Special Needs Plan (SNP) through a Medicare Advantage program.
- This individual should speak to an insurance agent to discuss whether a Special Needs Plan (SNP) through a Medicare Advantage program would best fit their needs.

No Health Insurance Coverage

- An individual turning 65 with no health insurance coverage must enroll in Medicare Part A and B during their 7-month IEP and pay the standard monthly Part B premium of $170.10 (as of 2022).

Conclusion When It Comes To No Health Insurance

- This individual must enroll in Medicare Part A and B since this will be the only form of insurance available to them.
- This individual should speak to an insurance agent to discuss whether a $0 premium Medicare Advantage plan or investing around $100 into a Medigap Supplement plan would best fit their needs.

Chapter 8

Medigap Supplements — Everything You Need To Know

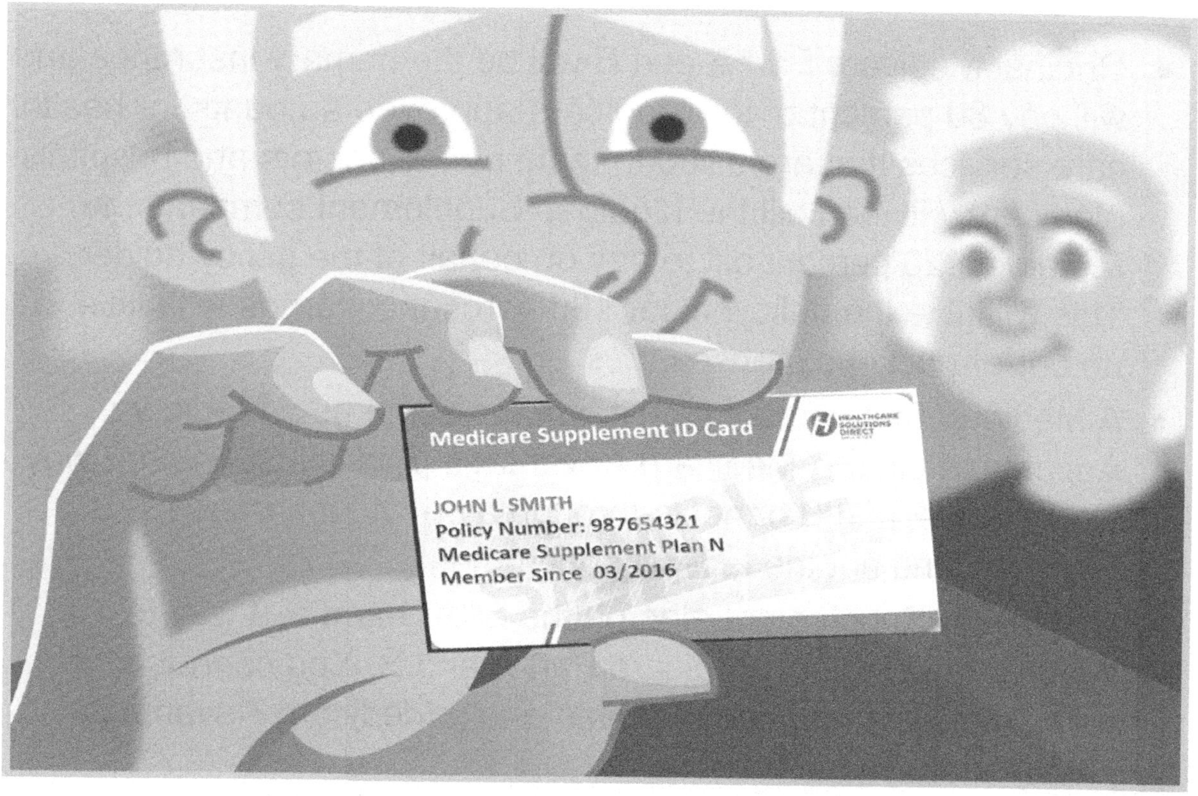

Basics of Medigap Supplement Plans

- A Medigap Plan is a Medicare Supplement plan that will help fill the "gaps" of Original Medicare Parts A and B.
- These plans are sold by private insurance companies, but are standardized by the federal government with alphabet letters to offer the same coverage and benefits no matter what insurance company sells it.
- Effective July 1, 1993, the federal government standardized Medigap plans using alphabet letters. The alphabet letter being

offered by one company will have identical coverage and benefits as the other company based on that alphabet letter. This helps make it easy to shop for a Medigap plan since the plan is the same with every company.

Original Medicare Is Primary And Medigap Secondary

- Original Medicare Part A and B will be the primary insurance and will pay 80 percent of the Medicare-approved amounts for health care services that are billed to them by the doctors and hospitals. Medicare will then bill the Medigap Supplement company the remaining 20 percent bill to pay on behalf of the policy holder. This will give the policyholder 100 percent coverage with little to no out-of-pocket expenses.
- A Medigap Supplement plan is *not* the same as a Medicare Advantage plan. A Medicare Advantage plan is just another way to get Part A and B benefits through a private insurance company and not the federal government.
- A Medigap Supplement plan on the other hand is a way to supplement Original Medicare Part A and B. You cannot have both a Medigap Supplement plan *and* a Medicare Advantage plan at the same time.

Learning More About Medigap Supplement Plans

- The individual will pay a private insurance company a monthly premium each month for the Medigap Supplement policy. This monthly premium cannot be deducted from the Social Security retirement benefits and will be in addition to the standard monthly Medicare Part B premium of $170.10 (as of 2022).
- Medigap Supplement plans can only cover one person since Medicare is provided to each person individually.

- Medigap Supplement plans are guaranteed renewable even if the individual experiences health problems in the future. If you pay, you stay; if you don't, you won't.

Medigap Supplement Company Is Billed Electronically

- Medicare Part A and B must be the primary insurance in order to purchase a Medigap Supplement plan. The Medigap Supplement company will be the secondary insurance to pick up the 20 percent where Medicare leaves off.

[redacted] **THIS IS NOT A BILL** | Page 3 of 12

Your Claims for Part B (Medical Insurance)

Part B Medical Insurance helps pay for doctors' services, diagnostic tests, ambulance services, and other health care services.

Definitions of Columns

Service Approved?: This column tells you if Medicare covered the service.

Amount Provider Charged: This is your provider's fee for this service.

Medicare-Approved Amount: This is the amount a provider can be paid for a Medicare service. It may be less than the actual amount the provider charged.

Your provider has agreed to accept this amount as full payment for covered services. Medicare usually pays 80% of the Medicare-approved amount.

Amount Medicare Paid: This is the amount Medicare paid your provider. This is usually 80% of the Medicare-approved amount.

Maximum You May Be Billed: This is the total amount the provider is allowed to bill you and can include a deductible, coinsurance, and other charges not covered. If you have Medicare Supplement Insurance (Medigap policy) or other insurance, it may pay all or part of this amount.

June 01, 2020

Service Provided & Billing Code	Service Approved?	Amount Provider Charged	Medicare-Approved Amount	Amount Medicare Paid	Maximum You May Be Billed	See Notes Below
[redacted]						
Eye and medical examination for diagnosis and treatment, established patient, 1 or more visits (92014)	Yes	$184.00	$124.78	$101.21	**$24.96**	A,B
Total for Claim # [redacted]		$184.00	$124.78	$101.21	**$24.96**	C

Continued →

Notes for Claims Above

A The approved amount is based on a special payment method.

B This claim shows a quality reporting program adjustment.

C We have sent your claim to your Medigap insurer. Send any questions regarding your benefits to them. Your Medigap insurer is BCBS OF [redacted] - SUPP.

Misconceptions About Medigap Supplement Plans

- There are two misconceptions many individuals have when it comes to Medigap Supplement plans that we will address. CMS used to call this coverage Medicare Supplement plans, but later transitioned to Medigap Supplement plans to try and eliminate the misconception that they were the same as a Medicare Advantage. One can argue if that was successful or not because most are still confused.

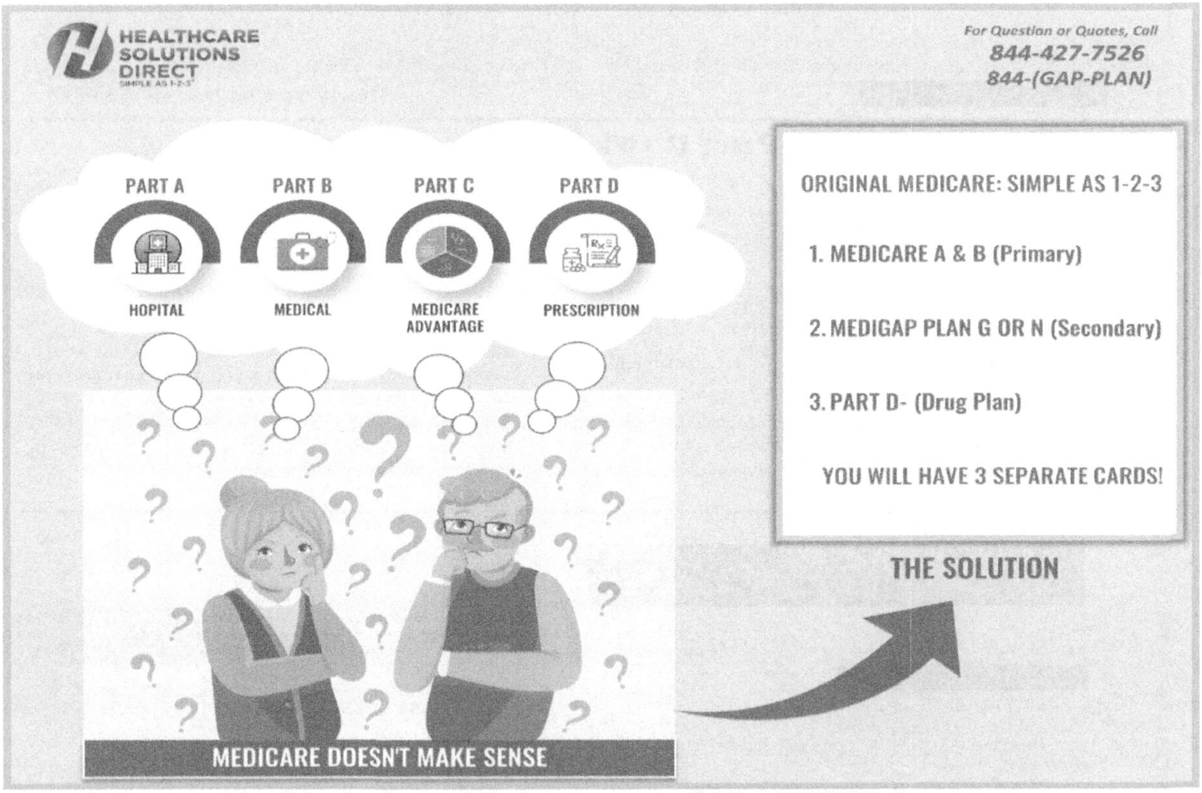

First Misconception About Medigap Supplement

- The first misconception individuals have about Medigap Supplement plans is that they are the same as a Medicare Advantage plan. This is incorrect because they are two different forms of insurance.

- Medicare Advantage plans are alternative health insurance plans to Original Medicare, which are provided by a private insurance company. They are similar to individual and group insurance plans.
- Medicare Advantage plans become the primary insurance and do supplement or fill the gaps of Original Medicare. Medicare Advantage plans have their own set of co-pays, coinsurance, and deductibles that differ from one company to the next.
- An individual *cannot* have a Medicare Advantage plan and a Medigap Supplement plan at the same time. An individual will choose either Original Medicare as their primary insurance or the Medicare Advantage plan as their primary.

Reasons Medicare Advantage Is Called A Supplement

- An individual who is enrolled into a Medicare Advantage plan will still commonly refer to it as their supplement plan and here are some reasons why they do that:
    - The individual must continue to pay the standard Medicare Part B monthly premium of $170.10 (as of 2022). This can make it can appear that they still have Medicare Part A and B as their primary insurance.
    - Many Medicare Advantage plans will also offer additional benefits that are not provided by Original Medicare so it could appear that the plan is supplementing Medicare Part A and B.

Second Misconception About Medigap Supplement

- The second misconception individuals have about Medigap Supplement plans is that they can switch or buy any plan from any company during the OEP, which runs from October 15 through December 7 of each calendar year. That is incorrect because they maybe turned down for coverage based on health conditions.

- An individual who has Original Medicare as their primary insurance *can* change or buy a Medigap Supplement plan from any company at any time during the calendar year.
- If an individual is outside of their 7-month IEP, they may need to medically qualify for the Medigap Supplement and could be potentially turned down for coverage based on health conditions.

Reasons Why Someone Can Be Declined For Medigap

- An individual who is outside of their 7-month IEP may lose the protection of being guaranteed for a Medigap Supplement. The following are some reasons for that:
    - The Medigap Supplement companies do not get any federal funding for offering the plan and assume all liability for the 20 percent coinsurance. A Medicare Advantage plan on the other hand does get federal funding for offering an alternative plan to Original Medicare.
    - The rule set forth by CMS is that anyone that is newly eligible to Medicare or losing their coverage involuntarily cannot be turned down for a Medigap Supplement plan. Outside of those parameters a company can evaluate health conditions and decide to not offer the coverage.

When Is The Best Time To Buy A Medigap Supplement?

- The best time for an individual to buy a Medigap Supplement plan is during the 6-month Medigap OEP, which is when an individual is turning 65 or picking up their Medicare Part B for the first time.

- During this period, an individual can purchase a Medigap Supplement plan from any company regardless of their health conditions and will be automatically approved for the coverage.
- If an individual is looking to keep Original Medicare Part A and B as their primary insurance, this will be the best time to enroll into a Medigap Supplement plan.

Reasons Those First Eligible Should Buy Medigap

- Medicare states that when an individual is first eligible for Medicare or picking up their Part B for the first time the individual will typically get better prices and have more choices available to them, which is correct. The following are some reasons for that, which we have discussed earlier.
    - Medigap Supplement plans do *not* get any federal funding from the federal government like that of a Medicare Advantage plan.
    - Medigap Supplement plans are allowed to not offer coverage outside of a Medigap OEP or Guaranteed Issue based on health conditions in order to minimize claims and maximize profits.
- If an individual is healthy, it would be smart to shop their Medigap Supplement plan ever couple of years since the plans are standardized and the alphabet letter will be identical coverage and benefits from any another company.

Medigap Supplement Plans Use Alphabet Letters

- Since July 1, 1993, Medigap Supplement insurance plans have been standardized by the federal government so now all plans offer the same coverage and benefits based on that alphabet letter.

- Medigap Supplement plans are each assigned an alphabet letter like Original Medicare assigns Part A for hospital and Part B for medical.
- However, an individual can still get confused because Original Medicare will refer to the alphabet letter as a 'part' and the Medigap Supplement plan will refer to the alphabet letter as a 'plan.'
- If an individual is looking at the Medigap Supplement chart, they will see that the basic plan offered is Medigap Plan A, which is not the same Medicare Part A. These differences are confusing to someone who does not completely understand Medicare, which can make it seem like it all does not make any sense.

Medigap Plans Have Been Eliminated In The Past

- Starting on June 1, 2010, the federal government decided to stop the sale of Plans E, H, I and J (including the high-deductible J) and added two new alphabet letters Plan M and N.
- Anyone who had Plan E, H, I or J (including the high-deductible J) prior to that date could keep it and were grandfathered indefinitely, but no one new could purchase it.
- The reason these plans were eliminated was because some of the additional benefits that were offered under these plans would now be provided by Original Medicare.

Two Benefits Eliminated From Medigap Plans

- Medigap plans E and J provided an additional benefit of up to $120 a year that the policyholder could use toward preventative care. Original Medicare did not cover preventative care 100 percent at that time.

- Starting on January 1, 2011, Original Medicare was required to cover preventative services at 100 percent. This made the $120 year benefit of Plans E and J obsolete.
- Another benefit that was removed from Medigap plans D, G, I, and J was a benefit of up to $1,600 a year toward personal home health care recovery.

Reason Home Health Care Recovery Was Removed

- It is important to understand what the home health care recovery benefit was used for and why it was removed. The $1,600 benefit could be used for personal home health care services such as dressing, laundry, cooking, etc. Original Medicare does not cover personal care; they will only cover skilled care.
- The individual could get a maximum of $40 per visit for personal care with up to 40 visits a year when the skilled home health care services were no longer needed.
- CMS decided that it would remove the $1,600 personal home health care recovery on the Medigap plans after June 1, 2010 because it was only used seldomly by any individual.

Prescription Coverage Removed From Medigap Plans

- The last benefit that was removed from Medigap plans was prescription drug coverage. Prescription coverage is not covered under Original Medicare Part A and B. For those needing prescription coverage, they could get it as a benefit included in the Medigap Supplement plan H, I, and J.
- When CMS implemented the Medicare Part D on January 1, 2006, it made Medigap Supplement plans H, I, and J no longer necessary to cover the additional benefit of prescription benefits.

- The most popular plan prior to June 1, 2010, was Medigap Supplement Plan J because it offered the most comprehensive benefits such as preventative care, personal home health care recovery, and prescription drug coverage.

Plan F Became The Most Popular Plan After 2010

- Once Plan J was no longer available for anyone to purchase after June 1, 2010, everyone began to focus their attention on Plan F. Plan F offered the most comprehensive coverage and was the most similar in benefits to the discontinued Plan J.
- For the next decade, Plan F was enjoyed as the most comprehensive plan that Medigap offered until CMS decided to start making some changes again to the coverage options available to new beneficiaries to Medicare.
- Beginning on January 1, 2020, CMS decided that they would do something slightly different than they had done in the past to Medigap plans, which created much confusion.
- Instead of eliminating alphabet letters, the federal government stopped the sale of Plan C and Plan F (including the high-deductible F) to anyone new to Medicare. Any individual who was eligible for Part A prior to January 1, 2020, was still able to continue to purchase Plan F.

Plan G and N Emerge As The Most Popular After 2020

- Those eligible for Medicare Part A prior to January 1, 2020, could keep Plan F or Plan C and would always be grandfathered into purchasing these plans.
- CMS did not eliminate these two plans; they just made them no longer available for purchase to anyone new to Medicare after 2020.
- The most comprehensive plan now available for purchase for those newly eligible for Medicare after January 1, 2020, are Plans G and N.

The Centers For Medicare And Medicaid Services Wanted To Eliminate First Dollar Coverage

- CMS made these changes to Plans C and F effective on January 1, 2020 because they offered first dollar coverage. This means that Plans C and F would pay the small Part B deductible ($233 as of 2022), leaving the policy holder without any out-of-pocket expenses.

- By requiring all newly eligible Medicare beneficiaries after 2020 to be responsible for the small Part B deductible, Congress felt it would help reduce medical overuse.

Medigap Supplement Plan Chart Availability

HEALTHCARE SOLUTIONS DIRECT
SIMPLE AS 1-2-3

For Question or Quotes, Call
844-427-7526
844-(GAP-PLAN)

MEDICARE SUPPLEMENT INSURANCE (MEDIGAP) PLANS
PLANS AVAILABLE TO ALL APPLICANTS

MEDICARE PART A FIRST ELIGIBLE BEFORE 2020 ONLY

BENEFITS	A	B	D	G[1]	K[2]	L[2]	M	N[3]	C	F[1]
Hospitalization: (Medicare Part A Coinsurance plus coverage for 365 additional days after Medicare benefits end.)	✓	✓	✓	✓	✓	✓	✓	✓	✓	✓
Medical Expenses: (Medicare Part B Coinsurance generally 20% of Medicare-approved expenses or copayments for hospital outpatient services. Plans K and L require insured to pay a portion of Part B Coinsurance or copayments.)	✓	✓	✓	✓	50%	75%	✓	✓ Copay[3]	✓	✓
Blood (First 3 pints of blood each year.)	✓	✓	✓	✓	50%	75%	✓	✓	✓	✓
Hospice Care: (Part A Coinsurance or copayment.)	✓	✓	✓	✓	50%	75%	✓	✓	✓	✓
Skilled Nursing Facility Care Coinsurance			✓	✓	50%	75%	✓	✓	✓	✓
Medicare Part A Deductible: $1556		✓	✓	✓	50%	75%	50%	✓	✓	✓
Medicare Part B Deductible: $233									✓	✓
Medicare Part B Excess Charges				✓						✓
Foreign Travel Emergency Care 4 (Up to plan limits)			✓	✓			✓	✓	✓	✓
Out-of-pocket limit in 2022					$6,620	$3,310				

1 Plans F and G also offer a high-deductible plan in some states. With this option, you must pay for Medicare-covered costs (coinsurance, copayments, and deductibles) up to the deductible amount of $2,490 in 2022 before your policy pays anything. (You can't buy Plans C and F if you were newly eligible for Medicare on or after January 1, 2020.)
2 For Plans K and L, after you meet your out-of-pocket yearly limit and your yearly Part B deductible ($233 in 2022), the Medigap plan pays 100% of covered services for the rest of the calendar year.
3 Plan N pays 100% of the Part B coinsurance. You may pay a copayment of up to $20 for some office visits and up to a $50 copayment for emergency room visits that don't result in an inpatient admission.
4 Benefit is 80% and beneficiaries are responsible for 20% after the $250 annual deductible with a $50,000 lifetime maximum. Benefits are defined as medically necessary emergency care services beginning during the first 60 days of each trip outside the U.S.

- The only three plans that the majority of individuals will purchase are Plans F, G or N. Even those individuals who are grandfathered into purchasing Plan F, are looking at Plans G or N for cost saving reasons.
- Anyone newly eligible to Medicare will only be looking to supplement Medicare A and B with Plan G or Plan N.

Medigap Supplement Plan F

- Medigap Supplement plan F offers:
  - No Deductibles
  - No Coinsurance
  - No Co-payments
- Plan F offers the most comprehensive coverage of any of the plans available.
- An individual must have been eligible for Medicare Part A prior to January 1, 2020, in order to enroll into Plan F.
- Many would refer to Plan F as the "full coverage" plan.
- Plan F will cover everything that Medicare A and B approved will not cover. There are no deductibles, no coinsurance, and no co-payments! All that the individual will pay is the monthly premium to the Medigap Supplement company for Plan F.

Medigap Supplement High Deductible Plan F

- Medigap Supplement high deductible Plan F (HDF) is a type of Medigap Supplement plan that covers everything that the traditional Medigap Plan F covers, after the individual has met the high deductible on the plan, which is $2,490 as of 2022.
- Those who are newly eligible to Medicare after January 1, 2020, will have the high deductible plan G (HDG) available to them with the same $2,490 limit.

Medigap Supplement Plan G

- Medigap Supplement plan G offers:
    - Responsible for Part B Deductible ($233 in 2022)
    - No Coinsurance
    - No Co-payments
- Plan G offers the same identical coverage as Plan F except that the individual is only responsible for the small Part B medical deductible ($233 as of 2022).
- Many referred to Plan G as the "great value" or "go-to-plan." Once the individual met the Part B medical deductible, Plan G would be identical to Plan F.
- Over the last decade, Plan G became a popular choice over Plan F due to the monthly cost savings in comparison to the Part B deductible.
- Those looking to save on monthly premiums would choose to pay the small Part B deductible ($233 as of 2022) under Plan G, which would give them a better cost savings compared to the monthly premium on Plan F.

Medigap Supplement Plan N

- Medigap Supplement plan N offers:
    - Responsible for Part B Deductible ($233 in 2022)
    - $20 doctor co-pay
    - $50 emergency room co-pay (Only if emergency room visit does not result in an inpatient admission.)

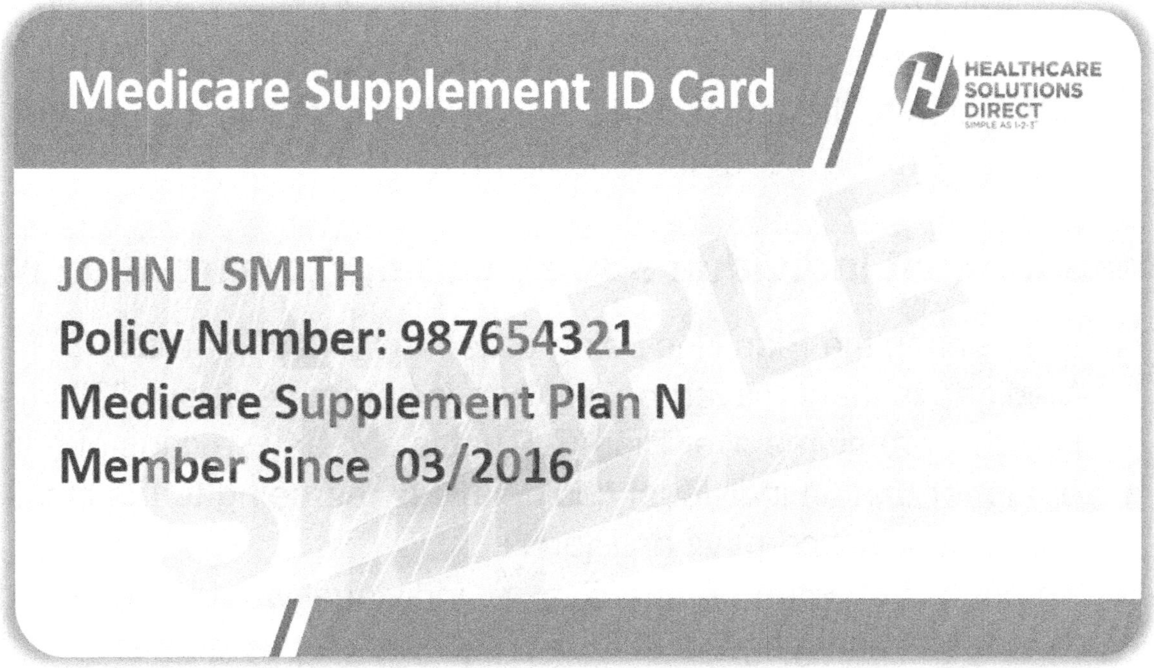

- Plan N offers the same identical coverage as Plan G with a couple of minor differences.
- Many refer to Plan N as the “now” plan.
- In recent years, this plan has become popular because it offers one of the least expensive monthly premiums compared to Plan G and Plan F.

Minor Cost Sharing On The Plan N Make It “Now” Plan

- An individual is responsible for the small Part B deductible ($233 as of 2022) just like Plan G.
- Only after the Part B deductible ($233 as of 2022) has been met for that calendar year, can doctors charge up to a $20 discretionary co-pay for an office visit. This co-pay cannot be charged for any preventive care visits.

- An individual will also be responsible for a $50 co-pay for a trip to the emergency room that does not result in an inpatient admission to the hospital. If the individual is admitted, they will not be responsible for the $50 co-pay.

Reason Most Individuals Are Leaning Toward Plan N

- The reason the Plan N is being called the "Now" plan for Medigap is that on average it will save someone about $30 in monthly premiums over Plan G. That is a yearly savings of $360 or higher that an individual could save by agreeing to the small cost sharing of co-pays on Plan N.
- To put this in better perspective, an individual would need to go to a doctor charging the $20 discretionary co-pay almost 18 times in one year to equal what they would have paid in premiums for Plan G.
- In looking at the Medigap chart, you will notice that Plan N will not cover something called "excess charges." This has been poorly explained by insurance agents, which has caused confusion that will be cleared up for you.
- Excess charges are extremely rare, which you will learn, that will make this almost a non-discussion. In many states, it is not even permitted for doctors to charge it.

What Is Medicare Excess Charges?

- Medicare excess charges fall under Part B medical of Medicare and are for doctor visits. This will occur when a doctor does not accept what is called "Medicare assignment."
- If a doctor chooses not to accept Medicare assignment, it means that they do not agree with what Medicare will pay them for the doctor visit.

- Doctors who do not accept Medicare assignment are allowed to charge 15 percent more than what Medicare will pay them, which is called an excess charge.

It Benefits Doctors To Accept Medicare Assignment

- It is estimated that over 97 percent of doctors and physicians do accept Medicare assignments.
  Courtesy: https://www.kff.org/medicare/issue-brief/how-many-physicians-have-opted-out-of-the-medicare-program/Page
- It *benefits* the doctor to accept Medicare assignments because they will be paid 100 percent of Medicare's approved amount. Those doctors who choose not to accept an assignment will only receive 95 percent of the approved amount.
- If a doctor chooses not accept Medicare's approved amount, they will receive 5 percent less reimbursement from Medicare. That doctor will be responsible for additional paperwork and billing to collect only an additional 10 percent for a doctor's visit. Most doctors choose to accept Medicare assignment.

Reason Medicare Excess Charges Are No Big Deal

- It is illegal for any doctor to charge an excess charge for those who live in either Connecticut, Massachusetts, Minnesota, New York, Ohio, Pennsylvania, Rhode Island, or Vermont.
- Plans F or G are the only two Medigap Supplement plans that cover excess charges at 100 percent. Medigap Supplement companies that offer Plans F and G are responsible for any excess charges that are billed.
- In August 2016, Aetna reported that 99.34 percent of the claims received had no excess charges they needed to pay out, which means that only .066 percent — less than 1 percent — had an excess charge, which they were responsible to pay for under

either Medigap Plan F or Plan G. The average was less than $20.

Courtesy: https://www.myprimetimenews.com/medicare-beneficiairies-who-switch-to-plan-g-could-save-hundreds-of-dollars/

What Are Medigap Select Plans?

- A Medigap Select plan is a Medigap Supplement plan that has a network. This is an excellent example of Medicare not making any sense.
- The insurance provider will determine a network of doctors, facilities, and hospitals that are approved for services. The individual must get their services at those approved doctors' offices, facilities, or hospitals or the policy will not pay anything.
- The Medigap Select plan will cover out-of-network emergency care like that of a Medicare Advantage plan.
- There are not many insurance companies that still offer these Medigap Select plans or insurance agents who offer them.

Medigap in Minnesota, Wisconsin, and Massachusetts

- Medigap Supplement plans offered in Wisconsin, Minnesota, and Massachusetts do *not* follow the standard alphabet letters as outlined in the Medigap Supplement charts.
    - Wisconsin has just a "Basic Plan" available. The individual can then select some optional riders to help cover certain parts of Medicare Part A and B they feel are important to them. The plan operates like an a la carte system.
    - Minnesota has a "Basic Plan" or "Extended Basic Plan." The Basic Plan offers select riders to help cover certain parts of Medicare Part A and B. The Extended Basic Plan will automatically cover some of these additional riders and provide some unique features such as an extra 20 days of

skilled nursing facility care beyond Medicare's 100 days as well as some additional foreign travel benefits.

Compare these plans side-by-side

If a "yes" appears, the plan covers the described benefit 100%. If a row lists a percentage, the policy covers that percentage of the described benefit. If a "no" appears, the policy doesn't cover that benefit.

Medigap Benefits	Medigap Plans	
	Basic Plan	Extended Basic Plan
Basic benefits	Yes	Yes
Part A: inpatient hospital deductible	No	Yes
Part A: skilled nursing facility coinsurance	Yes (Provides 100 days of SNF care)	Yes (Provides 120 days of SNF care)
Part B: deductible**	No	Yes**
Foreign travel emergency	80%	80%*
Outpatient mental health	50%	50%
Usual and customary fees	No	80%*
Medicare-covered preventive care	Yes	Yes
Physical therapy	20%	20%
Coverage while in a foreign country	No	80%*
State-mandated benefits (diabetic equipment and supplies, routine cancer screening, reconstructive surgery, and immunizations)	Yes	Yes

* The plan pays 100% after you spend $1,000 in out-of-pocket costs for a calendar year.

**Coverage of the Part B deductible will no longer be available to people who are new to Medicare on or after January 1, 2020. However, if you were eligible for Medicare before January 1, 2020 but not yet enrolled, you may be able to get this benefit

- Massachusetts has three plans to choose from which are the "Core Plan", "Supplement 1 Plan", or the "Supplement 1A Plan:"

- The Core Plan is like Plan A.
- The Supplement 1 Plan is like Plan F.
- The Supplement 1A Plan is like Plan G.

Compare these plans side-by-side

If a "yes" appears, the plan covers the described benefit 100%. If "no" appears, the policy doesn't cover that benefit.

Medigap Benefits	Medigap Plans		
	Core Plan	Supplement 1	Supplement 1A
Basic benefits	Yes	Yes	Yes
Part A: inpatient hospital deductible	No	Yes	Yes
Part A: skilled nursing facility coinsurance	No	Yes	Yes
Part B: deductible*	No	Yes*	No
Foreign travel emergency	No	Yes	Yes
Inpatient days in mental health hospitals	60 days per calendar year	120 days per benefit year	120 days per benefit year
State-mandated benefits (yearly Pap tests and mammograms. Check your plan for other state-mandated benefits.)	No	Yes	Yes

*Supplement 1 Plan (which includes coverage of the Part B deductible) will no longer be available to people who are new to Medicare on or after January 1, 2020. These people can buy Supplement 1A Plan. However, if you were eligible for Medicare before January 1, 2020 but not yet enrolled, you may be able to buy Supplement Plan 1.

Medigap Enrollment Periods Explained

- An individual who is eligible for Medicare can sign up for a Medigap Supplement plan anytime during the year if they have Original Medicare as their primary insurance.
- During OEP or a Guaranteed Issue, the insurance companies offering the Medigap Supplement plan cannot ask any medical

questions. The individual is guaranteed coverage by virtue of enrolling.

- If an individual is looking to buy a Medigap Supplement plan outside of these two periods, they will need to be what is referred to as underwritten.

Open Enrollment Period

- The best time to buy a Medigap Supplement policy is during the 6-month Medigap OEP.
- The individual will typically get the best prices and choices and will be automatically approved for the coverage.
- An individual can purchase any plan that is offered in their state regardless of their health conditions. Many who are eligible for Medicare will find that, due to their health, this might be the only time that they can get a Medigap Supplement.
- This period starts when the individual is either turning 65 or enrolling for the first time in Medicare Part B. This period cannot be changed when it starts and cannot be duplicated again.

Turning 65

- An individual who is turning 65, regardless if they are eligible for Medicare for the first time or have been on Medicare early for a disability, can buy any plan that is offered in their state regardless of their health conditions.
- The individual will automatically be approved for the coverage once they enroll into the plan.

Part B First Time Enrollment

- For many individuals, Part B first time enrollment will coincide with them turning 65.

- An individual who decided to delay their Part B when they turned 65 and will be enrolling into Part B for the first time through a Medicare SEP, or GEP will also be eligible for a Medigap OEP.
- Any individual who is enrolling into Medicare Part B for the first time will receive a Medigap OEP to purchase a Medigap Supplement plan without any medical questions.

Medigap Open Enrollment Window

- The Medigap OEP lasts for a full 12 months. It begins 6 months before the first day of the persons 65th birth month (or first-time taking Part B) and lasts 6 months after that effective date.
- The individual is given a full year to purchase a Medigap Supplement policy without any medical questions or preexisting conditions taken into consideration. They can make any changes to their Medigap Supplement plan during this 12-month period.

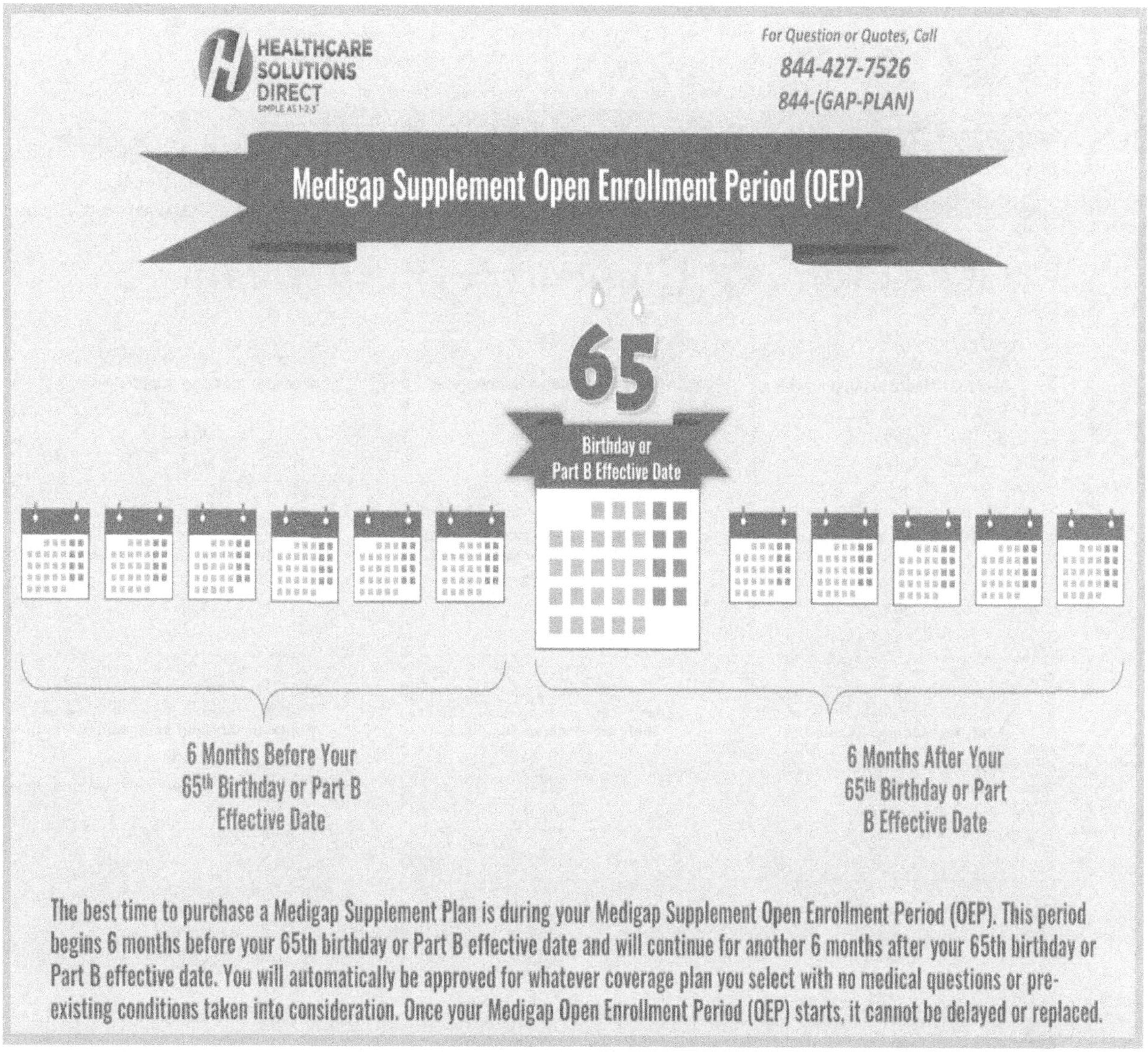

Medicare Card Is Not Required To Enroll In Medigap

- The individual is *not* required to have their Medicare A and B card in place in order to sign up and purchase their Medigap Supplement plan. If the individual knows that their Part B effective date will be within the next 6 months, they are allowed to enroll into the Medigap Supplement plan.
- This chart is a good reference on how early an individual can apply for their Medigap Supplement plan based on when they will be turning 65 or picking up Part B for the first time.

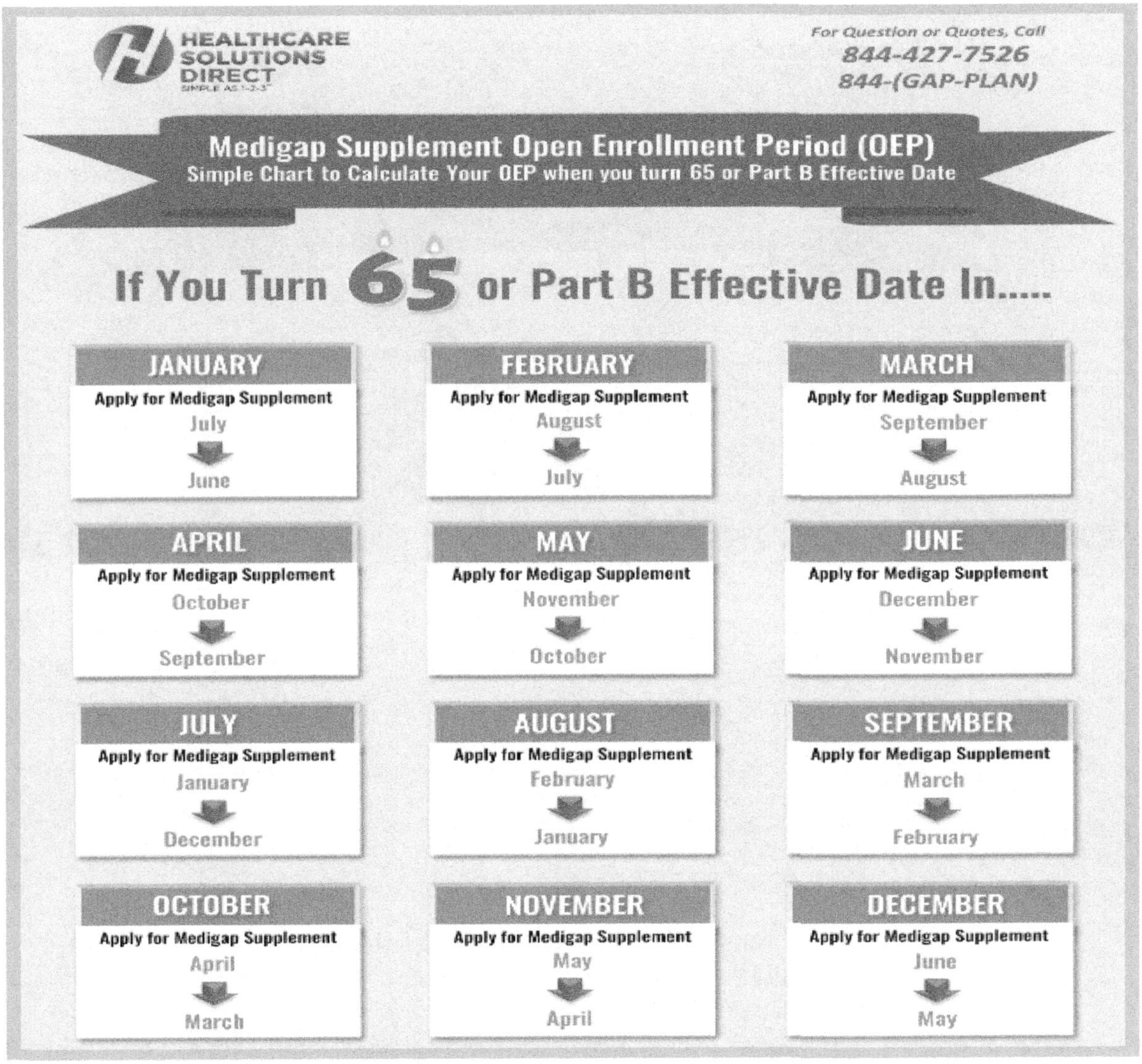

Once Enrolled Medigap It Is Guaranteed Renewable

- An individual who enrolls in a Medigap Supplement plan during their Medigap OEP does not need to reenroll in the coverage every year.
- The policy can *never* be cancelled by the insurance company for any reason other than for nonpayment. The plan will just auto renew every month for as long as the policyholder pays the monthly premium for the coverage.

- The best way to think about a Medigap Supplement plan is that if you pay, you stay; if you don't, you won't.

Applying For Coverage Outside OEP Is Not Automatic

- Since most health insurance plans today do not take into consideration preexisting conditions, many are surprised to find out that Medigap Supplement companies can still deny coverage outside of the Medigap OEP.
- We discussed earlier that private companies that offer the Medigap Supplement plans currently do not get any financial incentives from the federal government. They must operate with the monthly premium that they are charging for the Medigap Supplement plan and assume all risks.
- The federal government requires that during the Medigap OEP, the insurance company must offer the coverage without any medical questions. Outside of that period, they are allowed to evaluate the persons health to see if they pose a financial risk to the insurance company. The goal of every insurance company is to make money.

Guaranteed Issue

- Outside of the Medigap OEP, there is one other way to get a Medigap Supplement guaranteed without any medical questions, which is referred to as Guaranteed Issue.
- There are seven Guaranteed Issue rights that someone who is Medicare eligible will have available to get a Medigap Supplement plan with no medical underwriting.

HEALTHCARE SOLUTIONS DIRECT
SIMPLE AS 1-2-3

For Question or Quotes, Call
844-427-7526
844-(GAP-PLAN)

Medigap Guaranteed Issue Rights
7 Special Guaranteed Issue Situations

Guaranteed Issue Situation	Medigap Plans You Can Buy
Your Medicare Advantage plan is leaving the Medicare program, stops servicing your area, or you move out of the plan's service area. (Ex: You have an MA plan in TX and move to FL)	If you became eligible for Medicare prior to 01/01/2020: A, B, C, F, K or L (Plan F is the most popular) If you became eligible for Medicare after 01/01/2020: A, B, D, G, K, or L (Plan G is the most popular)
Trial Right #1- You joined a Medicare Advantage plan when you were first eligible for Medicare Part A at the age 65 and within the first 12-months of joining decide you want to switch back to Original Medicare.	Any Medigap plan that you are eligible for that is sold in your state by any insurance company.
Trial Right #2- You dropped a Medigap policy to enroll in a Medicare Advantage plan for the very first time and within the first 12-months of joining want to switch back to your Medigap policy. You must go back to the same company and plan you had before you joined the Medicare Advantage plan.	You must obtain the same plan from the Medigap company that you dropped it from.
You have Original Medicare Part A and B as your primary insurance and you have an employer group health plan (including retiree or Cobra coverage) that pays after Medicare pays and that coverage is ending of no fault of your own.	If you became eligible for Medicare prior to 01/01/2020: A, B, C, F, K or L (Plan F is the most popular) If you became eligible for Medicare after 01/01/2020: A, B, D, G, K, or L (Plan G is the most popular)
You have Original Medicare Part A and B and you have a Medigap Select policy. You have decided to move out of the plan's service area.	If you became eligible for Medicare prior to 01/01/2020: A, B, C, F, K or L (Plan F is the most popular) If you became eligible for Medicare after 01/01/2020: A, B, D, G, K, or L (Plan G is the most popular)
Your Medigap insurance company goes bankrupt or your Medigap policy coverage ends of no fault of your own. (This is extremely rare)	If you became eligible for Medicare prior to 01/01/2020: A, B, C, F, K or L (Plan F is the most popular) If you became eligible for Medicare after 01/01/2020: A, B, D, G, K, or L (Plan G is the most popular)
You request to leave your Medicare Advantage plan and are granted this request because the company has either not followed the rules, or you felt you were misled by marketing materials or the quality standard of the plan were not satisfactory. (This is extremely rare)	If you became eligible for Medicare prior to 01/01/2020: A, B, C, F, K or L (Plan F is the most popular) If you became eligible for Medicare after 01/01/2020: A, B, D, G, K, or L (Plan G is the most popular)

*Must apply as early as 60 calendar days before the coverage will end, but no later than 63 calendar days after the coverage ends.

The Most Commonly Used Medigap Guaranteed Issue Rights

- #1: Your Medicare Advantage plan is leaving the Medicare program, stops servicing your area, or you move out of the plan's service area. For example, you have a Medicare Advantage plan in Florida and move to Texas.

- #2: Trial Right #1: You joined a Medicare Advantage plan when you were first eligible for Medicare Part A at the age of 65 and within the first 12 months of joining, you decided you want to switch back to Original Medicare.
- #3: Trial Right #2: You dropped a Medigap policy to enroll in a Medicare Advantage plan for the first time and within the first 12 months of joining and want to switch back to your Medigap policy. You must go back to the same company and plan you had before you joined the Medicare Advantage plan.
- #4: You have Original Medicare Part A and B as your primary insurance and you have an employer group health plan (including retiree or COBRA coverage) that pays after Medicare pays and that coverage is ending of no fault of your own.

The Least Commonly Used Medigap Guaranteed Issue Rights

- #5: You have Original Medicare Part A and B, and you have a Medigap Select policy. You decided to move out of the plan's service area.
- #6: Your Medigap insurance company goes bankrupt or your Medigap policy coverage ends due to no fault of your own. (This is extremely rare!)
- #7: You request to leave your Medicare Advantage and are granted this request because the company has either not followed the rules, you felt you were misled by marketing materials, or the quality standard of the plan were not satisfactory. (This is extremely rare!)
- Must apply as early as 60 calendar days before coverage will end, but no later than 63 calendar days after the coverage ends in order to get a Guaranteed Issue.

Underwritten

- An individual can apply for a Medigap Supplement plan anytime during the calendar year if they have Original Medicare or during the OEP, which runs from October 15 through December 7.
- In order to apply for a Medigap, there is no need for a physical in order to qualify. The individual just needs to complete a short medical questionnaire over the phone.
- There are general questions for an individual to consider that need to be medically underwritten for a Medigap plan.

Basic Questions To Consider For Medigap Approval

- How is your current health? (Ok/Bad) What type of health issues do you have?
- Do you have any pending medical treatment that has been advised or not yet scheduled? (Y/N)
- When is your next doctor's appointment, what is it for?
    - Examples of a decline due to these questions might be as follows: You're advised to see a dermatologist to remove basal cells from your face, you have an appointment to see a doctor because your knee is hurting, you've scheduled cataract surgery, you need physical therapy, etc. These appointments must be completed *before* submitting an application.
    - Examples of an acceptance might be as follows: Annual mammogram, annual wellness physicals, routine semiannual/annual visits for cancer or heart attack checkups after 2 years of remission, etc. These will be viewed as preventative if there are no complications.
- How many medications are you taking? What are they for?
    - Example of ok: 2-4 meds normal for preventative.
    - Example of caution: 5+ medications

- Example of decline: Narcotics like Vicodin, Percocet, Oxycodone, etc., if filled more than once in 6 months.

Diabetes Is The Most Common Reason For A Decline

- Do you have diabetes or been diagnosed as prediabetic (elevated A1C level)? Diabetes is not an automatic decline, but if the answer is yes to any of the following 4 questions, the individual will typically not qualify for coverage:
  - "Have you ever in your lifetime had any heart issues for example heart attack, stent placement, diagnosed with congestive heart, or diagnosed with atrial fibrillation?"
  - "Have you ever had a stroke or transient ischemic attack or TIA (mini stroke) in your lifetime?"
  - "Have you ever been diagnosed with neuropathy or retinopathy?"
  - "Are you prescribed or taking either Gabapentin or Lyrica?"
- The two top Medigap Supplement companies can be strict about either the combination of blood pressure and diabetic medications and the use of insulin. Here are some examples:
  - Must have no changes in blood pressure/diabetes medication combination up or down over the last two years and must be stable for 24 months, which is called the 2/2/2 Rule.
  - Example of a decline: blood pressure medication + 1 diabetic medication or 2 blood pressure medications+ 3 diabetic medications.
  - Some companies will decline for the use of insulin.

Major Issues Will Not Be Accepted By Most Medigap

- In the last two years (24 months), have you experienced any major issues, which are declinable:

  - Heart attack or any heart issues,
  - Stent placement,
  - Stroke, or
  - Internal cancer (other than basal or squamous cell).
- Any major issues in an individual's lifetime, which are declinable:
  - Congestive obstructive pulmonary disease or COPD;
  - Kidney disease;
  - Parkinson's disease;
  - Lou Gehrig's disease or ALS;
  - Hepatitis;
  - Cirrhosis;
  - Alzheimer's;
  - Currently using oxygen or nebulizer; or
  - Diagnosed with major depression (anxiety and depression are okay), bi-polar, or schizophrenia.

Medigap Pricing Methods

- There are three ways that the Medigap Supplement plan determines how it will charge its monthly premium:
  - Attained-age rated,
  - Issue-age rated, or
  - Community rated.
- The top-rated companies are in the business to keep their customers. They will be careful to keep the rate increase acceptable, so their current customers are happy with their decision in choosing them for coverage.
- Regardless of what pricing method the Medigap Supplement company is using, they will have rate increases as they get older based on changes to Medicare, health care inflation, as well as other factors.

Attained-Age Rated

- This is what most Medigap Supplement companies will use for their pricing method.
- This pricing method is based on the current "attained" age and will continue to increase as an individual gets older.
- The premiums will be lower for the individual when they first enroll at a younger age. Those who are older will pay more under this pricing method.
- Under this pricing model, the individual will start out with a lower premium than the other two pricing methods, which may or may not benefit the policyholder over time.

Issue-Age Rated

- This pricing method is the most misunderstood and sometimes extremely misleading.
- This pricing method is based on the age when the individual was first issued the coverage. The premium will not increase based on age as the individual gets older like that of attained-age rating. The premium can only be increased if the insurance company decides to raise rates for everyone in the state.
- This rating is different than an attained-age rating because the monthly premium is typically higher in the beginning than that of an attained-age rated policy. Since age will not be a factor, the insurance companies will typically charge more at the beginning, which may or may not benefit the policyholder over time.
- There are some states that encourage every company to adopt this pricing model. These states include: *Arizona, Florida, Georgia, Idaho, Missouri, and New Hampshire.*

Community Rated

- This pricing method is the least offered of the three pricing methods. It is sometimes referred to as the "no age-rated" pricing model. With this pricing model, all policyholders in the area will pay the same premium regardless of their age.
- If someone purchases a community rated policy when they are older, this could be an attractive model. They will pay the same price as some who is 65.
- Since age will not be a factor like that of an issue-age policy, the premium can only be increased if the insurance company decides to raise rates for everyone in the state, which may or may not benefit the policyholder over time.
- There are some states that encourage every company to adopt this pricing model. These states include: *Arkansas, Connecticut, Maine, Massachusetts, Minnesota, New York, Vermont, and Washington.*

Medigap Supplement Costs

- When an individual is shopping for the Medigap Supplement plan, the monthly premium will come down to their zip code.
- The current monthly premium for a Medigap Supplement Plan G will cost on average approximately $125 a month, and the Medigap Supplement Plan N will cost on average approximately $95 a month.
- In some areas, such as Florida, where there is a larger population of retirees and the state uses an issue-age rating method, the monthly premium tends to be a little higher. The average cost is approximately $180 a month for Plan G, and around $145 a month for Plan N.

When Can I Expect Rate Increases?

- If an individual is due for a rate increase by their Medigap Supplement company, they can expect to receive a letter about a month or two before their policy anniversary date.
- The anniversary date can coincide with the individual's birth month, but it can also be different if they started their policy later.
    - For example, if they purchased a Medigap Supplement plan when they retired or shopped their policy during the calendar year, the effective date might be different than their birth month.
- If the policy is with a mutually owned company, they may not see a rate increase because the profits are given back to its members in the form of reduced premiums.
- If claims are down, they could see their premiums stay the same or they may see their premiums go down.
- On average, the person can expect to receive approximately a $7 rate increase every year, which is normal.

How Do I Pay For My Medigap Supplement Plan?

- Since the Medigap Supplement companies do not get any financial incentives from the federal government, the individual must pay them directly for their monthly premium.
- The monthly premium will not be drafted from the individual's Social Security check like it is with their Part B premium.
- The Medigap Supplement companies will require the policyholder to set up the monthly reoccurring draft payment from a checking or savings account similar to when someone gets a car loan.

Reasons Medigap Companies Require Auto Draft

- Only a few Medigap companies will allow the policyholder to use a credit card for their monthly premium. There are two reasons that they do not allow this.
  - The first reason is that the insurance companies would have to charge a higher premium in order to cover the interest fees on the credit card transactions.
  - The second reason is that credit cards are constantly updated for security purposes and new cards mailed to its customer. If the policyholder did not remember to update their credit card with the insurance company, their policy could lapse, and they could find themselves without coverage when they needed it the most.

Medicare Summary Notice

- Once the individual is on Medicare, they will get in the mail every three months a "Medicare Summary Notice," which is a summary of their Medicare claims from CMS.
- It is important to review the bill even if you do not owe anything to ensure that Medicare is not being billed for services that you are not receiving.
- On the Medicare Summary Notice, you will see what was billed to Medicare and how much they approved. It will also show you the 80 percent that they paid, and the 20 percent left over that you may have been billed. If you have a Medigap Supplement plan, it will show that the remaining bill was sent directly to your Medigap Supplement company.

Medicare Summary Notice
for Part B (Medical Insurance)

Page 1 of 12

The Official Summary of Your Medicare Claims from the Centers for Medicare & Medicaid Services

THIS IS NOT A BILL

Notice for	
Medicare Number	
Date of This Notice	**September 2, 2020**
Claims Processed Between	**June 4 — September 2, 2020**

Your Deductible Status

Your deductible is what you must pay for most health services before Medicare begins to pay.

Part B Deductible: You have now met your **$198.00** deductible for 2020.

Be Informed!

We can send you, upon request, Medicare information for free in accessible formats like Braille and large print. Learn more at Medicare.gov/about-us/accessibility-nondiscrimination-notice.

Your Claims & Costs This Period

Did Medicare Approve All Services? N

Number of Services Medicare Denied
See claims starting on page 3. Look for NO in the "Service Approved?" column. See the last page for how to handle a denied claim.

Total You May Be Billed $264.2

Providers with Claims This Period

June 1, 2020

June 9, 2020

June 11 — July 24, 2020

June 16, 2020

June 16, 2020

Create MyMedicare.gov Account As Soon As Possible

- It is important that every individual who gets their Medicare number create their own MyMedicare.gov account right away and go paperless.
- With a MyMedicare.gov account, the individual can view their Medicare Summary Notice online in almost real time when Medicare gets the bills. They will be able to see claims in a matter of weeks instead of every three months.

- Another benefit to creating a MyMedicare.gov account is that an individual can request a new Medicare ID card, and even print a copy of their card immediately if they lost it.

Chapter 9

Medicare Advantage — Everything You Need To Know

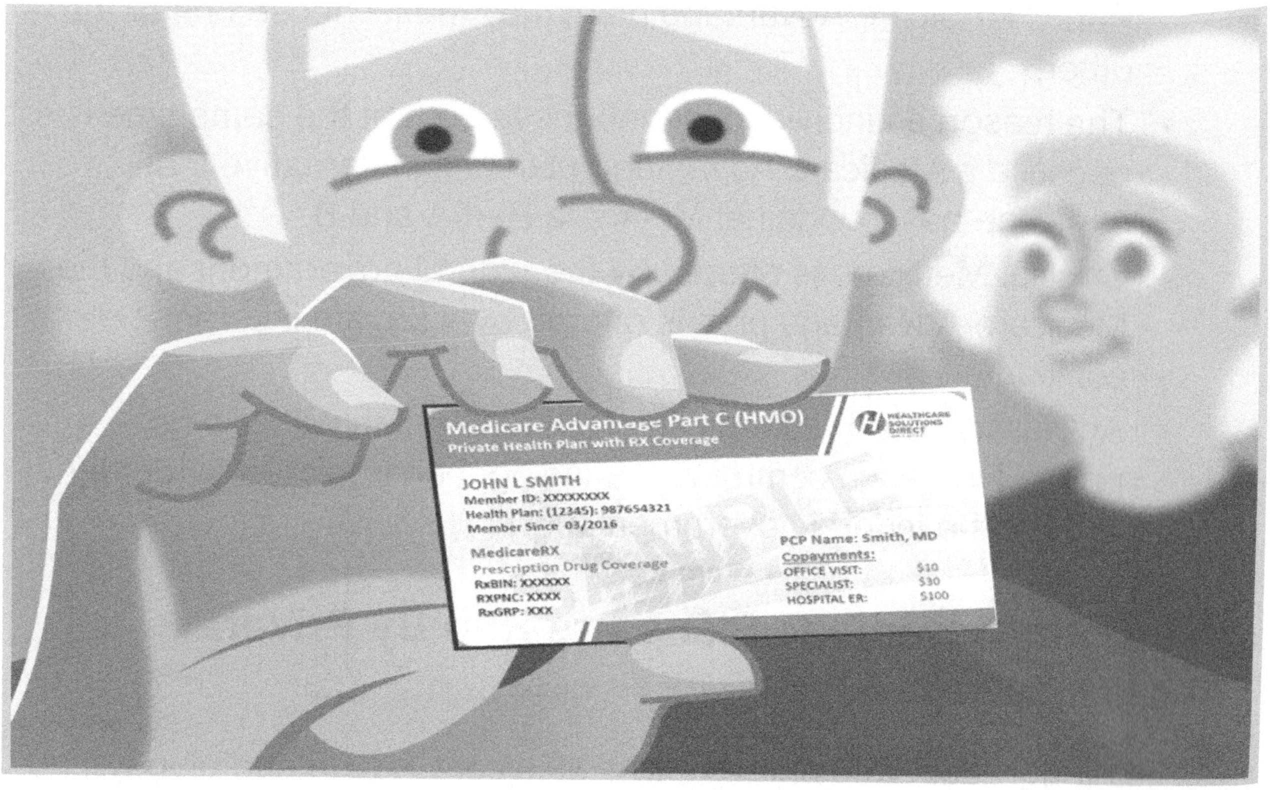

Basics of Medicare Advantage Plans

- Part C Medicare Advantage is another option that someone will have to choose from for their health care needs when they are eligible for Medicare.
- Medicare Advantage plans are like HMO or PPO that are provided by private insurance companies and not by the federal government.
- Although Medicare Advantage plans will vary by plan, they must all provide the same if not better coverage as Original Medicare

Part A and B. Most plans will give some additional benefits not provided by the federal government.

Medicare Advantage Is An Alternative Option

- An individual *cannot* have both Medicare Part A and B and a Part C Medicare Advantage plan; they must choose one or the other.
- The reason an individual cannot have both at the same time is because a Medicare Advantage plan is an alternative that someone has to Original Medicare Part A and B.
- Original Medicare is offered by the federal government and the Medicare Advantage plan is offered by a private insurance company.
- An individual with a Medicare Advantage plan will now have a private insurance company managing their health care for them and not the federal government.

Medicare Advantage Plans Are Run By Private Insurance

- An individual who enrolls into a Medicare Advantage plan will no longer be enrolled in Original Medicare Part A and B.
- Since an individual is no longer enrolled in Original Medicare Part A and B, they cannot purchase a Medigap Supplement to cover the cost sharing associated with the Medicare Advantage plan.
- The private insurance company will send the individual their own card to use at a hospital and for medical services such as individual and group insurance. This new card will be used instead of the red, white, and blue Medicare card.

Medicare Advantage Are Advertised As $0 Premium

- Medicare Advantage plans are commonly advertised as a $0 premium. An individual will continue to be marketed these $0 premium plans, so it is important to fully understand them.
- The reason Medicare Advantage plans typically offer $0 premium plans are because they form a network with doctors and hospitals in order to help manage costs.
- Medicare Advantage plans are like group and individual HMO or PPO plans and advertise as "all-in-one" plans.

Misconceptions About Medicare Advantage Plans

- There are two misconceptions many individuals have when it comes to Medicare Advantage plans that we will address.
- An individual who can understand the following two misconceptions will have a much easier time being able to navigate their options and make the best decision for their health care needs.

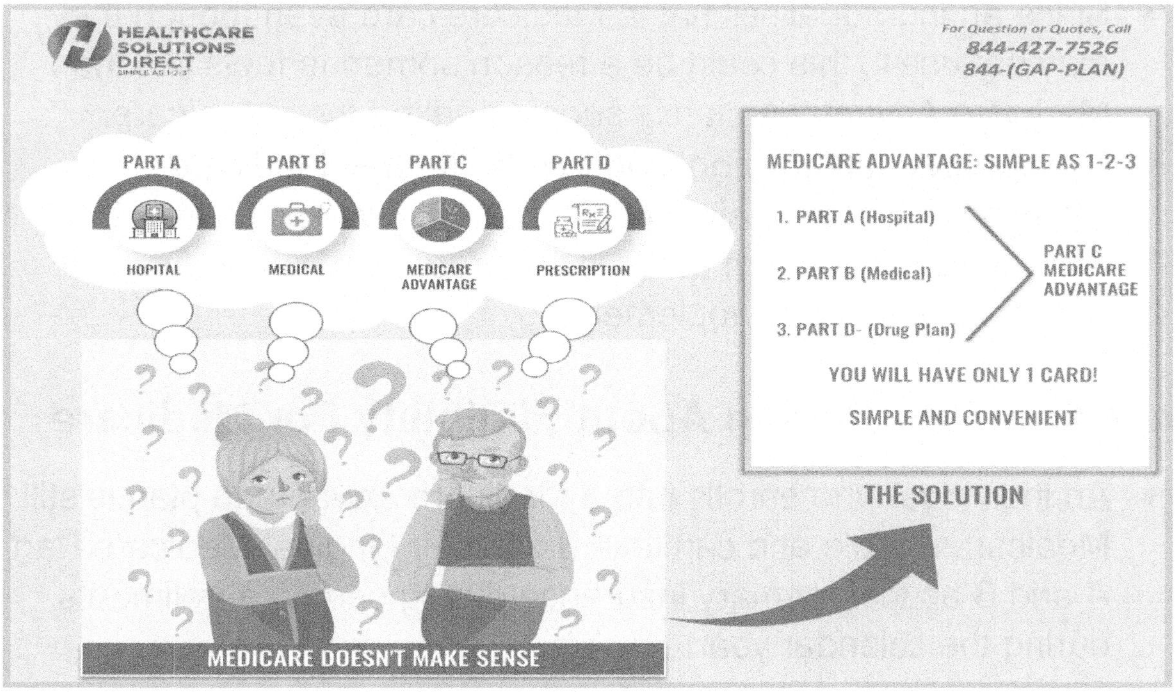

First Misconception About Medicare Advantage

- The first misconception individuals have about Medicare Advantage plans is that they are the same as a Medigap Supplement plan. That is incorrect because they are two different forms of insurance.
- It is easy for anyone to assume that a Medicare Advantage plan is a supplement plan based on the name. The Part C of Medicare has the word Medicare and the word Advantage in the title.
- This is where much of the confusion begins. This contributes to the misconception that a Medicare Advantage plan is a supplemental plan.

Reasons Medicare Advantage Still Create Confusion

- Individuals who enroll into a Medicare Advantage plan will still receive their Medicare Part A and B card in the mail. The individual does not need to send it back to Social Security.
- Since an individual still has a Medicare card even though they may not use it, this could be a reason someone feels like the Medicare Advantage plan is supplementing their Medicare.
- Many individuals will continue to refer to their Medicare Advantage plan as their supplement and few agents take the time to explain to them that it is an *alternative* plan to Original Medicare and not a supplement.

Important Information About Eligibility For Medicare

- An individual who enrolls into a Medicare Advantage plan is still Medicare eligible and can take back their Original Medicare Part A and B as their primary insurance during certain enrollments during the calendar year.

- Medicare Advantage plans will typically require the policyholder to enter into an annual contract with the plan.
- An individual can always take back Original Medicare Part A and B; however, if they do not have a Medigap OEP or a Guaranteed Issue, they may need to medically qualify for a Medigap Supplement.
- Taking back Original Medicare Part A and B without the protection of a Medigap Supplement plan may not be in the best interest for someone with a Medicare Advantage plan.

Example Showing Medicare Advantage Is Not A Supplement

- As of 2022, a Medicare Advantage plan will not pay the Part A hospital deductible of $1556 if an individual is admitted to the hospital, or the daily coinsurance if it is past 60 consecutive dates. A Medicare Advantage plan will also not pay the Part B medical coinsurance of 20 percent for medical bills.
- A Medicare Advantage plan will instead replace those Part A and Part B hospital and medical bills with their own set of deductibles, co-pays, and coinsurance charges.
- Since a Medicare Advantage will not pay the Part A and Part B deductibles, co-pays, or coinsurance, it cannot be a supplement plan to Original Medicare Part A and B.

Medicare Advantage Has Its Own Charges That Vary

- Each Medicare Advantage plan will have its own set of deductibles, co-pays, coinsurance, and network. This makes comparing plans sometimes a little challenging for an individual without the help of an experienced insurance agent.

- Some Medicare Advantage plans will have some incredible benefits such as no co-pay for a primary care doctor and maybe a small to no co-pay for a specialist visit. The individual may need to take into consideration the network associated with that plan compared to another plan with higher out-of-pocket co-pays.
- Medicare Advantage plans can offer some incredible benefits and protection, but an individual needs to make sure that they review the plan and how it affects their health care needs since each plan varies in coverage options.

Examples Of Medicare Advantage Hospital Charges

HOSPITAL SERVICES	
Inpatient hospital coverage	$300 per day for days 1 through 6 $0 per day for days 7 through 90

HOSPITAL SERVICES	
Inpatient hospital coverage	$150 per day for days 1 through 4 $0 per day for days 5 through 90

HOSPITAL SERVICES	
Inpatient hospital coverage	$350 per stay

HOSPITAL SERVICES	
Inpatient hospital coverage	$0 copay per stay

Courtesy: https://www.medicare.gov/plan-compare

- Since Medicare Advantage plans do not follow the same rules when it comes to deductibles and daily coinsurance like Medicare Part A, each plan will vary in the out-of-pocket responsibility if the policyholder was admitted to the hospital.

- Some Medicare Advantage plans will charge the individual $300 a day for the first 6 days in the hospital. An individual only admitted for 2 days could pay less if they had Original Medicare Part A as their insurance. If the individual were in the hospital for 6 days, it could be more expensive than the $1,556 Medicare Part A deductible.
- Some Medicare Advantage plans can offer a flat co-pay per inpatient hospital stay, and some may have no charge at all for an inpatient hospital stay.

Second Misconception About Medicare Advantage

- The second misconception individuals will have about a Medicare Advantage plan is that it will cost them nothing to join the plan since many are advertised as $0 premium.
- Many individuals can be surprised to learn that they must still pay the standard monthly Part B premium of $170.10 (as of 2022) to Social Security. The Part B premium never goes away when someone enrolls into a $0 premium or any Medicare Advantage plan.
- This goes back to the fact that even though the individual is no longer enrolled in Original Medicare they are always Medicare eligible no matter what option they choose.

Part B Premium Requirement For Medicare Advantage

MONTHLY PREMIUM

$0.00 Includes: Health & drug coverage

Doesn't include: $148.50 Standard Part B premium

YEARLY DRUG & PREMIUM COST

$0.00 Only includes premiums for the months left in this year when you don't enter any drugs

Courtesy: https://www.medicare.gov/plan-compare *Standard Part B Premium $170.10 for 2022

- When an individual enrolls into a Medicare Advantage plan, the standard Part B monthly premium of $170.10 (as of 2022) a month that is collected by Social Security is now given to the private insurance company. This helps offset the cost in managing that individual's health care instead of to Original Medicare.
- Once an individual is eligible for Medicare, they must always continue to contribute to the Medicare system no matter if they keep Original Medicare or choose a Medicare Advantage plan as their primary insurance.
- Medicare Advantage companies rely almost entirely on what the federal government gives them to manage someone's health care and the Part B premium plays a large part in that.

Medicare Advantage Same Price As Original Medicare

- When an individual compares Original Medicare Parts A and B to that of a Part C Medicare Advantage plan, they are exactly the same cost.
- However, the individual must still pay the standard Part B monthly premium of $170.10 (as of 2022) to Social Security regardless of if they keep the federal government program or go to a private insurance company.
- One of the benefits an individual will see with a Medicare Advantage plan when comparing the monthly cost to Original Medicare is that it will come with an out-of-pocket maximum where, unfortunately, Medicare does not.

Medicare Advantage Plans Get More Than Part B Premium

- Although it varies from state to state, it appears the average fixed amount a Medicare Advantage plan company receives is approximately $900 a month per person in reimbursement from CMS to cover the individuals Part A and B cost.

- Since Medicare Advantage plan companies rely almost entirely on federal funding, some plans will get more from CMS based on the needs of that individual.
- These are known as a Special Needs Plan (SNP) that an individual can qualify for, which offers benefits designed to meet the specific needs of that individual.

The Centers For Medicare And Medicaid Services Sets A Benchmark To Determine Funding

- Each year, CMS will determine what is called a "benchmark" for what it will give in federal funding to a Medicare Advantage company. Some of this funding is from the Medicare Part B premium; however, most of the funding comes from CMS.
- In determining the benchmark, CMS looks at each geographical area and compares what they would have paid on average in regular Medicare costs for that individual. CMS will then set up a bidding process that the Medicare Advantage companies will then submit.
- If the bid comes at or under the benchmark from the Medicare Advantage company, you will see the plan typically offered as a $0 premium. If the bid is above the benchmark, then many times the plan will charge a monthly premium in addition to the standard Medicare Part B premium.

Medicare Advantage Plan Benefits

- Medicare Advantage plans can offer some incredible benefits. The first benefit that makes a Medicare Advantage plan attractive is that the individual will have a calendar year out-of-pocket maximum limit for their hospital and medical expenses.

This is a benefit that is not provided to an individual who has Original Medicare as their primary insurance.

Medicare Advantage Out-Of-Pocket Maximum Benefit

- In 2022, all Medicare Advantage plans are required to have an out-of-pocket limit for hospital and medical expenses not to exceed $7,550 for in-network expenses and $11,300 for a combined in-network and out of network.
- According to the Kaiser Family Foundation, they reported that in 2020 the average out-of-pocket limit is $4,925 for in-network services and $8,828 for both in-network and out-of-network services, which can be found in PPO plans.
- Here is an example from the Kaiser Family Foundation in 2020, showing the average out-of-pocket limits across all Medicare Advantage plans.

8. For Medicare Advantage enrollees, the average out-of-pocket limit is $4,925 for in-network services and $8,828 for both in-network and out-of-network services (PPOs)

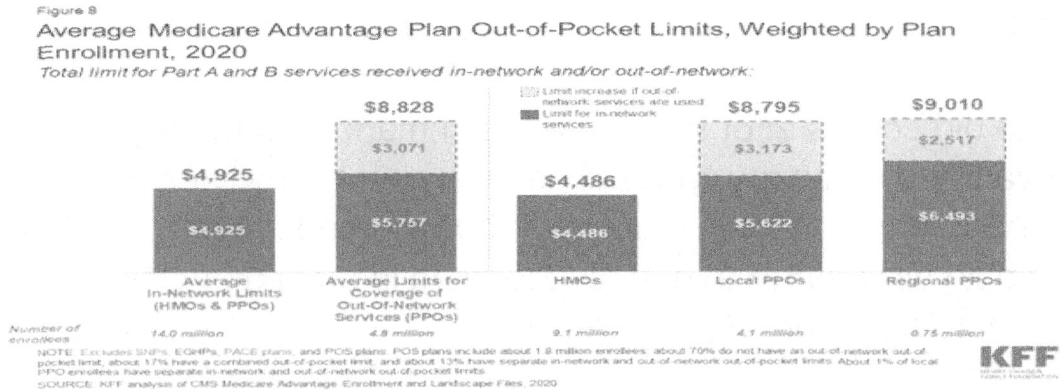

Figure 8: Average Medicare Advantage Plan Out-of-Pocket Limits, Weighted by Plan Enrollment, 2020

In 2020, Medicare Advantage enrollees' average out-of-pocket limit for in-network services is $4,925 (HMOs and PPOs) and $8,828 for out-of-network services (PPOs). For HMO enrollees, the average out-of-pocket (in network) limit is $4,486; these plans do not cover services received from out-of-network providers. For local and regional PPO enrollees, the average out-of-pocket limit for both in-network and out-of-network services are $8,795, and $9,010, respectively. These out-of-pocket limits apply to Part A and B services only, and do not apply to Part D spending.

Courtesy of the Kaiser Family Foundation: https://www.kff.org/medicare/issue-brief/a-dozen-facts-about-medicare-advantage-in-2020/

Example of Meeting Medicare Advantage Out-Of-Pocket Expenses

- Medicare Advantage plans will typically have a co-pay for doctor visits or services during the calendar year. Medicare Advantage plans operate on the premise of 'pay as you go'.
- Medicare Advantage plans will typically have a coinsurance responsibility for out-of-network services or if the individual needs services such as durable medical equipment, chemotherapy, dialysis, or they receive other Part B drugs such as infusions, vaccinations, or injections.
- Medicare Advantage plans on the market will typically charge 20 percent for these services up to the out-of-pocket limit.
- The following example on a popular Medicare Advantage plan shows in the summary of benefits the 20 percent responsibility on these services up to the out-of-pocket limit.

MAXIMUM YOU PAY FOR HEALTH SERVICES		
Maximum you pay for health services ∨		$5,500 In-network
OTHER SERVICES		
Durable medical equipment (like wheelchairs & oxygen)	20% coinsurance per item	Limits apply ∨
Prosthetics (like braces, artificial limbs)	20% coinsurance per item	Limits apply ∨
Dialysis	In-network: 20% coinsurance	Limits apply ∨
PART B DRUGS ∨		
Chemotherapy drugs	20% coinsurance	Limits apply ∨
Other Part B drugs	20% coinsurance	Limits apply ∨

Courtesy: https://www.medicare.gov/plan-compare

Most Medicare Advantage Plans Are $0 Premium

- In 2020, the Kaiser Family Foundation, a non-profit organization, reviewed Medicare Advantage plans across the country and reported that most enrollees *do not pay* a monthly premium other than the standard Medicare Part B premium.
- Almost 60 percent of individuals who have a Medicare Advantage plan are only responsible for the standard monthly Part B premium of $170.10 (as of 2022).

6. Nearly two-thirds of Medicare Advantage enrollees pay no supplemental premium (other than the Part B premium) in 2020

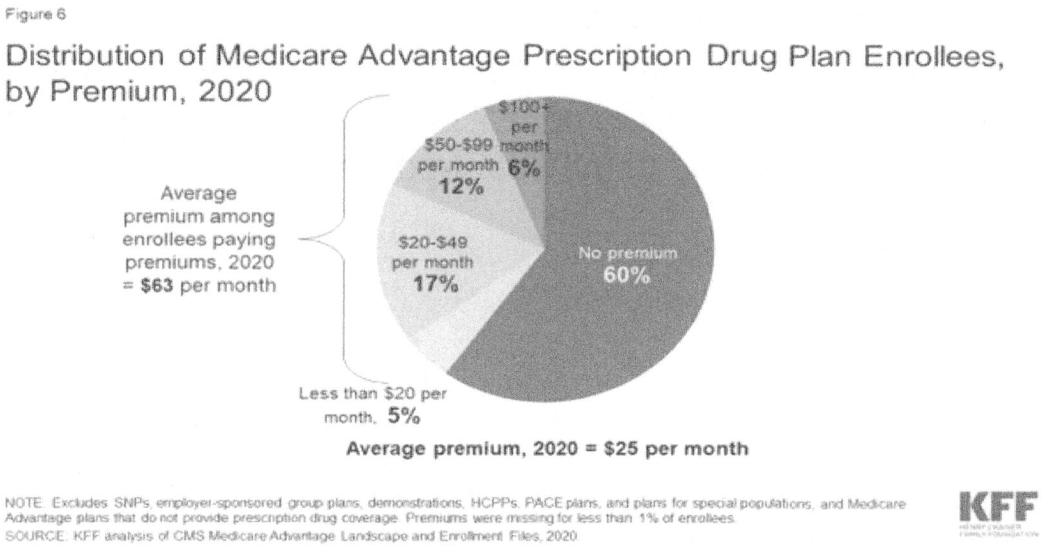

Figure 6: Distribution of Medicare Advantage Prescription Drug Plan Enrollees, by Premium, 2020

In 2020, 90% of Medicare Advantage plans offer prescription drug coverage (MA-PDs), and most Medicare Advantage enrollees (89%) are in plans that include this prescription drug coverage. Nearly two-thirds of these beneficiaries (60%) pay no premium for their plan, other than the Medicare Part B premium ($144.60 in 2020). However, 18 percent of beneficiaries in MA-PDs (2.8 million enrollees) pay at least $50 per month, including 6 percent who pay $100 or more per month, in addition to the monthly Part B premium. The MA-PD premium includes both the cost of Medicare-covered Part A and Part B benefits and Part D prescription drug coverage. Among MA-PD enrollees who pay a premium for their plan, the average premium is $63 per month. Altogether, including those who do not pay a premium, the average MA-PD enrollee pays $25 per month in 2020.

Courtesy of the Kaiser Family Foundation: https://www.kff.org/medicare/issue-brief/a-dozen-facts-about-medicare-advantage-in-2020/

Medicare Advantage Offers "All-In One" Coverage

- Another incredible benefit with a Medicare Advantage plan is the convenience of having all the benefits of hospital, medical, and prescription drug coverage all in one plan.
- Most Medicare Advantage plans on the market will provide the convenience of just one card for the individual to carry with them, which will include hospital, medical, and prescription drug coverage.
- The card will show the co-pay responsibility for primary care doctors, specialists, and emergency room visits.
- An individual with Original Medicare who purchased a Medigap Supplement and a PDP standalone would need to carry three separate cards.

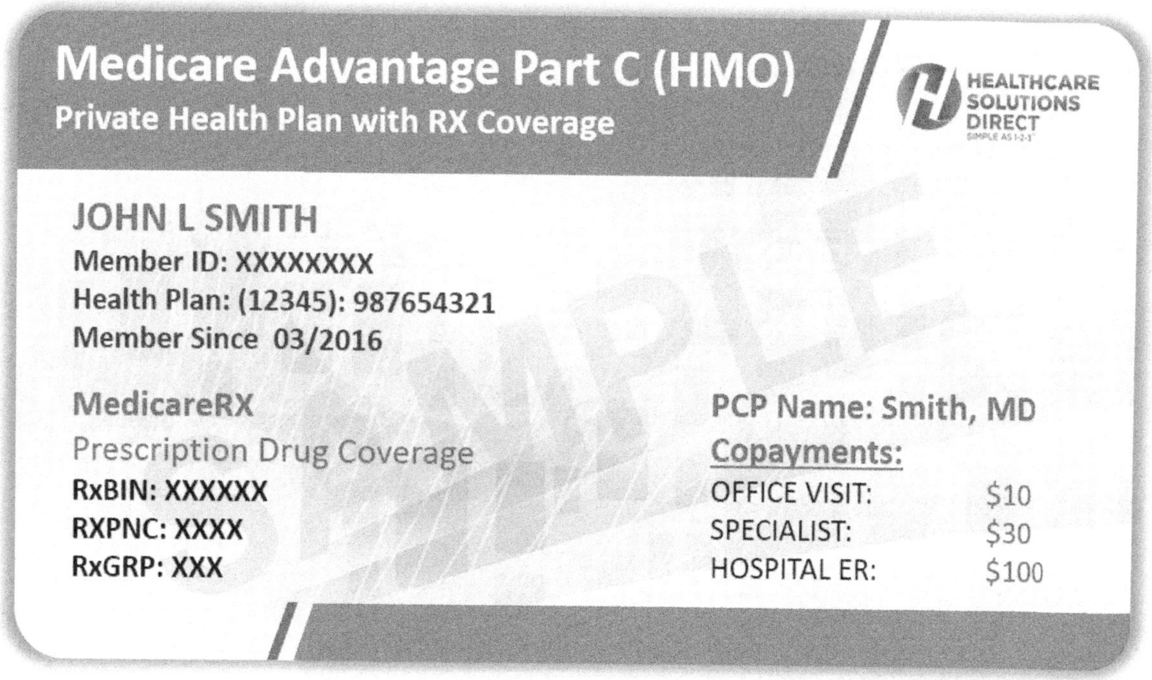

Added Benefits Not Covered By Original Medicare

- Medicare Advantage plans will offer some incredible additional benefits that Original Medicare does not offer.
- The three big benefits that most people who are eligible for Medicare want are dental, vision, and hearing coverage. Most Medicare Advantage plans will include some sort of coverage for these benefits.
- In 2020, the Kaiser Family Foundation which is a non-profit reviewed additional benefit that were currently offered by Medicare Advantage plans.
- Besides the additional benefit of dental, vision and hearing, an individual also will have access many times to telehealth, fitness, and over-the-counter benefits with most plans.

9. Most Medicare Advantage enrollees have access to some benefits not covered by traditional Medicare in 2020

Figure 9

Share of Medicare Advantage Enrollees in Plans with Extra Benefits by Benefit Type, 2020

NOTE: Dental includes plans that only provide preventive benefits, such as cleanings.
SOURCE: KFF analysis of CMS Medicare Advantage Enrollment and Benefit Files, 2020

Figure 9: Share of Medicare Advantage Enrollees in Plans with Extra Benefits by Benefit Type, 2020

Medicare Advantage plans may provide extra ("supplemental") benefits that are not offered in traditional Medicare, and can use rebate dollars to help cover the cost of extra benefits. Plans can also charge additional premiums for such benefits. Beginning in 2019, Medicare Advantage plans have been able to offer additional supplemental benefits that were not offered in previous years. These supplemental benefits must still be considered "primarily health related" but CMS expanded this definition, so more items and services are available as supplemental benefits.

Courtesy of the Kaiser Family Foundation: https://www.kff.org/medicare/issue-brief/a-dozen-facts-about-medicare-advantage-in-2020/

Fitness, Transportation, and Over-The-Counter Benefits

- Most Medicare Advantage plans will offer free fitness memberships at local gyms or the YMCA. This is an excellent feature to help someone stay healthy without the added cost of a fitness membership.
- Another benefit that has become popular among Medicare Advantage offerings is transportation to and from medical appointments. The plans will offer the individual a certain number of trips toward medical appointments at no cost.
- Over-the-counter benefits are offered by many Medicare Advantage plans. The individual will be able to get over-the-counter items such as allergy medications, cough drops, pain relievers, vitamins and so much more. These benefits can be ordered online, over the phone, or by going to a participating store.

Medicare Advantage Benefit Called The Giveback

- Some Medicare Advantage companies will offer a benefit called a "giveback" or "buydown" program. This is where a Medicare Advantage company will pay the individual to join their plan.
- When a Medicare Advantage plan bids below the benchmark we spoke of earlier, they will get what is called a rebate from CMS. Most plans will take the rebate to provide additional benefits to the plan while others will use the rebate to "giveback" or "buydown" someone's standard Part B premium.
- The giveback is where the Medicare Advantage plan will give back either the full standard Part B $170.10 (as of 2022) a month, or a portion of that toward someone's Social Security check.

- Most Medicare Advantage plans will use the rebate to offer additional benefits to its members instead of a giveback.

Medicare Advantage Drawbacks To Be Aware Of

- Medicare Advantage plans can offer some incredible benefits that are hard to pass up, but there are some drawbacks to be aware of when someone unenrolls from the federal government's Original Medicare Part A and B.
- An individual may find it hard to purchase a Medigap Supplement in the future if they do not have a Medigap OEP or Guaranteed Issue due to health conditions.
- Original Medicare operates on a private fee-for-service, which means there are no networks. Currently, it is estimated that 93 percent of all doctors and specialist in the U.S. accept Original Medicare.

Medicare Advantage Plans Most Offered Network Is Health Maintenance Organization (HMO)

- According to research done in 2019 by the Kaiser Family Foundation, they reported that over 60 percent of plans offered are HMO plans, which will typically not cover anything out of network unless it is an emergency.
- This could be a problem if someone is traveling or they want to see a doctor, facility, or hospital out of network.
- Over the last decade, Medicare Advantage plan networks have become better with many plans offering the ability to switch the network to the local area of where the person is traveling.
- An individual who may be concerned about network restrictions should consider either a local or regional PPO that might give them more access to care in or out of network.

Medicare Advantage May Require Referrals

- An individual with an HMO network may be required to get a referral from their primary care doctor to see a specialist.
- The reason behind needing to get a referral under an HMO Medicare Advantage plan is to prevent misuse of the plan and to manage costs.
- An individual who may be concerned about needing to get referrals should consider either a local or regional PPO that typically does not require referrals much like Original Medicare.

Medicare Advantage May Require Prior Authorizations

- Much like group and individual insurance plans, most all Medicare Advantage plans will typically require prior authorizations for services or procedures. This is not required by Original Medicare.
- Most type of surgeries, procedures, or medical equipment will require a prior authorization from the Medicare Advantage plan before being able to schedule or obtain it.
- There are benefits and drawbacks to both Original Medicare and Medicare Advantage plans; therefore, it's important that an individual takes into consideration what is best for their health care needs.

Medicare Advantage Plan Types

- An individual has different Medicare Advantage plan types they can choose from in their area when they are eligible for Medicare.
- It is important to understand the fundamental differences between an HMO and a PPO network since these are the two

most offered networks when it comes to Medicare Advantage plans.

- It is also important to understand that the individual must live in the plans service area to enroll into the plan.

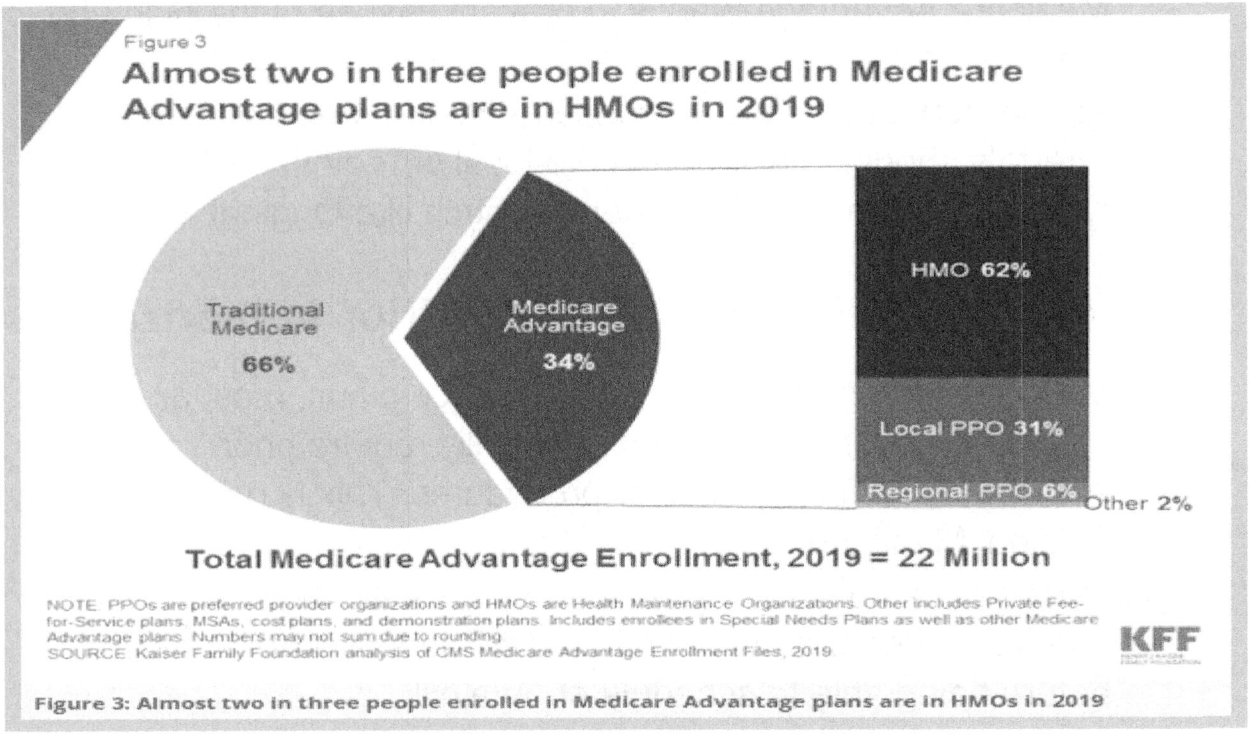

Figure 3: Almost two in three people enrolled in Medicare Advantage plans are in HMOs in 2019

Courtesy of: https://www.kff.org/medicare/fact-sheet/medicare-advantage/

Health Maintenance Organization (HMO)

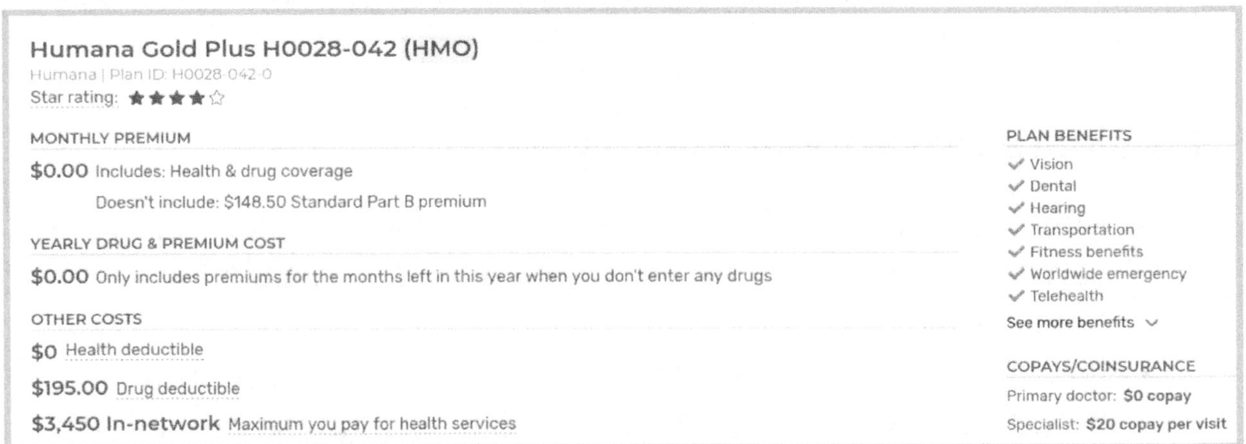

Humana Gold Plus H0028-042 (HMO)
Humana | Plan ID: H0028-042-0
Star rating: ★★★★☆

MONTHLY PREMIUM
$0.00 Includes: Health & drug coverage
Doesn't include: $148.50 Standard Part B premium

YEARLY DRUG & PREMIUM COST
$0.00 Only includes premiums for the months left in this year when you don't enter any drugs

OTHER COSTS
$0 Health deductible
$195.00 Drug deductible
$3,450 In-network Maximum you pay for health services

PLAN BENEFITS
- ✓ Vision
- ✓ Dental
- ✓ Hearing
- ✓ Transportation
- ✓ Fitness benefits
- ✓ Worldwide emergency
- ✓ Telehealth

See more benefits

COPAYS/COINSURANCE
Primary doctor: **$0 copay**
Specialist: **$20 copay per visit**

Courtesy: https://www.medicare.gov/plan-compare *Standard Part B Premium $170.10 for 2022

- The HMO network plans will typically require the individual to get care and services from certain doctors and hospitals that are contracted within that plans' network.
- The individual will typically be required to select a primary care physician (PCP) within the plan's network who will help to coordinate their care. If they do not select one at the time of enrollment, one will typically be assigned to them.
- Most HMO plans will require referrals from the PCP to see a specialist.
- An individual will typically be responsible for all costs if they see a provider outside of the network. Certain exceptions would be if they needed emergency care or dialysis treatments outside of the plan's network.
- Most HMO plans will require prior approval for certain services when they are needed.

Health Maintenance Organization — Point of Service (HMO-POS)

WellCare Value (HMO-POS)
WellCare | Plan ID: H0174-005-0
Star rating: ★★★½☆

MONTHLY PREMIUM
$0.00 Includes: Health & drug coverage
Doesn't include: $148.50 Standard Part B premium

YEARLY DRUG & PREMIUM COST
$0.00 Only includes premiums for the months left in this year when you don't enter any drugs

OTHER COSTS
$0 Health deductible
$0.00 Drug deductible
$4,500 In and Out-of-network
$4,500 In-network
$4,500 Out-of-network Maximum you pay for health services

PLAN BENEFITS
✓ Vision
✓ Dental
✓ Hearing
✗ Transportation
✓ Fitness benefits
✓ Worldwide emergency
✓ Telehealth
See more benefits

COPAYS/COINSURANCE
Primary doctor: $0 copay
Specialist: $30 copay per visit

DRUGS
Add your prescription drugs

Courtesy: https://www.medicare.gov/plan-compare *Standard Part B Premium $170.10 for 2022

- A health maintenance organization — point of service (HMO-POS) network plans will give more freedom and flexibility to the individual with their HMO Medicare Advantage plan. Think of an HMO-POS plan as an HMO plan, which allows someone to see out of the network providers for certain or all benefits at a higher cost. They will typically have separate out-of-pocket limits for in-network and out-of-network services.

- The out-of-network provider is not required to accept the plans' terms and conditions of payment. The individual must make sure before they see the provider that they agree to the terms and conditions of payment from the plan.
- An HMO-POS plan will typically require the individual to select a PCP within the plans network who will help to coordinate their care.
- A benefit of an HMO-POS plan is that the individual may not be required by the plan to get a referral to see a specialist.
- Most HMO-POS plans will require prior approval for certain services when they are needed.

Preferred Provider Organization (Local PPO)

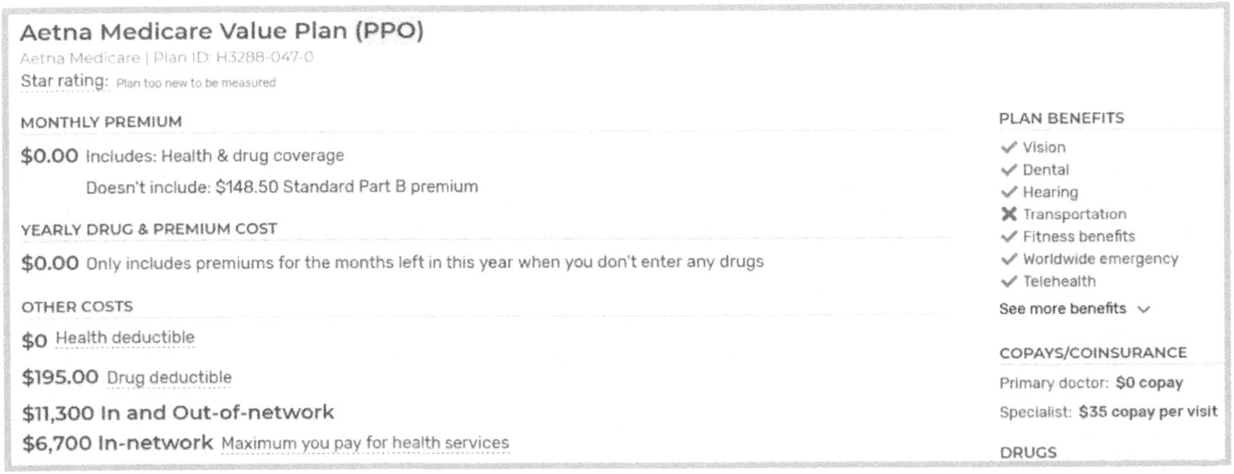

Courtesy: https://www.medicare.gov/plan-compare *Standard Part B Premium $170.10 for 2022

- The PPO network plans are offered as either a local PPO or regional PPO. The local PPO is the most offered Medicare Advantage plan that an individual will see available to them.

- The PPO network plans have an established network of doctors and hospitals in the local area. Individuals will typically pay less if they use the providers in the plans' network.
- The individual will have separate out-of-pocket limits for in-network and out-of-network services.
- The PPO network plans make it easy for the individual to simply log on to the carrier site and search for a PPO provider at generally a higher cost to them out of network. These types of plans are great for someone that travels.
- The PPO network plans will typically not require the individual to select a PCP or need to get a referral to see a specialist.
- When they are needed, most PPO network plans will require prior approval for certain services.

Regional Preferred Provider Organization (RPPO)

HumanaChoice R4182-001 (Regional PPO)
Humana | Plan ID: R4182-001-0
Star rating: ★★★½☆

MONTHLY PREMIUM
$0.00 Includes: Only health coverage
Doesn't include: $148.50 Standard Part B premium

YEARLY DRUG & PREMIUM COST
$0.00 Only includes premiums for the months left in this year when you don't enter any drugs

OTHER COSTS
$975 annual deductible Health deductible
Drug deductible: This plan doesn't cover prescription drugs, so you'll pay for the drug's full cost under this plan. Other Medicare Advantage Plans offer drug coverage.
$6,700 In and Out-of-network
$5,700 In-network Maximum you pay for health services

PLAN BENEFITS
✓ Vision
✓ Dental
✓ Hearing
✗ Transportation
✗ Fitness benefits
✓ Worldwide emergency
✓ Telehealth
See more benefits

COPAYS/COINSURANCE
Primary doctor: **$15 copay per visit**
Specialist: **$40 copay per visit**

DRUGS

Courtesy: https://www.medicare.gov/plan-compare *Standard Part B Premium $170.10 for 2022

- The RPPO plans will have a network that will consist of a region instead of a local area. These plans were originally designed for those who lived in rural areas so they could have access to a region and not be limited to just one state like a local PPO.

- Medicare has set up 26 regions, which are comprised of one or more states that the individual will have in-network access.
- The RPPO network plans allow the individual to go out of network to anyone who accepts the plan at generally a higher cost to them and will follow the same rules and guidelines of a local PPO. They will typically have separate out-of-pocket limits for in-network and out-of-network services.
- The RPPO network plans will typically not require the individual to select a PCP or need to get a referral to see a specialist.
- Most RPPO network plans will require prior approval for certain services when they are needed.

Private Fee for Service (PFFS)

Humana Gold Choice H8145-084 (PFFS)
Humana | Plan ID: H8145-084-0
Star rating: ★★★½☆

MONTHLY PREMIUM
$96.00 Includes: Health & drug coverage
Doesn't include: $148.50 Standard Part B premium

YEARLY DRUG & PREMIUM COST
$864.00 Only includes premiums for the months left in this year when you don't enter any drugs

OTHER COSTS
$0 Health deductible
$250.00 Drug deductible
$6,700 In and Out-of-network Maximum you pay for health services

PLAN BENEFITS
✓ Vision
✓ Dental
✓ Hearing
✗ Transportation
✗ Fitness benefits
✓ Worldwide emergency
✓ Telehealth
See more benefits

COPAYS/COINSURANCE
Primary doctor: **$15 copay per visit**
Specialist: **$45 copay per visit**

Courtesy: https://www.medicare.gov/plan-compare *Standard Part B Premium $170.10 for 2022

- A private fee-for-service (PFFS) plans are different in many ways than any of the other Medicare Advantage plans. These types of plans may or may not have a network.
- Original Medicare operates as a private fee-for-service, so in PFFS plans the individual can go to any Medicare-approved provider if they agree to the terms and conditions of payment from the Medicare Advantage plan.
- PFFS plans will not require the individual to select a PCP or need to get a referral to see a specialist.

- PFFS plans are not prevalent and there may not be one available in the individual's zip code. If one is offered, it will typically cost more than $100 a month to enroll in the plan.
- The benefit to a PFFS plan is that the individual will have an out-of-pocket limit to their health care.

Medical Savings Account (MSA)

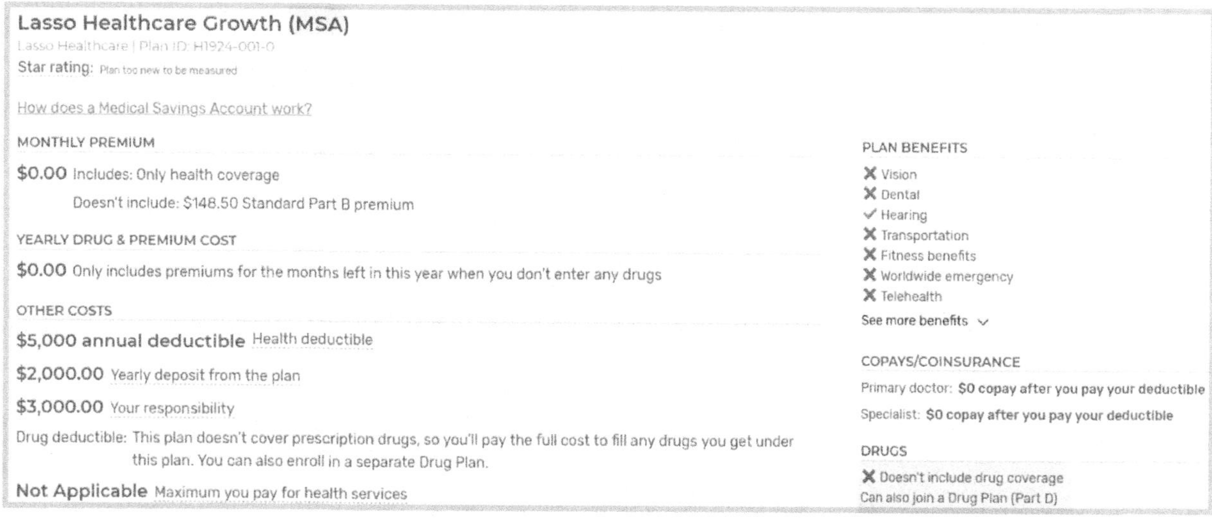

Courtesy: https://www.medicare.gov/plan-compare *Standard Part B Premium $170.10 for 2022

- The Medicare Saving Account plans are like HSA plans available outside of Medicare. These types of plans are a private-fee-for service so the individual can go to any Medicare-approved provider.
- The MSA plans will not require the individual to select a PCP or need to get a referral to see a specialist.
- The MSA plans will incorporate a high-deductible insurance plan with a MSA that the individual can use to pay for their health care costs.
- The individual is responsible for all costs up to the annual deductible; however, the plan will typically deposit a certain dollar amount into a savings account. This can be used to pay for health care costs before meeting the annual deductible. Any

money not used in the MSA will roll over to the following calendar year.

- The MSA plans do *not* offer prescription coverage so this is one of the only Medicare Advantage plans where the individual can purchase a standalone PDP.

Special Needs Plan (SNP)

- These types of plans will only be available to an individual who is eligible for Medicare and meets the following requirements because the plans' benefits are designed to meet the specific needs of that individual:
    - D-Special Needs Plan (SNP): Dual eligible for Medicare and Medicaid because of low income or resources.
    - I-SNP: Institutionalized in a nursing home or assisted living facility.
    - C-SNP: Serious chronic or disabling condition.

Requirements for Special Needs Plan

- A SNP plan generally requires that the individual gets services from doctors and hospitals that participate in the SNP network. The network will contract with specialists who are experts in the disease or condition that affects the individual.
- The individual will normally be required to select a PCP within the plans' network who will help to coordinate their care. Most plans will require a referral to see a specialist.

Special Needs Plan Enrollment Period

- If an individual has a disabling condition such as chronic heart failure, cancer, diabetes, ESRD, HIV, or dementia, they should explore this type of Medicare Advantage plan.

- An individual can enroll in this type of plan any time during the year if they meet the requirements. If the individual is currently enrolled in a SNP, they can switch once during each of the first three calendar quarters of the year.
- A SNP can be a great option for an individual who meets the requirements since the plan gets more money from the federal government because they will typically require more for the individual's health care needs.

Medicare Advantage Enrollment Periods

- There are only certain times during the year that an individual can either enroll or switch a Medicare Advantage plan.
- Medicare Advantage plans will not require an individual to medically qualify to join the plan. No matter what their health conditions, they can enroll into a Medicare Advantage plan.
- Prior to 2021, anyone who was diagnosed with ESRD could not qualify for a Medicare Advantage plan. However, this requirement has since been removed.
- There are only two requirements that someone must meet to enroll in a Medicare Advantage plan which is as follows:
    - Must be enrolled in Medicare Part A and B and
    - Must have a valid enrollment period to join the Medicare Advantage plan.

Initial Coverage Enrollment Period

- The initial coverage enrollment period (ICEP) is the first time an individual can choose a Medicare Advantage plan instead of Original Medicare Part A and B.
- An individual who is turning 65 and taking Medicare Part A and B for the first time, their 7-month IEP will also be their ICEP to enroll into a Medicare Advantage plan.

- An individual eligible for Medicare Part A and B because of a disability that is turning 65 will also get an ICEP to join a Medicare Advantage plan.
- An individual who received their Medicare Part A and B prior to the age of 65 due to a disability, will also be eligible for an ICEP after receiving SSDI benefits for 24 months.
- An individual with an SEP or GEP for Medicare Part A and B, will also get an ICEP and can apply three months before their Medicare Part B effective date.

Medicare Open Enrollment Period

- The Medicare OEP will *always* run from October 15 through December 7.
- During this time, the individual can join a Medicare Advantage plan for the first time or make changes to their current Medicare Advantage plan for the next calendar year.
- The individual will need to make their selections by December 7 so their coverage will take effect on January 1.

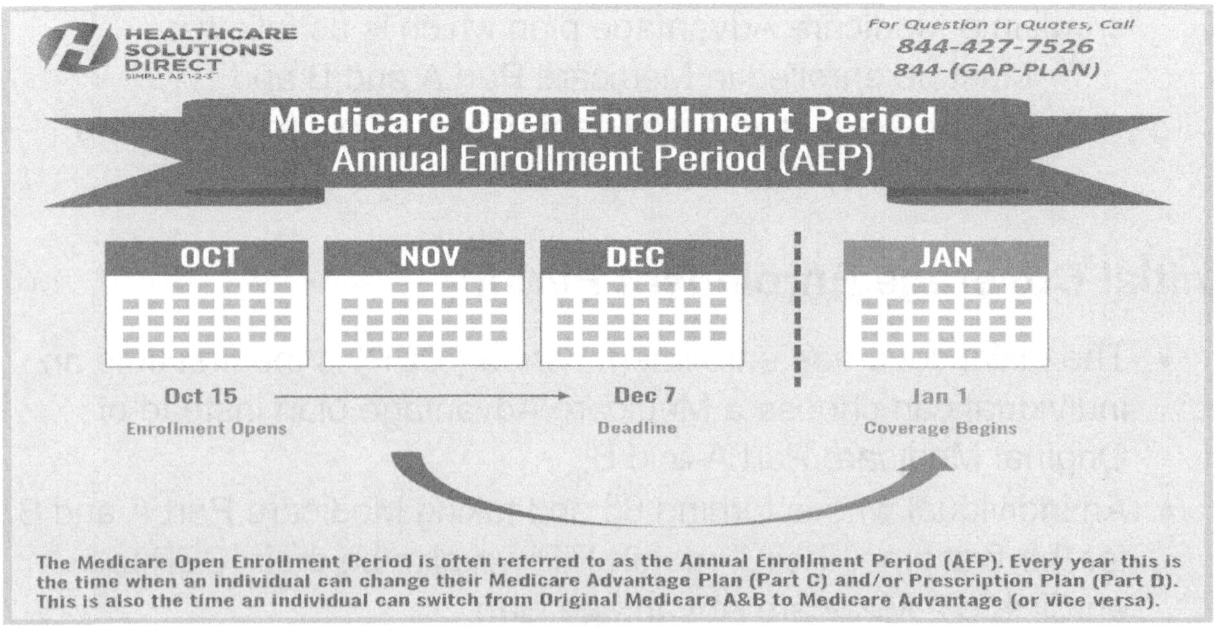

Changes Available During Medicare Open Enrollment Period

- During the Medicare OEP, the individual can make these following changes:
    - Change to a Medicare Advantage plan from Original Medicare,
    - Change to Original Medicare from a Medicare Advantage plan,
    - Change from one Medicare Advantage plan to another regardless if they have drug coverage, and/or
    - Enroll or drop a standalone PDP.

Only Requirements During Medicare Open Enrollment Period

- If an individual would like to enroll in a Medicare Advantage plan during the Medicare OEP, there are only two requirements:
    - The individual must have both Medicare Part A and B and
    - They must live within the plans service area or network.
- If the individual's Medicare Advantage plan or standalone PDP is still available in their area and they do not want to make any changes during the Medicare OEP, the plan will auto renew for the next calendar year at midnight on December 7.

Medicare Advantage Open Enrollment Period

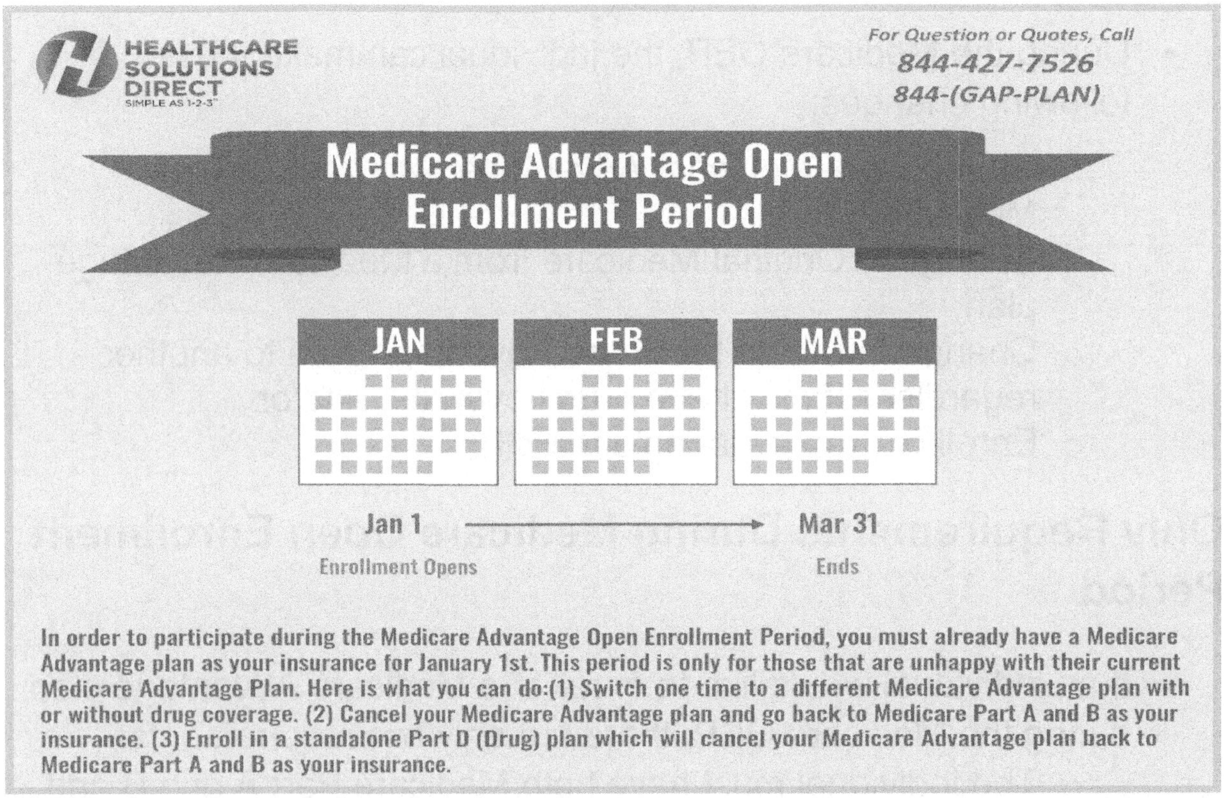

- The Medicare Advantage OEP is only for individuals who are already enrolled into a Medicare Advantage plan with or without drug coverage, which could be referred to as the "buyer's remorse" period.
- This period is set aside for those that would like to still make some changes to their current Medicare Advantage plan.

Prior To 2019 It Was Called Medicare Disenrollment Period

- Up until 2019, the Medicare Advantage OEP was called the Medicare Disenrollment Period, which ran from January 1 through February 14.

- The Medicare Disenrollment Period only allowed an individual with a Medicare Advantage plan to enroll into a standalone PDP. This would disenroll the individual from their current Medicare Advantage plan back to Original Medicare as their insurance.
- In 2019, the enrollment period was renamed the Medicare Advantage OEP and currently runs from January 1 through March 31.

Available Changes Between January 1-March 31

- If an individual is satisfied with their current coverage, they do *not* need to make any changes during this period.
- During the Medicare Advantage OEP, the individual can make the following changes:
    - Change one time to a different Medicare Advantage plan with or without drug coverage,
    - Cancel their Medicare Advantage plan and return to Original Medicare, or
    - Enroll in a standalone PDP, which will cancel their Medicare Advantage plan and return them to Original Medicare.

More Options Now Available After January 1

- The Medicare Advantage OEP provides an individual with more options after the Medicare OEP ends on December 7. Any changes made during the Medicare Advantage OEP will take effect on the first of the month.
- If an individual makes any changes to their coverage in the month of February, the new coverage will start on March 1.
- No changes can be made to their Medicare Advantage plan after the March 31 midnight deadline until the next year's calendar Medicare OEP.

Medicare Special Enrollment Period

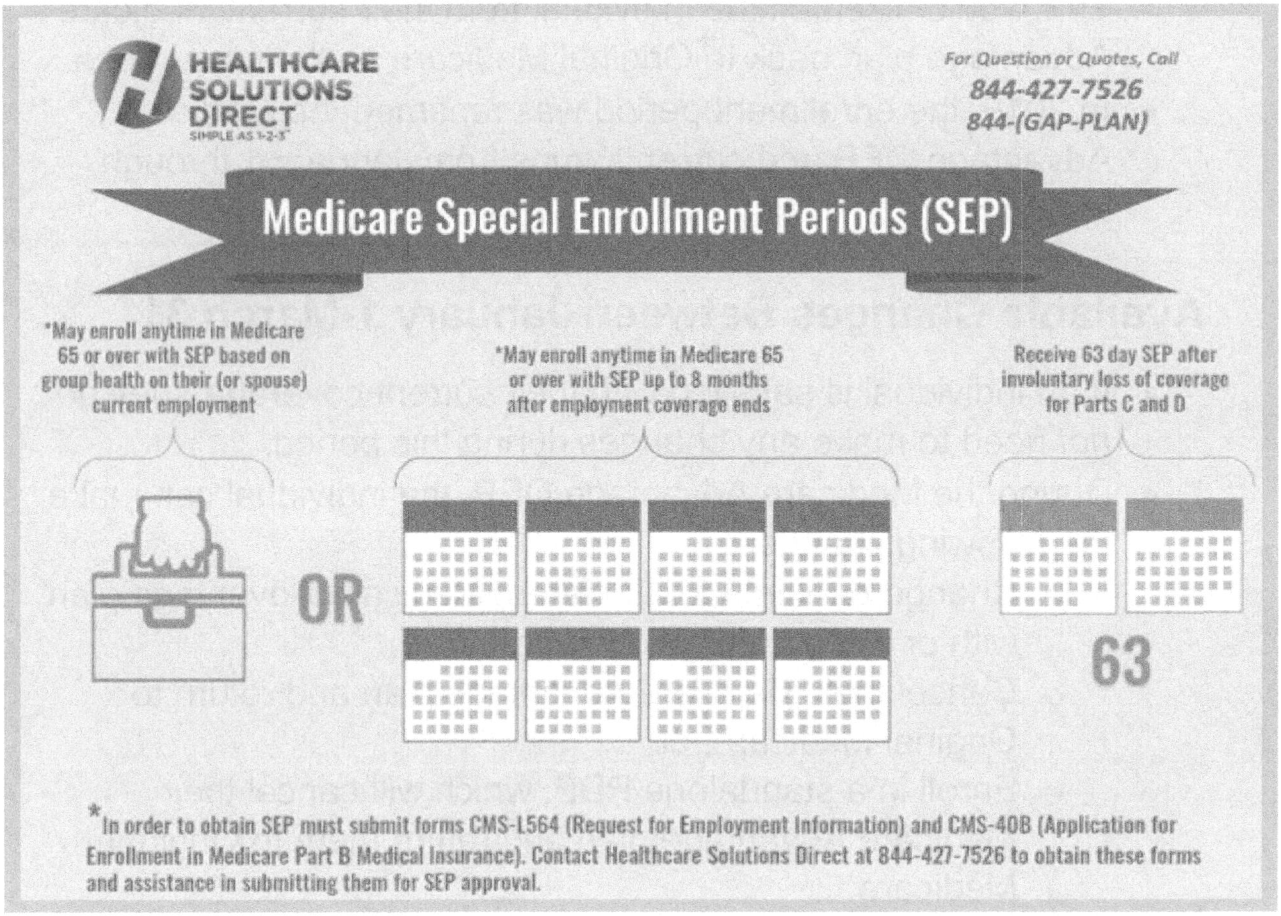

- An individual may also be eligible to receive a 63-day Medicare SEP after an involuntary loss of coverage for their Medicare Advantage plan or standalone PDP.
- If an individual's Medicare Advantage plan is no longer servicing the area or they have moved out of the coverage area, they will be eligible for a 63-day SEP to enroll into another plan.
- If someone has a standalone PDP and move out of the coverage area, they will be eligible for a 63-day SEP even if they are outside of the Medicare OEP.

Five Star Special Enrollment Period

- Since the rating was introduced in 2007, Medicare Advantage plans that achieve a 5-star rating are not that common.
- CMS rates Medicare Advantage plans on a 5-star system based on quality of care and customer service.
- If a 5-star plan is available in the individual's area, they will have a onetime opportunity to enroll into that plan anytime during the calendar year for any reason.
- These plans will continue to market themselves throughout the calendar year and can be an incredible opportunity because anyone who is eligible for Medicare can enroll into one.

Medicare Advantage Star Rating System

- Medicare Advantage plans and Part D plans are assigned a star rating from CMS to help evaluate how well they are performing.
- A plan will get a rating that will range from one to five stars. They use five different categories to determine the overall star rating. Starting in 2021, CMS will be putting more focus on the member experience and complaints when assigning the star rating.
- In 2012, CMS introduced bonus payments and rebate adjustments as an incentive to encourage improved performance so that Medicare Advantage plans focus on getting as close as possible to a 5-star rating. Any plans that achieved a 4-star rating or higher will be eligible for this incentive.

Scope of Appointment

- A Scope of Appointment (SOA) gives the insurance agent or agency Permission to Contact (PTC) to discuss the products that the individual has originally requested. It is designed to protect all parties involved in the discussion.

- An SOA is required by CMS to ensure that the individual is protected from being solicited for a product like a Medicare Advantage plan or standalone PDP that they did not originally express any interest in discussing.

Scope of Appointment Protects Everyone Involved

- CMS requires an SOA to ensure that the individual is fully aware of what they will be discussing when it comes to the marketing and sale of a Medicare Advantage plan or standalone PDP. This is also aimed at keeping complaints down by the individual to CMS.
- Medicare Advantage plans are annual contracts with the private insurance company; therefore, CMS wants to ensure someone is not calling unsolicited without permission.
- Many companies will accept an SOA either verbally over the phone, or through a text or email.

Statement of Understanding and Disclosures

- If an individual has decided that the Medicare Advantage plan is going to be their best option, the insurance agent must review the "Summary of Benefits" of the plan with them and go over some disclosures. They must clearly point out the benefits of the plan along with the cost that are associated with the plan.
- Toward the end of the enrollment, the individual will be read and will need to acknowledge what is called a "Statement of Understanding," which will go over some basic acknowledgements from the individual.

Basic Statement of Understanding Acknowledgments

- The individual will acknowledge that they are enrolling into a Medicare Advantage plan that has a contract with the federal government, but is not a Medigap supplement plan.
- The individual will acknowledge that they must keep their Medicare Part A and B and continue to pay the Part B premium unless that premium is paid for by someone else such as Medicaid.
- The individual will acknowledge that they can only be enrolled in one Medicare Advantage plan or standalone PDP at a time. They will lose the plan if they enroll in another plan.
- The individual will acknowledge that they are joining the plan for the entire calendar year.
- The individual will acknowledge that the plan only will cover a specific area and that if they move out of the area, they can join a new plan in that area.

Chapter 10

Medicare Part D —
Everything You Need To Know

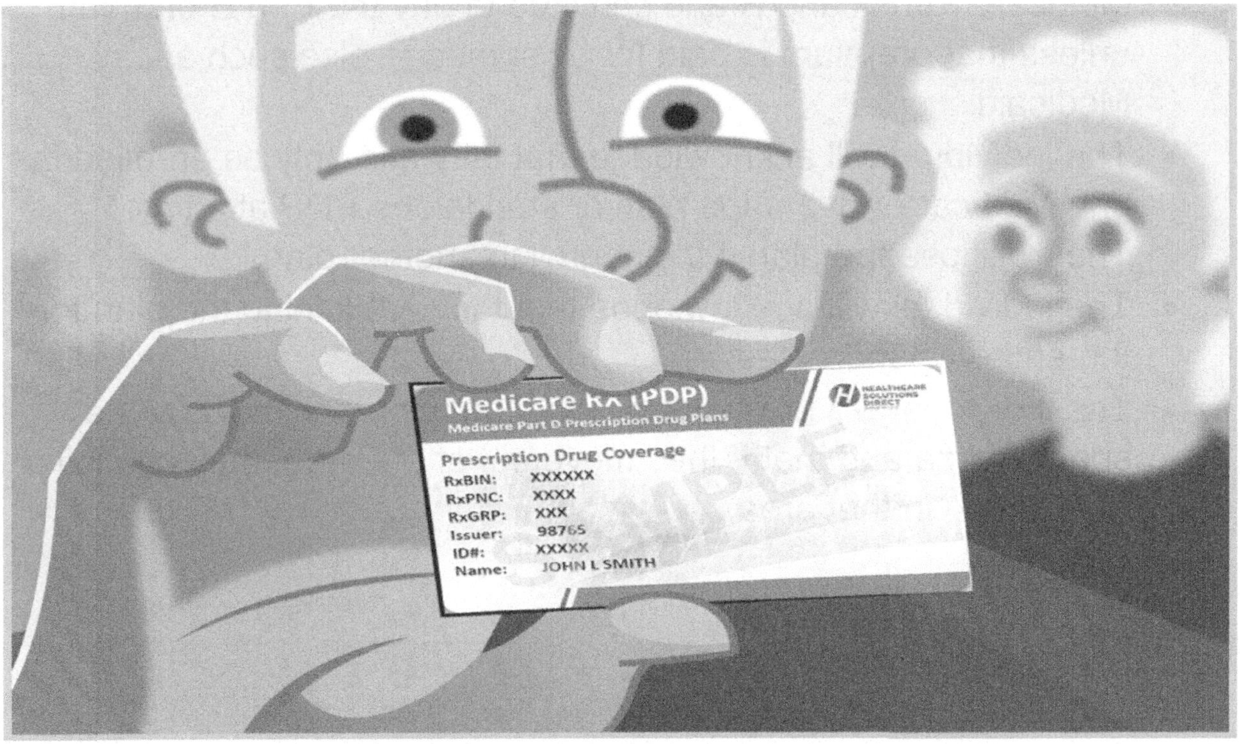

Everything About Prescription Drug Coverage

- This is the part of Medicare that will help an individual pay for medications that are prescribed by a doctor.
- Medicare added outpatient prescription drugs to its coverage on January 1, 2006, which is known as Part D.
- This was one of the biggest benefits to Medicare, but it also led to much confusion because some prescriptions can still come at a high cost.
- An individual transitioning from an individual or group insurance plan will not see much of a difference when it comes to generic

medications, but they could be in for a shock when it comes to how brand name medications are handled under Part D.

Brand Name Medications Can Still Be Costly

- Most individuals on Part D will find themselves being prescribed generic medication, which could result in little to no out-of-pocket co-pay. Most brand name medications have a generic alternative, which can keep costs manageable.
- An individual coming off an individual or group plan where they were prescribed a costly brand name medication might need to move to a generic equivalent for cost reasons.
- A problem an individual could encounter on Medicare Part D is if there is *not* a generic equivalent to the medication prescribed, or the generic version does not work as well for their situation.

Group Plans Can Offer Great Prescription Coverage

- Employer group insurance plans can offer some incredible prescription drug benefits to their employees. This is because the employer contributed financially to ensure the prescription coverage offered was robust.
- An individual coming from that employer group insurance plan will *not* have the same benefits when it comes to their Part D prescription coverage since the employer is no longer contributing to their drug plan.
- We discussed earlier that if an individual is still working and taking high-cost brand name medication(s), it is important for them to compare the employer group coverage with Medicare Part D. The individual could be paying a $10 co-pay for their brand name, but find that the same medication could cost them over $200 through a Medicare Part D plan.

Most Retirees Are Prescribed Generic Medication(s)

- The good news is that most prescribed brand name medications have a generic version, which are prescribed to those on Medicare.
- Generic medications should be inexpensive and affordable under the Part D drug plan if someone uses the plans preferred pharmacy network or mail order program.
- By the end of this section, you will understand each of the four stages of the Part D. You will know how the coverage gap “donut hole” works when an individual is prescribed some brand name medications.
- You will know everything about Part D to make you a Medicare expert when it comes to outpatient prescriptions.

Basics of Medicare Part D

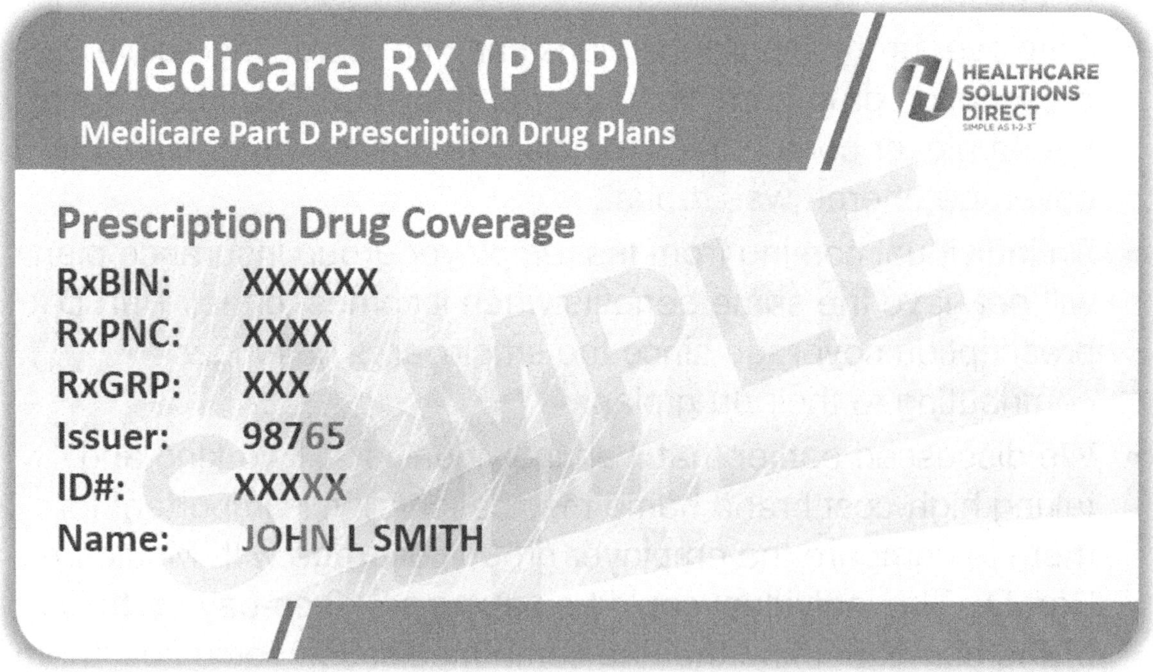

- Medicare Part D is provided by private insurance companies and not by Medicare. CMS never got into the prescription drug market, but does oversee it and has rules in place that every company must follow.
- CMS focused their attention on both Part A and Part B, making those the foundation of the federal health insurance program for those eligible for Medicare.
- Parts C and D are provided by private insurance companies, and each company and plan must be approved by CMS before it can be offered in someone's zip code.
- Parts C and D are awarded a star system by CMS in order to rate its efficiency and customer service. If the star system falls below a certain threshold, CMS will step in and sanction the company and plan.

There Are Two Ways To Get Prescription Coverage

- There are only two ways that an individual can get their prescription drug coverage when they are eligible for Medicare. If they have Original Medicare as their primary insurance, the individual can purchase a standalone plan or have it included as a benefit to their Medicare Advantage plan.
    - PDP: A standalone plan that an individual eligible for Medicare will purchase through a private insurance company approved by CMS. They must be enrolled in Medicare Part A and/or B in order to have a separate PDP or
    - A Medicare Advantage plan approved by CMS that offers prescription drug coverage included in the plan offering. They must be enrolled in both Medicare A and B in order to enroll into a Medicare Advantage plan.

Standalone PDP Will Disenroll Medicare Advantage

- An individual enrolled in a Medicare Advantage plan that decides to enroll in a standalone PDP plan will automatically be disenrolled from their Medicare Advantage plan and back to Original Medicare.
- A standalone PDP can *only* go with Original Medicare Part A and B. An individual cannot have a standalone PDP and a Medicare Advantage plan. They must have one or the other.
- The only Medicare Advantage plans that allow someone to have a standalone PDP plan is a MSA because they do *not* provide prescription drug coverage. This is the only exception to the CMS rule.

Everyone Eligible For Medicare Should Have Part D

- An individual who is eligible for Medicare should enroll into either a standalone PDP or a MAPD, which includes prescription drug coverage when they are first eligible for Medicare during their 7-month IEP.
- Even if the individual is *not* taking any prescribed medication, they will need to pick a Part D plan in order to avoid Medicare's late enrollment penalty.
- Although prescription drug coverage is voluntary for those who are eligible for Medicare, an individual will owe a late enrollment penalty if they do not have credible prescription drug coverage after their 7-month IEP.
- An individual who delays Medicare Part B because they are working with employer group coverage that includes credible prescription drug coverage will not owe a late enrollment period when enrolling in a SEP.

How Much Is the Part D Penalty?

- If an individual does not enroll in either a PDP or MAPD during their 7-Month IEP and they do not have a SEP, they will have a late enrollment penalty for Part D of 1 percent per month for as long as they did not have credible prescription drug coverage. This will be a lifetime penalty added to their Part D drug plan.
- The only time an individual can buy or change a PDP or MAPD is during the Medicare OEP that runs from October 15 through December 7.
- If someone is responsible for a Part D penalty, here is how the late enrollment penalty is calculated.
- In 2022, the “national base beneficiary premium” is set at $33.37. In order to calculate the late enrollment penalty, CMS would take the $33.37 times the number of months that the individual was without credible prescription coverage and round it to the nearest $0.10.
- In an individual went 3 years without credible prescription coverage they would have a 36 percent penalty. Here is how CMS would calculate the late enrollment penalty.
    - .36 (36% penalty) x $33.37 (2022 national base beneficiary premium) = $12.01
- CMS would round that to the nearest $0.10 which would make the late enrollment penalty an additional $12.10 a month. This would be permanently added to the individuals Part D prescription drug plan.

Understanding The Medicare Part D 63-day Rule

- Medicare’s rule is that after the 7-month IEP, the individual cannot go more than 63 days *without* credible prescription drug coverage.

- A prescription discount card will not count as credible prescription coverage. Credible prescription drug coverage must either be through an employer sponsored plan, VA coverage, standalone PDP, or an MAPD.
- A prescription discount card will *not* be considered credible prescription drug coverage and may not help someone who is taking a high-cost brand name medication.
- A popular discount card like GoodR$_X$ provides discount drug coupons, but would not give much financial assistance for a commonly prescribed blood thinner to prevent blood clotting such as Xarelto. For an individual in this situation, a Part D drug plan would be an enormous help financially.

GoodR$_X$ Discount Drug Coupon

Your prescription	Pharmacist info
Xarelto 20mg 30 tablets	Member ID **ER105662**
	Group **06340003**
Discounted price with this coupon	Bin **600428**
$524.17 at CVS Pharmacy This is your estimated price. The pharmacy will provide exact pricing.	PCN **05100000**
Customer questions call: **1-855-426-4465**	Pharmacist questions call: **1-855-782-3703**

Courtesy: https://www.goodrx.com/xarelto

Part D (Drug) Tiers

Tiers	Initial coverage phase
Preferred Generic	$2.00 copay
Generic	$7.00 copay
Preferred Brand	$35.00 copay
Non-Preferred Drug	50%
Specialty Tier	28%

Courtesy: https://www.medicare.gov/plan-compare

- Medicare Part D plans will have a list of covered drugs that are listed on what is called a "formulary" and broken down by "tiers." The lower that the drug appears on the tier, the less the individual will pay out of pocket for that prescribed medication.
- There are generally five tiers that a prescribed medication will fall under with Part D.

Become Familiar With The Five Part D Tiers

1. Preferred generic: This will be for common generic medications, which are prescribed. These will have a small co-pay of $1 to $3 or it may be even free.
2. Non-preferred generic: This will be for generic medications the plan did not negotiate a lower cost to be considered a preferred drug under the plan. These will typically have a $7 to $13 co-pay.
3. Preferred brand: This will be for a brand name medication that does not currently have a generic equivalent. Typically, these will have a co-pay around $35, which will probably move someone into what is called the Coverage Gap "Donut Hole." A medication like Xarelto would usually fall under this tier.
4. Non-preferred brand: This will be for a brand name medication that does not have a generic equivalent and was not negotiated as preferred by the drug plan. These will have a co-pay of $95 to 50 percent cost sharing, depending on the plan.

5. Specialty tier: This will be for the most expensive drugs, which are typically used to treat severe conditions such as cancer or multiple sclerosis. Typically, these will not have a co-pay, but will have cost sharing of around 25 percent. This type of medication will have an individual move into the Catastrophic Coverage phase of Part D.

Medicare Part D Network Pharmacies

CVS PHARMACY #17201	✓	Preferred in-network pharmacy
WALGREENS #13824	✓	Standard in-network pharmacy
WALMART PHARMACY 10-3197	✓	Preferred in-network pharmacy
Mail Order Pharmacy		Costs vary based on the specific mail-order pharmacy

Courtesy: https://www.medicare.gov/plan-compare

- When an individual is looking to keep their costs down for their prescriptions, there are three things that they can do.
    1. The first is to make sure that whenever possible be prescribed generic medications. Most medications now have a generic equivalent, which will keep costs down.
    2. The second is to use a preferred in-network pharmacy to fill medications. Part D drugs plans have a network of pharmacies that agree to discount the prescriptions to its members. This may require an individual to use a preferred in-network pharmacy in order to get the lowest out-of-pocket co-pay for that medication.
    3. The last thing an individual can do is to consider a mail-order program offered by the plan. This will typically provide lower costs and save the individual time from needing to go to a pharmacy to fill the medication.

Medicare Part D — The 4 Stages Of Coverage

- We will go over each of the four stages CMS has in place for outpatient prescription drug coverage. All four stages will be the same regardless if someone has a MAPD plan or a standalone PDP.
- When an individual is prescribed medication, they will have four stages: Deductible (if applicable), Initial Coverage, Coverage Gap Donut Hole, and Catastrophic Coverage.

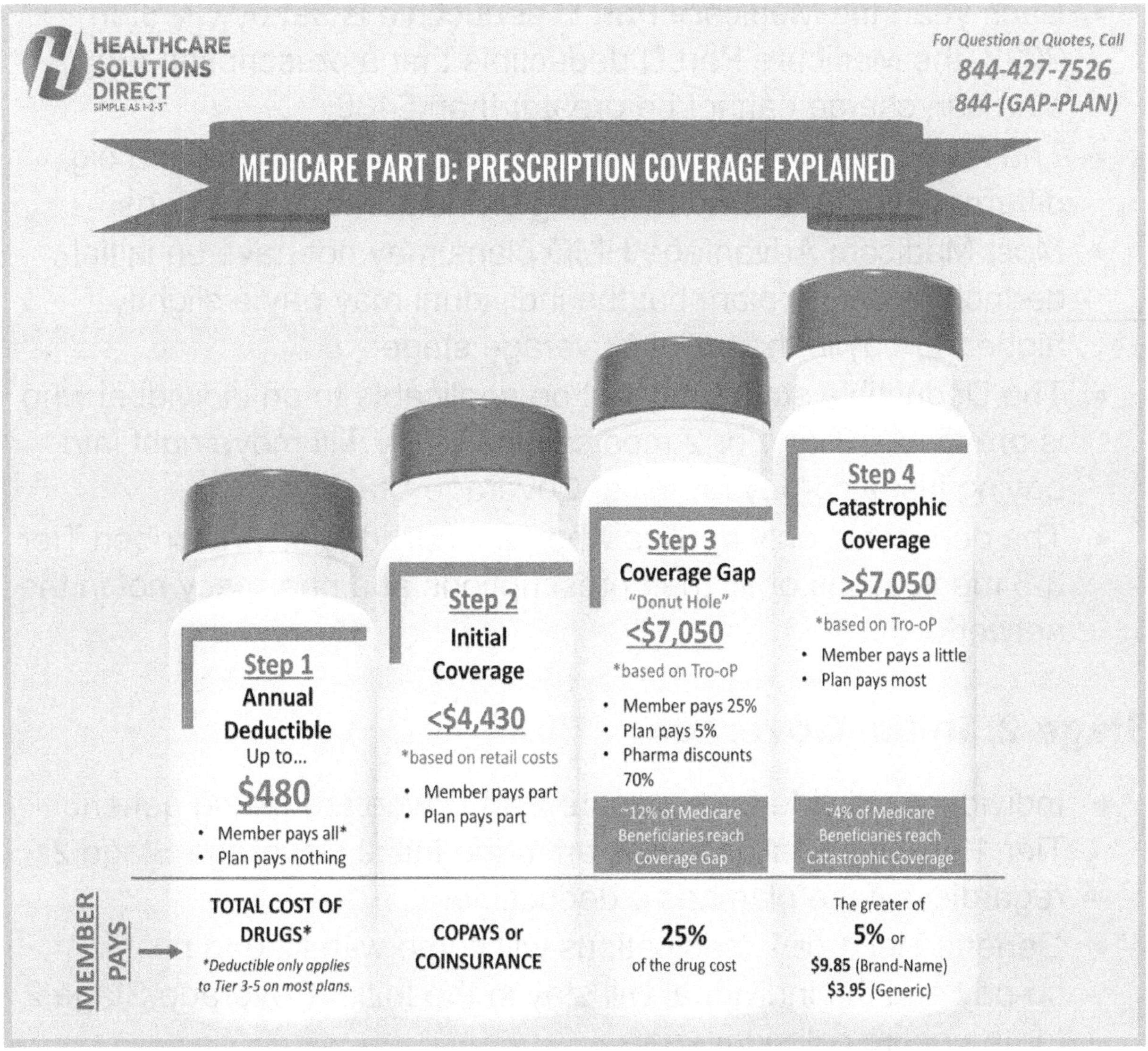

Stage 1: Deductible (If Applicable)

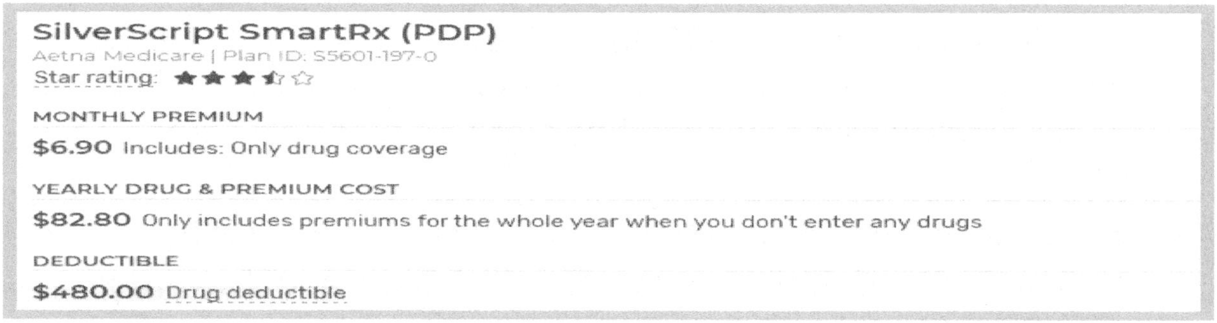

Courtesy: https://www.medicare.gov/plan-compare

- Each year, the Medicare Part D deductible is set by CMS. In 2022, the Medicare Part D deductible that a prescription drug plan can charge cannot be greater than $480.
- The Part D deductible will vary by plan, which can make a big difference for an individual taking brand name medications.
- Most Medicare Advantage HMO plans may not have an initial deductible on the plan, but the individual may pay a slightly higher co-pay in the Initial Coverage stage.
- The Deductible stage may not be applicable to an individual who is prescribed Tier 1 or 2 medications. They will move right into paying just a co-pay for Initial Coverage Stage 2.
- The deductible only applies when an individual is prescribed Tier 3-5 medications or fill their prescriptions at a pharmacy not in the network.

Stage 2: Initial Coverage

- Individuals eligible for Medicare Part D who are taking generic Tier 1 or 2 medications will start in the Initial Coverage Stage 2 regardless if the plan has a deductible.
- Generic Tier 1 or 2 medications will come with little to no co-pay and the individual will stay in the Initial Coverage Stage 2 for the entire calendar year.

- Under the Initial Coverage Stage 2, there will be cost sharing where the plan will pay part and the individual will pay part, usually in the form of a set dollar amount co-pay.
- An individual taking a common preventative Tier 1 or 2 medication should not need to pay the $480.00 deductible (as of 2022). They will pay a set dollar amount co-pay.

✔ Preferred in-network pharmacy

Selected drugs	Retail cost	Cost before deductible	Cost after deductible
Atorvastatin 40mg tablet	$13.15	$1.00	$1.00
Lisinopril 20mg tablet	$6.85	$1.00	$1.00
Metformin hcl 500mg tablet	$7.15	$1.00	$1.00
Omeprazole 20mg capsule delayed release	$7.45	$1.00	$1.00
Potassium chloride crys er 20meq tablet extended release	$11.65	$3.00	$3.00
Monthly totals	$46.25	$7.00	$7.00

Estimated total drug + premium cost

You will pay **$184.50** per year on drug + premium costs.
Based on current drug costs, it's estimated that:

- You won't meet your **$445.00 deductible** this year

Courtesy: https://www.medicare.gov/plan-compare *Medicare Part D deductible maximum is $480 for 2022

- The only time that someone would pay a coinsurance instead of a set dollar amount co-pay would be if they were taking a Tier 3-5 medication. This would move them into Stage 3 — the Coverage Gap Donut Hole.

Stage 3: Coverage Gap “Donut Hole”

- An individual who is prescribed a Tier 3-5 will more than likely move into Stage 3 Coverage Gap. In Stage 2 once the co-pays or coinsurance exceed the retail costs of $4,430 (as of 2022), the individual will move into the Coverage Gap referred to as the Donut Hole.

- The good news is that only 10 to 12 percent of individual's who have Part D will move into the Stage 3 Coverage Gap.
- During Stage 3, the individual will pay 25 percent of the retail cost of the medication. Most individuals who are prescribed brand name medication will stay in Stage 3 for the rest of the calendar year.

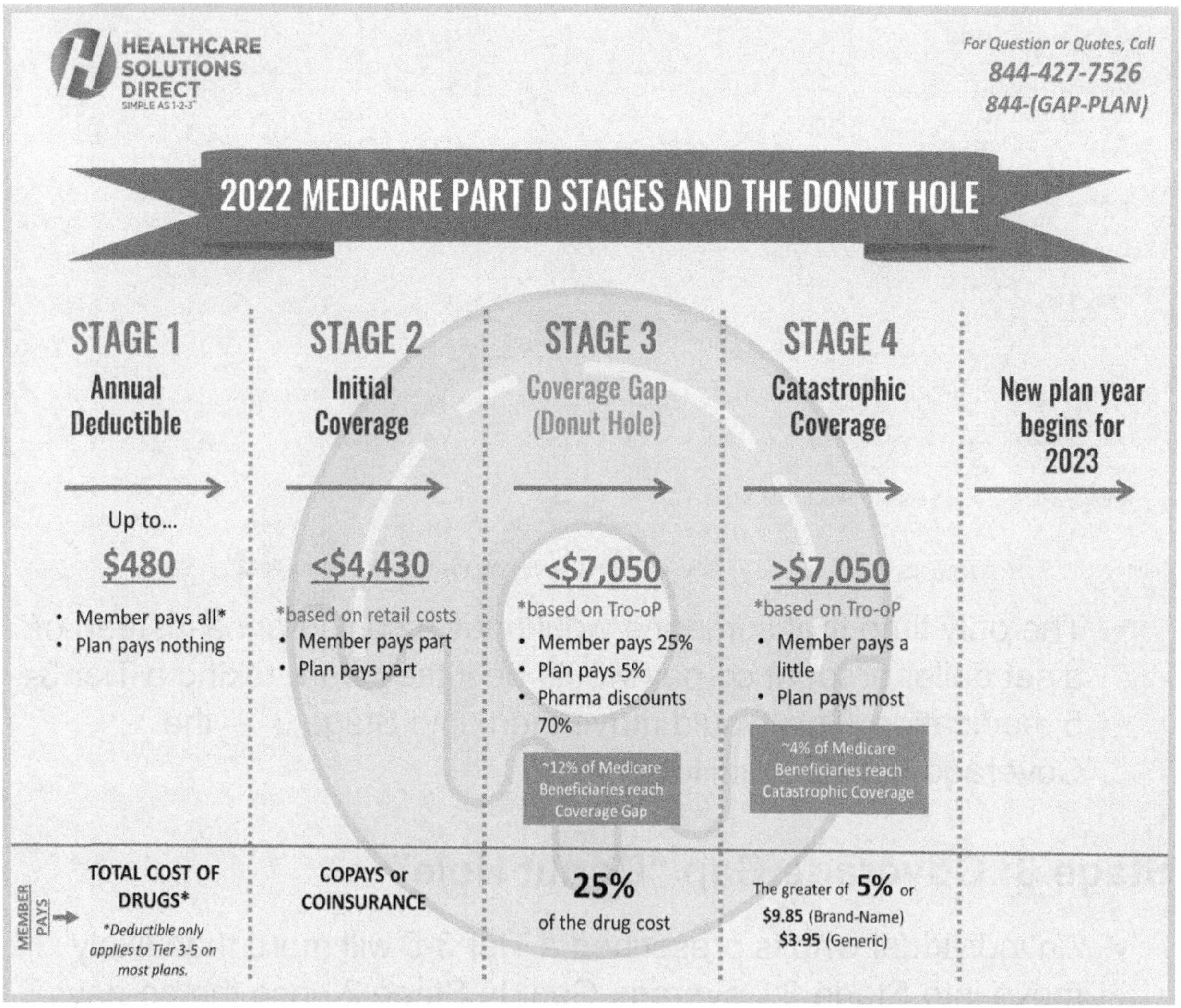

Understanding The 25 Percent (As Of 2022) Under Stage 3

- A brand name medication with a retail cost of approximately $375 a month or higher will cause an individual to move into Stage 3 Coverage Gap Donut Hole.
- If an individual were prescribed a $375 retail brand name medication, over 12 months the retail costs would be $4,500. This would exceed the $4,430 (as of 2022) set forth by CMS.
- Once the retail costs exceed the $4,430 (as of 2022), the individual will be responsible for 25 percent of the cost of that medication.

Popular Brand Name Xarelto Would Move To Stage 3

- Popular brand name medications such as Xarelto, Pradaxa, and Eliquis, which currently do not have generic alternatives, are used to prevent blood clotting. They have a retail cost of approximately $500 a month.
- If the retail cost of a medication such as Xarelto was $520.48 a month, the individual would pay the Part D deductible right away if there was one on the plan.
- Once the deductible was satisfied under Stage 1, the individual would pay a co-pay for Xarelto, which is approximately $35 a month during Stage 2, the Initial Coverage stage.
- Once the retail costs exceed the $4,430 set by CMS (as of 2022), the individual would pay 25 percent of the retail cost of that medication, which would be in this example around $130.

✔ Preferred in-network pharmacy

Selected drugs	Retail cost	Cost before deductible	Cost after deductible	Cost in coverage gap
Atorvastatin 40mg tablet	$0.42	$0.00	$0.00	$0.11
Lisinopril 20mg tablet	$0.41	$0.00	$0.00	$0.10
Metformin hcl 500mg tablet	$0.42	$0.00	$0.00	$0.11
Omeprazole 20mg capsule delayed release	$4.66	$4.66	$4.66	$1.17
Potassium chloride crys er 20meq tablet extended release	$5.20	$5.00	$5.00	$1.30
Xarelto 20mg tablet	$520.48	$520.48	$35.00	$130.12
Monthly totals	$531.60	$530.14	$44.66	$132.91

Estimated total drug + premium cost

You will pay **$1,049.07** per year on drug + premium costs.
Based on current drug costs, it's estimated that:

- You'll meet your **$305.00 deductible** in April
- You'll enter the **coverage gap** in November
- You won't exit the **coverage gap**

Courtesy: https://www.medicare.gov/plan-compare *Medicare Part D deductible maximum is $480 for 2022

Stage 4: Catastrophic Coverage

- If the true out-of-pocket costs where to exceed $7,050 (as of 2022) in a calendar year, the individual would move to Stage 4 Catastrophic Coverage.
- Currently, less than 5 percent of individuals on Part D will make it to the Catastrophic Coverage stage.
- An individual would only enter this stage if they were taking a lot of brand name medications or some specialty drugs used to treat a chronic condition such as cancer, multiple sclerosis, etc. These conditions might require a tier 5 drug.
- If an individual entered Stage 4 Catastrophic Coverage, the cost of each medication will be the greater of 5 percent or it will be capped at $9.85 for a brand name or $3.95 for a generic medication (as of 2022).

Specialty Medications Contribute To Stage 4

- Let's look at a medication called Copaxone, which is used to treat multiple sclerosis. This brand name medication does have a less expensive generic version; however, the generic version is still listed as a Tier 5 medication.
- Currently, the brand name Copaxone has a retail cost of around $6,200 a month, and the less expensive generic version glatiramer acetate is around $2,200 a month.
- An individual prescribed this medication would pay the Part D deductible right away in Stage 1 if there was one on the plan. Almost immediately the next month, they would then enter the Coverage Gap and be responsible for 25 percent.
- A specialty medication like this one would have the true out-of-pocket cost that exceeds the $7,050; therefore, the individual would enter Stage 4 Catastrophic Coverage.

✓ Preferred in-network pharmacy

Selected drugs	Retail cost	Cost before deductible	Cost after deductible	Cost in coverage gap	Cost after coverage gap
Atorvastatin 40mg tablet	$2.38	$1.00	$1.00	$0.60	$2.38
Glatiramer acetate 40mg/ml solution prefilled syringe	$2,170.18	$2,170.18	$542.55	$542.55	$108.51
Lisinopril 20mg tablet	$1.48	$0.00	$0.00	$0.37	$1.48
Metformin hcl 500mg tablet	$1.78	$0.00	$0.00	$0.45	$1.78
Omeprazole 20mg capsule delayed release	$8.38	$8.38	$4.19	$2.10	$3.70
Potassium chloride crys er 20meq tablet extended release	$4.48	$3.00	$3.00	$1.12	$3.70
Xarelto 20mg tablet	$522.88	$522.88	$30.00	$130.72	$26.14
Monthly totals	$2,711.56	$2,705.44	$580.74	$677.91	$147.69

Estimated total drug + premium cost

You will pay **$5,310.87** per year on drug + premium costs.
Based on current drug costs, it's estimated that:

- You'll meet your **$445.00 deductible** in April
- You'll enter the **coverage gap** in May
- You'll exit the **coverage gap** in October

Courtesy: https://www.medicare.gov/plan-compare *Medicare Part D deductible maximum is $480 for 2022

Avoiding The Coverage Gap or Catastrophic Stage

- There are *no* Part D plans that offer full coverage protection against the high out-of-pocket costs of brand name or specialty drugs, which would prevent individuals from entering the Coverage Gap or Catastrophic Coverage.
- There are some things that an individual who is eligible for Part D can do to keep the prescription costs down.
- An individual should consult with their doctors about making sure they are prescribed generic medications as much as possible. Not all doctors will think to prescribe a generic equivalent unless requested by the individual.
- An individual should be aware that some Part D plans will classify the drug tier differently. One plan might classify the prescription as a Tier 4 and another plan will classify it as a Tier 3 or possibly a Tier 2.

Formulary Exception and Step Therapy To Lower Cost

- The individual can also ask the Part D plan representative for what is called a formulary exception. A formulary exception is where the individual is asking for a non-preferred drug at a better cost, have the drug covered on the formulary list, and not require them to complete a step therapy. This request is not an easy process for a drug plan representative to agree to for the individual.
- Step therapy is where the plan will require an individual to try a less expensive drug before covering the more expensive medication at a lower cost. The individual would need to consult with their doctor to find out what is the best course of action for their high-cost medication if they feel that the less expensive medication is not appropriate for their condition.

- There are also some pharmaceutical assistance programs that might be available to an individual that will help pay for high-cost medications and provide financial assistance.

Pharmaceutical Assistance Might Be Available

- Pharmaceutical programs can be found on Medicare's website, or an individual can call the drug manufacturer directly and see if there are any programs available to them.

- There are also some states that offer pharmaceutical programs through the state, which can help the individual get assistance for high-cost medications. Not all states offer this, but the ones that do will be listed on Medicare's website.

Extra Help Part D

This is a program that many individuals could qualify for, but either they do not know about it or they are taking generic medications that are already relatively inexpensive; therefore, they do not apply.

- Extra Help Part D is offered through Medicare and Social Security as a benefit to help an individual with limited income or resources who might not qualify for Medicaid.
- If the individual qualifies for Extra Help Part D, they will pay no more than $3.95 for generics and $9.85 for brand name medications (as of 2022). The individual could also get their Part D plan premium covered and any deductibles waived.

Qualifications For Extra Help Part D

- Here are the qualifications for Extra Help Part D (as of 2022):
    - The annual income is below $19,320 ($26,130 for a married couple) and financial assets are below $14,790 ($29,520 for a married couple).
    - Financial assets would include liquid cash in a checking or savings account, stocks, or bonds. Items such as their home, car, and personal items are not considered resources or assets; therefore, these will not count against them.

Medicare Savings Programs

- If an individual is receiving full Medicaid, Supplemental Security Income benefits, or assistance from their state Medicaid program that is paying for their Part B premiums, they will automatically qualify for Extra Help on their Part D. There is nothing they need to do.

- An individual who is not currently getting the assistance they feel that they are entitled to will have the opportunity to apply for financial assistance through one of four MSPs.

Qualified Medicare Beneficiary (QMB)

- Qualified Medicare Beneficiary program: If the monthly income (as of 2022) is below $1,094 ($1,472 married couple) and financial assets are below $7,970 ($11,960 married couple), an individual could get help paying their Part A and/or B monthly premiums and will not be charged any of Medicare's deductibles, coinsurance, or copayments.

Specified Low-Income Medicare Beneficiary (SLMB)

- Specified Low-Income Medicare Beneficiary program: If the monthly income (as of 2022) is below $1,308 ($1,762 married couple) and financial assets are below $7,970 ($11,960 married couple), and the individual has Part A, they could get help paying their Part B premiums only with this program.

Qualified Individual (QI)

- Qualified Individual program: If the monthly income (as of 2022) is below $1,469 ($1,980 married couple), financial assets are below $7,970 ($11,960 married couple), and the individual has Part A, they could get help paying their Part B premiums only with this program. This program must be applied for every year to get help paying the Part B premium only. This program is on a first come, first served basis. Priority will be given to someone who qualified for this program the previous year.

Qualified Disabled and Working Individuals (QDWI)

- Qualified Disabled and Working Individuals program: If the monthly income (as of 2022) is below $4,379 ($5,892 married couple) and financial assets are below $4,000 ($6,000 married couple), this program will help pay for the Part A premium only. This program is for someone who is disabled and working under the age of 65, lost their premium-free Part A because they went back to work, and is not getting medical assistance from their state.

Commonly Prescribed Medications

- It is important for an individual, as well as insurance agents, to become familiar with the most prescribed medications.
- The top 10 medications are common medications taken for preventative conditions such as high cholesterol, high blood pressure, acid reflux, diabetes, and pain relieve.

Top 10 Prescription Medications Filled in the U.S.

1. **Atorvastatin calcium** *(generic for Lipitor)*

• Atorvastatin is used to treat high cholesterol, and to lower the risk of stroke, heart attack, or other heart complications in people with type 2 diabetes, coronary heart disease, or other risk factors.

2. **Levothyroxine** *(generic for Synthroid)*

• Levothyroxine treats hypothyroidism (low thyroid hormone). It is also used to treat or prevent goiter (enlarged thyroid gland), which can be caused by hormone imbalances, radiation treatment, surgery, or cancer.

3. **Lisinopril** *(generic for Prinivil)*

• Lisinopril is used to treat high blood pressure (hypertension) or congestive heart failure. It is also used to improve survival after a heart attack.

4. **Omeprazole** *(generic for Prilosec)*

• Omeprazole is used to treat symptoms of gastroesophageal reflux disease, which is abbreviated as GERD, and other conditions caused by excess stomach acid. It is also used to promote healing of erosive esophagitis (damage to your esophagus caused by stomach acid).

5. **Metformin** *(generic for Glucophage)*

• Metformin is used to improve blood sugar control in people with type 2 diabetes. It is sometimes used in combination with insulin or other medications, but this medicine is not for treating type 1 diabetes.

6. Amlodipine besylate *(generic for Norvasc)*

• Amlodipine is used to treat high blood pressure (hypertension), or chest pain (angina) and other conditions caused by coronary artery disease. This medication is for use in adults and children who are at least 6 years old.

7. Simvastatin *(generic for Zocor)*

• Simvastatin is used to lower cholesterol and triglycerides (types of fat) in the blood.

8. Hydrocodone/acetaminophen *(generic for Lortab)*

• This combination medication (hydrocodone and acetaminophen) is used to relieve moderate to moderately severe pain.

9. Metoprolol succinate ER (*generic for Toprol XL)*

• Metoprolol succinate ER is used to treat angina (chest pain) and hypertension (high blood pressure). It is also used to treat or prevent a heart attack.

10. Losartan *(generic for Cozaar)*

• Losartan is used to treat high blood pressure (hypertension). It is also used to lower the risk of stroke in certain people with heart disease.

Conclusion

We have now come to the end of this Medicare journey. I know that we have gone through a lot, and my hope is that you have a much better understanding of Medicare. As simple as Medicare sometimes seems to me after more than a decade in this business, I still find myself sometimes saying: Medicare just does not make any sense.

I will find myself telling a complete stranger I meet that Medicare is made up of only two options: Original Medicare or Medicare Advantage. That's all there is, pretty simple right? However as much as it is simple to me, I will still see the confused look on their face. To me, this is as simples as tying your shoes, but to the other person I am speaking to it might seem like decoding hieroglyphics.

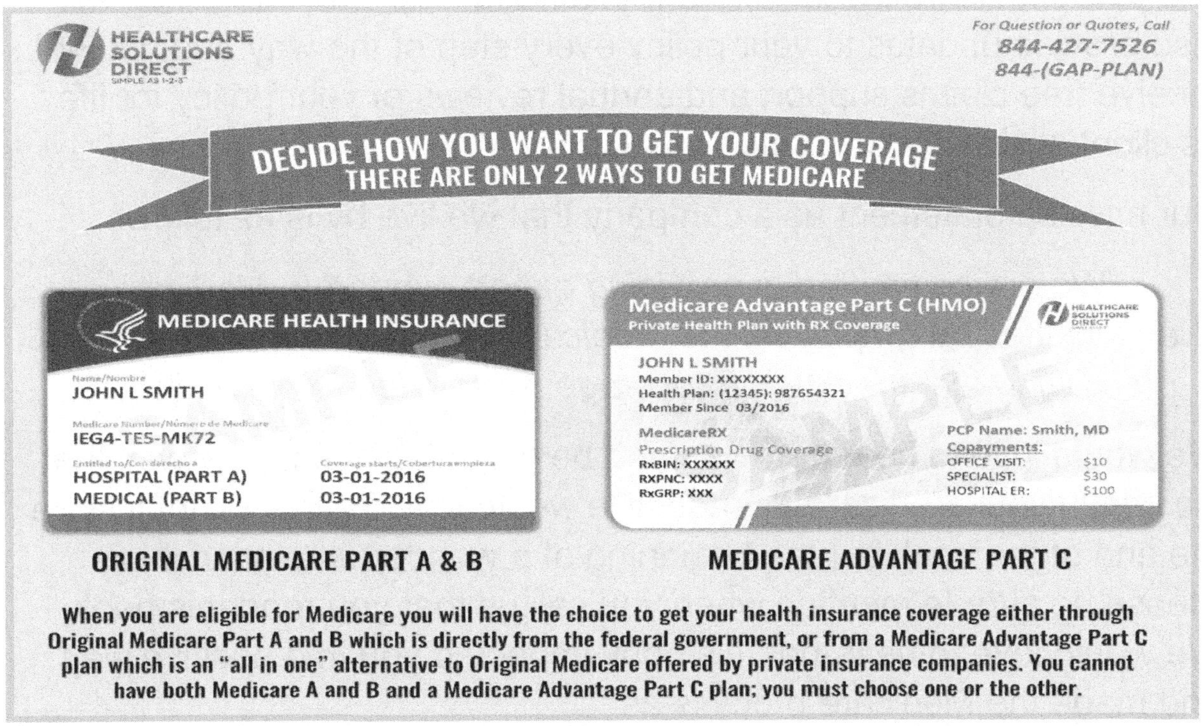

At the end of the day when trying to decide on which option is best for you, it comes down to what works best for your needs. My goal with this book was to give you an unbiased opinion of the facts. Medicare is not a one size fits all, so it is best to take the time to talk to an experienced licensed agent. They can help talk to you about your particular situation and make sure you are getting all the benefits that you are entitled to.

We would love to hear from you at **Healthcare Solutions Direct** to see what we can do to help you. Our consultation and services are free to you. We have a dedicated staff that is well versed in all the Medigap Supplement, Medicare Advantage, and PDP prescription drug plans in your area. We work with all the top A+ rated companies so we can give you an unbiased opinion and make the enrollment process easy and simple for you right over the phone.

We also have an entire department called the Client Experience Group that is dedicated to helping you with the process of enrolling into your Medicare Part A and B if you need help with that. They will also provide updates to your policy every step of the way and you will receive free claims support and annual reviews of your policy for life as client of **Healthcare Solutions Direct**.

Our mission statement as a company that we live by is as follows:

"We are committed to providing expert support to Medicare Beneficiaries by simplifying the Medicare process from start to finish, ensuring that the RIGHT coverage is provided to each client."

We would love to hear from you and be of assistance in any way that we can in your Medicare journey. We would love for this to not just be the end of the book but the beginning of a wonderful relationship. Please be sure to mention when you call us that you read this book. We would love to hear that this book impacted you in a positive way and made the Medicare process as

Simple as 1-2-3

WANT MORE?

Be sure to subscribe to our Healthcare Solutions Direct YouTube Channel and hit the notification bell so you never miss a Medicare video.

SCAN ME

Our mission in providing expert support does not stop with this book. We want to be there throughout your Medicare journey as your trusted resource. We understand Medicare sometimes does not make sense so we have created amazing video content that will keep you updated on everything related to Medicare.

If you have questions, we probably have a video that will help answer it for you. If not, please reach out to us toll free at 844-427-7526. The call is free, but your financial security is priceless.

You can also visit us at www.healthcaresolutionsdirect.com so we can help make Medicare As Simple As 1-2-3 for you! Look forward to joining you on your Medicare journey.

Made in the USA
Middletown, DE
08 March 2022

62343650R00150